I WILL TEACH YOU TO BE RICH

BY RAMIT SETHI

HODDER &
STOUGHTON

For my parents, Prab and Neelam Sethi, who taught me that being rich is about more than money

First published in the USA in 2009 by Workman Publishing

First published in Great Britain in 2010 by Hodder & Stoughton

An Hachette UK Company

13

ISBN 978 0340 998052

Cover illustrations by Peter Sucheski
Interior illustrations by Nora Krug
Author photo by Scott Jones
Printed and bound in Great Britain by
CPI Group (UK) Ltd, Croydon, CR0 4YY

Hodder & Stoughton policy is to use papers that are natural, renewable and recyclable products and made from wood grown in sustainable forests. The logging and manufacturing processes are expected to conform to the environmental regulations of the country of origin.

Hodder & Stoughton
338 Euston Road
London NW1 3BH

www.hodder.co.uk

Acknowledgments

The process of writing this book repeatedly made me wish I were dead. But once I was done, I felt great, my posture improved, my eyesight got clearer, and the world seemed great. I imagine this is what giving birth feels like.

I was fortunate to have a great team of people who helped me turn this book into its final form.

Jeff Kuo is simply the finest researcher I've ever worked with. He was instrumental in helping bring this book together.

I'm grateful to Chris Yeh, who's not only a brilliant marketer but perhaps the most frugal man I have ever met. And to Ben Casnocha, a deep thinker who forced me to dig deeper into everything I wrote.

Noah Kagan and Charlie Hoehn helped me spread the word about this book. Couldn't have done it without them.

Several friends helped immensely by reviewing drafts of this book, including Ben Abadi, Julie Nguyen, Vivek Sankaran, and Jen Tsang.

The folks at Workman were amazing: Margot Herrera, my editor, was incredibly skilled at helping me organize my thoughts into a coherent book. Plus, she's fun: In one of the first chapters, I wrote an over-the-top joke just to see how fast she'd cut it. She just said, "I think we should keep it. It's pretty funny." What more could I ask for? Cassie Murdoch, the perfect complement to Margot, is ultra-organized and constantly thinking two steps ahead

Many thanks to Peter Workman, who is brilliant and eccentric—exactly as rumored—and to all the people who helped tell the world about this book: Andrea Bussell, Kristin Matthews, David Schiller, Andrea Fleck, and Justin Nisbet. Kudos to Janet Parker, Beth Levy, Barbara Peragine, Doug Wolff, David Matt, and Nora Krug.

Lisa DiMona has now worked with me on two books. You couldn't ask for a better agent.

Seth Godin, who took a chance on a college kid with a cocky attitude and a lot of ambition, got me started in publishing.

BJ Fogg, my mentor and professor, first showed me that you can use psychology for pro-social uses, not just to get people to buy more stuff.

To my family, Prab and Neelam Sethi, Nagina, Ibrahim, Rachi, Haj, and Maneesh—thanks for keeping me motivated for the last two years of writing.

Finally, to my readers. I hope this book helps you on your way to being rich.

Foreword

To my UK readers,

Let's be honest. "I Will Teach You to Be Rich" sounds like a big fat scam. But it's not—so where did the name come from?

When I was in high school, coming from a middle-class family with four kids, my parents told me that if I wanted to go to college (which I had to, because I'm Indian), I'd have to get scholarships. Because I'm a big weirdo, I applied to over 70 scholarships. I still remember my first one: They wrote the $2,000 check to me, which I promptly invested, losing 50% of it right away.

After that, I decided to learn about money so I didn't lose the rest. I read the books and magazines, watched the TV shows, and realized there are a few simple steps to getting rich—and a lot of hype.

- *Getting started is more important than being the smartest person in the room.*

- *It's OK to make mistakes.*

- *Read a lot so you know when to call BS, but not too much—action is more important than reading.*

- *Ordinary actions get ordinary results.*

- *And there's a difference between being sexy and being rich.*

As my website grew, I knew that young people were looking for this kind of information. It's so easy to get overwhelmed, take the lazy road, and do nothing. That's why I decided to teach people that getting rich can be easy, if you're willing to put in a small amount of effort. But let's be clear: If you expect to get rich quick, go find another book. In fact, what does "rich" mean to you? Is it about buying £200 shoes? Or the latest Mac? Or travelling?

Unlike other personal-finance pundits, you won't find me wagging my finger, telling you to save on everything and count the number of grains of rice you can eliminate when cooking. Get a life. I *encourage* you to spend extravagantly on the things you love—if you can cut costs mercilessly on the things you don't. And perhaps earn a little extra money on the side.

When I was approached with the idea of turning my website into a book, I jumped at the opportunity. But instead of just turning the existing posts into a book, I spent two years of pure hell rewriting everything and putting my recommendations in a six-week program. I wanted this book to be *the* book you use to get started with your money, optimise it, and become expert enough to dominate.

A few weeks after the US edition of this book came out in March 2009, I flew to New York for a media tour. Just a few days later, my publishers took me out to a fancy dinner to celebrate the book launch. With about ten of the most senior people from the publishing house there, one of them made an announcement: "Ramit," she said, "we're thrilled to tell you that we've sold the UK rights for *I Will Teach You To Be Rich*!"

What a great feeling—I had no idea they'd been working on this, and we were all clapping at the terrific news. But then I asked a question: "Who's going to make sure everything is correct for the UK?" All of a sudden, the table got quiet. Selling an international edition is great, but nobody wants to be responsible for rewriting the book. Everyone at the table shrugged. I stared into the distance, deciding whether I should kill myself before or after dessert. I'd just spent two years writing the US edition and couldn't bear the thought of starting all over again and learning how finances work in another country. Would you want to?

I shouldn't have worried! Hodder & Stoughton put together a great team to help me with all the changes that were needed for the UK. My editor Lisa Highton had so much enthusiasm and assured me I could rest easy in her hands. Heather Rainbow helped me translate American financial terms into UK terms to make sure everything made sense, and Independent Financial Advisor Sarah Pennells took a look at the financial specifics, so I'd know I was offering the right advice for the UK.

However, there are a few things you need to know about to get the most out of my advice. I figured I should talk to you in the language of British Pounds Sterling, but whenever I refer to myself, or a friend over here, I've kept the dollar references because it doesn't make any sense to translate that. The principles in getting rich are the same no matter if you use $ or £. There were other things that got translated too:

"college/school" became "university"
"checking account" became "current account"
"mutual fund" became "actively managed fund"
"index fund" became "tracker fund"
and "popsicle" became "ice lolly" (this cracked me up)

However, this isn't to say I've changed everything. I'm afraid you'll have to put up with my American spelling! I've changed things where necessary and most important, but I've kept the core the same. There are some instances, however, where I couldn't change specific examples so I want to give you a heads up on a few American terms that you'll come across:

401(k) = a retirement account set up by the company you work for
IRA = Individual Retirement Account
Roth IRA / Roth 401(k) = the same thing, but with tax incentives

Basically, they are all different kinds of pensions. As I've said, it's the principles that matter, not the terms, so don't worry if you don't know the ins and outs of it all! When it comes to specifics, I've got lots of information and advice about UK pensions as well as ISAs.

Lots of people like to believe that personal finance is rational and we always make the best decisions for our personal situations. That's complete nonsense. We're profoundly influenced by culture, psychology, and personal biases.

That's why it's important to acknowledge that young people in the UK are generally more wary of investing than young people in the US. The US stock market has, historically, given higher returns than the UK market does. Perhaps this is why Americans are more ready to risk some cash. But lower returns shouldn't put you off—investing is still a great way to get earning more money and you'll still be earning much more than you would with only a savings account. In fact, this should just encourage you to get investing sooner. Start Investing today so you can earn far more than your friends and completely crush them over the long term, silently gloating all the while. I'll show you how.

I know student debt is an increasing worry for young Brits, especially as fees keep rising. It can feel unaffordable, but education is important—even with the added debt, it will help you increase your wealth. I've included specific recommendations for paying off student debt in the UK.

By going through this 6-week program, you'll be able to identify the best accounts, figure out what to do with your money, set up a spending plan that doesn't nag you for buying the things you love, and automatically invest for the future. Nobody wants to be a personal-finance expert—we just want to control our money to ensure it's doing the right thing so that we can get on with our lives. Being rich isn't just about how much money we have—but having more money helps.

I'm thrilled to pass along the system that has helped thousands of people in the US focus on living a rich life. Please let me know how this works for you.

Ramit

Contents

WOULD YOU RATHER BE SEXY OR RICH?

I've always wondered why so many people get fat after college. I'm not talking about people with medical disorders, but regular people who were slim in college and vowed that they would "never, ever" get fat. Five years later, they look like the Stay Puft Marshmallow Man after a Thanksgiving feast, featuring a blue whale for dessert.

Weight gain doesn't happen overnight. If it did, it would be easy for us to see it coming—and to take steps to avoid it. Ounce by ounce, it creeps up on us as we're driving to work and then sitting behind a computer for eight to ten hours a day. It happens when we move into the real world from a college campus populated by bicyclists, runners, and varsity athletes who once inspired us to keep fit (or guilted us into it). When we did the walk of shame back at school, at least we were getting exercise. But try talking about post-college weight loss with your friends and see if they ever say one of these things:

"Avoid carbs!"
*"Don't eat before you go to bed, because fat doesn't burn
efficiently when you're sleeping."*
"If you eat mostly protein, you can lose lots of weight quickly."
"Eating grapefruit in the morning speeds up your metabolism."

I always laugh when I hear these things. Maybe they're correct, or maybe they're not, but that's not really the point.

The point is that we love to debate minutiae.

When it comes to weight loss, 99.99 percent of us need to know only two things: Eat less and exercise more. Only elite athletes need to do more. But instead of accepting these simple truths and acting on them, we discuss trans fats, diet pills, and Atkins versus South Beach.

WHY ARE MONEY AND FOOD SO SIMILAR?

When it comes to food, we ...	When it comes to personal finance, we ...
don't track calorie intake	don't track spending
eat more than we know	spend more than we realize— or admit
debate minutiae about calories, diets, and workouts	debate minutiae about interest rates and hot stocks
value anecdotal advice over research	listen to friends, our parents, and TV talking heads instead of reading a few good personal-finance books

Most of us fall into one of two camps in regard to our money: We either ignore it and feel guilty, or we obsess over financial details by arguing interest rates and geopolitical risks without taking action. Both options yield the same results—none. The truth is that the vast majority of young people don't need a financial adviser to help them get rich. We need to set up accounts at a reliable no-fee bank and then automate savings and bill payment. We need to know about a few things to invest in, and then we need to let our money grow for thirty years. But that's not sexy, is it? Instead, we watch shows with talking heads who make endless predictions about the economy and "this year's hottest stock" without ever being held accountable for their picks (which are wrong more than 50 percent of the time). Sometimes they throw chairs, which drives up ratings but not much else. And we look to these so-called "experts" more than ever in turbulent times like the global crisis of 2008. "It's going up!" "No, down." As long as there is *something* being said, we're drawn to it.

Why? Because we love to debate minutiae.

When we do, we somehow feel satisfied. We might just be spinning our wheels and failing to change anyone's mind, but we feel as if we are really expressing ourselves, and it's a good feeling. We feel like we're getting somewhere. The problem is that this feeling is totally illusory. Focusing on these details is the easiest way to get nothing done. Imagine the last time you and your friend talked about finances or fitness. Did you go for a run afterward? Did you send money to your savings account? Of course not.

People love to argue minor points, partially because they feel it absolves them from actually having to do anything. You know what? Let the fools debate the details. I decided to learn about money by taking small steps to manage my own spending. Just as you don't have to be a certified nutritionist to lose weight or an automotive engineer to drive a car, you don't have to know everything about personal finance to be rich. I'll repeat myself: *You don't have to be an expert to get rich.* You *do* have to know how to cut through all the information and *get started*—which, incidentally, also helps reduce the guilt.

It's the first time since graduating a year ago that I'm earning enough to start paying back my student loan, so joining the company pension and saving for retirement was the last thing on my mind. However, when I noticed that my company would invest 5% for my 3%, I realised opting out would be throwing money away, and as Ramit says, it's better to start early. Because it comes out before I even see the money, I don't miss what I never had, so I can keep dreaming about cruising the world as soon as I retire.

—**FARAH SHAFIQ, 22**

Who wins at the end of the day? The self-satisfied people who heatedly debate some obscure details? Or the people who sidestep the entire debate and get started?

Why Is Managing Money So Hard?

People have lots and lots of reasons for not managing their money, some of them valid but most of them poorly veiled excuses for laziness. Yeah, I'm talking to you. Let's look at a few:

INFO GLUT

The idea that—gasp!—there is too much information is a real and valid concern. "But Ramit," you might say, "that flies in the face of all American culture! We need more information so we can make better decisions! People on TV say this all the time, so it must be true! Huzzah!" Sorry, nope. Look at the actual data and you'll see that an abundance of information can lead to decision paralysis, a fancy way of saying that with too much information, we do nothing. Barry Schwartz writes about this in *The Paradox of Choice: Why More Is Less:*

> . . . *As the number of investment funds in a pension plan offered to employees goes up, the likelihood that they will choose a fund—any fund—goes down. For every 10 funds added to the array of options, the rate of participation drops 2 percent. And for those who do invest, added fund options increase the chances that employees will invest in ultraconservative money-market funds.*

You read the papers and see ads about shares, pensions, ISAs, insurance, child trust funds, and international investing. Where do you start? Are you already too late? What do you do? Too often, the answer is nothing—and doing nothing is the worst choice you can make, especially in your twenties. As the table on the next page shows, investing early is the best thing you can do.

Look carefully at that chart. Smart Sally actually invests less, but ends up with about £15,000 more. She invests £100/month from age twenty-five to age thirty-five and then never touches that money again. Dumb Dan is too preoccupied to worry about money until he's thirty-five, at which point he starts investing £100/month until he's sixty-five. In other words, Smart Sally invests for ten years and Dumb Dan for thirty years—but Smart Sally has much more money. And that's just with £100/month! The single most important thing you can do to be rich is to start early.

HOW TO MAKE £15,000 MORE THAN YOUR FRIENDS (WITH LESS WORK)

	Smart Sally	Dumb Dan
When beginning to invest, the person is . . .	25 years old	35 years old
Each person invests £100/month for . . .	10 years	30 years
With a 7 percent rate of return, at age 65, their accounts are worth . . .	£135,044. Voilà—the value of starting early	£121,287. Even though he invested for three times as long, he's behind by £15,000

Source: www.thisismoney/calculators

THE MEDIA IS PARTIALLY TO BLAME (I LOVE CASTING BLAME)

Why does just about everything written about personal finance make me want to paint myself with honey and jump into a nest of fire ants? Personal-finance advice has been geared toward old white men and taught by old white men for far too long. I don't understand why newspaper columnists continue to write about tax-optimization strategies and spending less on lattes, hoping that young people will listen. We don't care about that. We care about knowing where our money's going and redirecting it to go where we *want* it to go. We want our money to

WE DON'T WANT TO HAVE TO BECOME FINANCIAL EXPERTS TO GET RICH.

grow automatically, in accounts that don't nickel-and-dime us with fees. And we don't want to have to become financial experts to get rich.

Now, I fully recognize that I'm a big fancy author (that's right, ladies) and am therefore part of the "media." Perhaps it's uncouth to mock my brethren. Still, I can't help myself. Pick up any major magazine and chances are you'll see an article called "10 No-Hassle Tips for Getting Ahead with Your Finances." Amusingly, the same writers who breathlessly encouraged us to buy real estate in 2007 are now advising us on "what to do in the downturn." I'm sick and tired of the same old boring, tired, and frankly horrible financial opinions that are paraded around as "advice." More on this in Chapter 6.

OTHER PEOPLE WE CAN BLAME FOR OUR MONEY PROBLEMS

There are other common excuses for why we don't manage our money. Most of them are complete B.S.:

- "Our education system doesn't teach this," people whine. It's easy for people in their twenties to wish that their colleges had offered some personal-finance training. Guess what? Most colleges *do* offer those classes. You just didn't attend!

- I also often hear the cry that "credit-card companies and banks are out to profit off us." Yes, they are. So stop complaining and learn how to game the companies instead of letting them game you.

- "I'm afraid of losing money," some of my friends say. That's fair, especially after market losses during the global financial crisis, but you need to take a long-term view. Also, you can choose among many different investment options—some aggressive, some conservative— it depends on how much risk you're willing to take. (Because of inflation, you're actually losing money every day your money is sitting in a bank account.) Fear is no excuse to do nothing with your money. When others are scared, there are bargains to be found.

- "What if I don't know where to get an extra £100 per month?" It doesn't have to be £100. And you don't need to earn another penny. I'll show you how to streamline your existing spending to generate that money to invest. Remember, £1 saved per day is £30 saved per month.

Too many of us are paralyzed by the thought that we have to get every single part of our personal finances in order before truly getting started managing our money. Should I use my pension from work or open an ISA? Should I go for pooled funds or individual stocks? Do I need a variable annuity? Here's my answer: Do you need to be the Iron Chef to cook a grilled-cheese sandwich? No, and once you make your first meal, it'll be easier to cook the next most complicated thing. The single most important factor to getting rich is getting started, not being the smartest person in the room.

Put the Excuses Aside

Listen up, crybabies: This isn't your grandma's house and I'm not going to bake you cookies and coddle you. A lot of your financial problems are caused by one person: you. Instead of blaming "the economy" and corporate America for your financial situation, you need to focus on what you can change yourself. Just as the diet industry has overwhelmed us with too many choices, personal finance is a confusing mess of overblown hype, myths, outright deception—and us, feeling guilty about not doing enough or not doing it right. But we can't just blame corporations and the media: With both food and money, we're not taking personal responsibility to step up, learn this stuff, and get started. The result is that many of us end up fat, consumption-minded, and poor. No, seriously: Two-thirds of Americans are overweight or obese, and the average American is nearly $7,000 in debt. In the UK the average debt is nearly £5,000, excluding mortgages.

BECAUSE OF INFLATION, YOU'RE ACTUALLY LOSING MONEY EVERY DAY YOUR MONEY IS SITTING IN A BANK ACCOUNT.

In 2008, when the global financial crisis really erupted in the stock market, the first thing many people did was pull their money out of the market. That's almost always a bad move. They compounded one mistake—not having a diversified portfolio—with a second: buying high and selling low. For all the people who blamed the government, CEOs, and evil banks, had any of them read *one* personal finance book? And yet they expected to get ahead with their money?

Let's put the excuses aside. What if you could consciously decide how to spend your money, rather than say, "I guess that's how much I spent last month"? What if you could build an automatic infrastructure that made all your accounts work together and automated your savings? What if you could invest simply and regularly without fear? Guess what? You can! I'll show you how to take the money you're making and redirect it to the places you want it to go—including substantially growing your money over the long term, no matter what the economy is like.

The Key Messages of
I Will Teach You to Be Rich

I believe in small steps. I want to reduce the number of choices that paralyze us. It's more important to get started than to spend an exhaustive amount of time researching the best fund in the universe. *I Will Teach You to Be Rich* is about taking the first step—understanding the barriers that keep us from managing our money—and then tearing them down and putting our money in the right places so we can achieve our goals. Frankly, your goal probably isn't to become a financial expert. It's to live your life and let money serve you. So instead of saying, "How much money do I need to make?" you'll say, "What do I want to do with my life—and how can I use money to do it?" And instead of being driven by fear, you'll be guided by what history has shown us about investing and growth.

I'll keep it simple: Too many books try to cover everything about money, leaving you holding a book that you "should" read but don't because it's overwhelming. I want you to know enough to get started setting up automated accounts and investing, even with just £50. So here are the essential messages of *I Will Teach You to Be Rich:*

The 85 Percent Solution: Getting started is more important than becoming an expert. Too many of us get overwhelmed thinking we need to manage our money perfectly, which leads us to do nothing at all. That's why the easiest way to manage your money is to take it one step at a time—and not worry about being perfect. I'd rather act and get it 85 percent right than do nothing. Think about it: 85 percent of the way is far better than 0 percent. Once your money system is good enough—or 85 percent of the way there—you can get on with your life and go do the things you really want to do.

It's okay to make mistakes. It's better to make them together now, with a little bit of money, so that when you have more, you'll know what to avoid.

Ordinary actions get ordinary results. Most people are, by definition, ordinary. Yet more than half of a group of college graduates surveyed said they plan to be millionaires by the age of forty, an expectation that is not in line with reality. Look around you: How many of our parents are millionaires? Not many. And if we follow the same ordinary route they did, we'll end up ordinary, too. To be extraordinary, you don't have to be a genius, but you do need to take some different steps than your folks did (like starting to manage your money and investing early).

There's a difference between being sexy and being rich. When I hear people talk about the stocks they bought, sold, or shorted last week, I realize that my investment style sounds pretty boring: "Well, I bought a few good funds five years ago and haven't done anything since, except buy more on an automatic schedule." But investment isn't about being sexy—it's about making money, and when you look at investment literature, buy-and-hold investing wins over the long term, every time. Forget what that money TV station or finance magazine says about the stock-of-the-month. Do some analysis, make your decision, and then reevaluate your investment every six months or so. It's not as sexy as those guys in red coats shouting and waving their hands on TV, but as an individual investor, you'll get far greater returns.

Spend extravagantly on the things you love, and cut costs mercilessly on the things you don't. This book isn't about telling you to stop buying lattes. Instead, it's about being able to actually spend *more* on the things you love by not spending money on all the knucklehead things you don't care about. Look, it's easy to want the best of everything: We want to go out all the time, live in a great apartment, buy new clothes, drive a new car, and travel any time we want. The truth is, you have to prioritize. My friend Jim once called to tell me that he'd gotten a raise at work. On the same day, he moved into a smaller apartment. Why? Because he doesn't care very much about where he lives, but he loves spending money on camping and biking. That's called conscious spending. (Learn how one of my friends consciously spends $21,000 per year going out on page 98.)

I Will Teach You to Be Rich is about sensible banking, saving, spending, and investing. I'll teach you how to set up your accounts to create an automatic financial infrastructure that will run smoothly with minimal intervention. You'll also learn what to avoid, some surprising findings from financial literature (is real estate really a good investment?), and how to avoid common financial mistakes. And you'll start taking action instead of debating minutiae. All this will take you just six weeks—then you'll be on the road to being rich. Doesn't that sound good?

When I was in high school, my parents told me that if I wanted to go to college, I'd need to pay for it with scholarships. So like a good Indian son, I started applying . . . and applying and applying. In the end, I'd applied for about seventy scholarships and had won hundreds of thousands of dollars.

But my best scholarship was the first one—an award for $2,000. The organization wrote a check directly to me. I took it and invested in the stock market—and immediately lost half my money.

Oops. That's when I decided that I really needed to learn about money. I read the personal-finance books, watched the TV shows, and bought the magazines. After a while, I also started sharing what I'd learned. I taught informal classes to friends at Stanford. Then, in 2004, I began writing a blog called "I Will Teach You to Be Rich," where I cover the basics of saving, banking, budgeting, and investing. The rest, as they say, is history.

Why Do You Want to Be Rich?

I've talked to more than a million young people about personal finance over the last four years through my website and speaking engagements. When I do, I always ask two questions:

Why do you want to be rich?

What does being rich mean to you?

Most people never spend even ten minutes thinking through what *rich* means to them. Suckers. Here's a hint: It's different for everyone, and money is just a small part of being rich. For example, my friends all value different things. Dan loves eating out at super gourmet restaurants where a meal might cost $100. Anton loves traveling. And Jen loves buying jeans. If you don't consciously choose what *rich* means, it's easy to end up mindlessly trying to keep up with your friends. I consider myself rich now that I can do these things:

- *Make career decisions because I want to, not because of money*

- *Help my parents with their retirement, so they don't have to work if they don't want to*

- *Spend extravagantly on the things I love and be relentlessly frugal about the things I don't (e.g., spend lots on visiting family in New York, but don't buy the flashiest sports car)*

- *Start a scholarship fund for young entrepreneurs (launched in May 2006!)*

Before you go further, I encourage you to set your goals today. Why do you want to be rich? What do you want to do with your wealth?

What You'll Get Out of This Book

I love to laugh at people when they talk about investing. People think that investing means "buying stocks," so they throw around fancy terms like *hedge funds, derivatives,* and *call options.* Sadly, they actually think you need this level of complexity to get rich because they see people talking about this stuff on TV each day. Guess what? For individual investors like you and me, these options are completely irrelevant.

It sounds sexy, but when individual investors talk about complicated concepts like this, it's like two elementary school tennis players arguing about the string tension of their racquets. Sure, it might matter a little, but they'd be much better tennis players if they just went outside and hit some balls for a few hours each day.

Simple, long-term investing works. This idea gets nothing but yawns and rolling eyes during a conversation. But you need to make a decision: Do you want to sit around impressing others with your sexy vocabulary, or do you want to join me on my gold-lined throne as we're fed grapes and fanned with palm fronds?

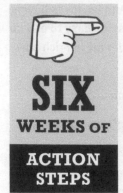

SIX
WEEKS OF
ACTION STEPS

I Will Teach You to Be Rich will help you figure out where your money is going and redirect it to where you *want* it to go. Saving for a vacation to China? A wedding? Just want to make your money grow? Here's the six-week program that will let you tackle it.

IN WEEK 1, you'll set up your credit cards and learn how to improve your credit history (and why that's so important).

IN WEEK 2, you'll set up the right bank accounts, including negotiating to get no-fee, high-interest accounts.

IN WEEK 3, you'll open a pension and an investment account (even if you have just £50 to start).

IN WEEK 4, you'll figure out how much you're spending. And then you'll figure out how to make your money go where you want it to go.

IN WEEK 5, you'll automate your new infrastructure to make your accounts play together nicely.

IN WEEK 6, you'll learn why investing isn't the same as picking stocks—and how you can get the most out of the market with very little work.

Plus, there's plenty more. You'll learn to choose a low-cost automatic portfolio that beats typical Wall Street portfolios, and how to maintain your investments by setting up a system that enables you to remain as hands-off as possible while your money accumulates automatically. There are even answers to many specific money questions, including how to buy a car, pay for a wedding, and negotiate your salary.

After reading this book, you'll be better prepared to manage your finances than 99 percent of other people in their twenties and early thirties. You'll know what accounts to open up, ways not to pay your bank extra fees, how to invest, how to think about money, and how to see through a lot of the hype that you see on TV and in magazines every day.

There aren't any secrets to getting rich—it just takes small steps and some discipline, and you can do it with just a little bit of work. Now let's get started.

CHAPTER 1

OPTIMIZE YOUR CREDIT CARDS

How to beat the credit card companies at their own game

You'll never see an Indian driving a two-door coupe. Seriously, think about it. If you have a neighborhood Indian—let's call him Raj—he's probably driving a four-door car, usually a Honda Accord or Toyota Camry. However, Indian people aren't just fanatical about driving practical four-door cars. We're absolutely nuts about hammering down the price to the last penny. Take my dad, for example. He'll bargain for *five straight days* just to buy one car. Dear God, it's not pretty. I've been along for the ride on these weeklong negotiating sessions with him before. Once, as he was literally about to sign the papers, he stopped, asked them to throw in free floor mats (a $50 value), and *walked away when they refused*. This, after he'd spent five days bargaining them down. As he dragged me from the dealership, I just stared straight ahead, shell-shocked.

As you can imagine, by the time I went to buy my own car, I had been steeped in a rich tradition of negotiating. I knew how to make unreasonable demands with a straight face and never take no for an answer. I took a more modern approach, however: Instead of spending a week going from dealership to dealership, I simply invited seventeen dealers in northern California to bid against one another for my business while I sat at home, watched *The Real World,* and calmly reviewed the e-mails and faxes as they came in. (For more about buying a car, see page 244.) In the end, I found a great deal in Palo Alto and walked in ready to sign the papers. Everything was going smoothly until the dealer went to check my credit. He came back smiling. "You know, you have the best credit of anyone I've ever seen at your age," he said.

"Thanks," I replied, actually wanting to say, "AWWW, YEAH, I KNEW IT." That is because I am a weird twentysomething Indian who chooses a four-door Accord for his dream car and prides himself on his credit score.

Then the dealer said, "Hmm."

"Hmm?" I asked.

"Well," he said, "it looks like you have great credit, but not enough credit sources." The bottom line, he told me, was that they couldn't offer me the low-interest option we had talked about. Instead of 1.9 percent interest, it would be 4.9 percent. That didn't sound like much, but I pulled out a notepad and did a quick calculation. The difference would be more than $2,200 over the life of my car loan. Because I was getting such a great deal on the car, I convinced myself that the higher interest rate was okay, and I signed the papers for the loan. But I was still pissed. Why should I have to pay an extra two grand when I had great credit?

How Credit Can Help You Be Rich

People love to pick sexy investments and use fancy words like *distressed securities* and *EBITDA* when they focus on getting rich. But they often ignore something that is so simple, so basic, that it just doesn't seem important: their credit. Ironically, credit is one of the most vital factors in getting rich, but because it's hard to wrap our minds around it, we often overlook it entirely. It's time to wake up and pay attention to it (and not just because of the credit crisis), because establishing good credit is the first step in building an infrastructure for getting rich. Think about it: Our largest purchases are almost always made on credit, and people with good credit save tens of thousands of pounds on these purchases. Credit has a far greater impact on your finances than saving a few pounds a day on a cup of coffee.

What you saw in 2008 was the unraveling of credit, including personal spending that relied on unaffordable credit from credit cards and remortgaging. Those days of easy credit are gone (at least for a while until we forget history and do it all over again). So understanding your credit is more important than ever.

There are two main components to credit (also known as your credit history): the credit report and the credit score. These boring terms can actually save you tens of thousands of pounds over your lifetime, so listen up. This is what will enable you to justify heading to Vegas and staying at the Hugh Hefner suite at the Palms.

CREDIT SCORE VS. CREDIT REPORT

What your credit score is based on:	What your credit report includes:
35% payment history (How reliable you are. Late payments hurt you.)	■ Basic identification information— if you're on the electoral roll, if your address is listed in the Royal Mail Postcode Address File and how long you've lived there
25% stability How old you are, how long you've lived in the same place and if you rent or own.	■ Court actions and insolvency history—County Court Judgments, bankruptcies and similar public records
2% court actions Legally, lenders cannot give loans to bankrupts and they aren't willing to lend to anyone taken to court for debt arrears.	■ Your credit history, or whom you've paid, how consistently, and any late payments over the last six years
5–7% credit activity People who aren't 'credit active' can be considered higher risk.	■ Fraud warnings—suspected fraudulent applications sent from your address by anyone, and 'goneaway' incidents recorded against you
8–10% other stuff This varies widely, but can include marital status, existing relationship with the lender and even information based on your postcode.	■ Credit inquiries, or who else has requested your credit (like other lenders)
Get your free credit score at www.checkmyfile.com.	Get your free credit report once a year at www.annualcreditreport.co.uk.

Source: www.checkmyfile.com

Your **credit report** gives potential lenders—the people who are considering lending you money for a car or home—basic information about you, your accounts, and your payment history. In general, it tracks all credit-related activities, although recent activities are given higher weight.

Your **credit score** is a single, easy-to-read number between 0 and 1000 that represents your credit risk to lenders. It's like Cliff's Notes for the credit industry. The lenders take this number (higher is better) and, with a few other pieces of information, such as your salary and age, decide if they'll lend you money for credit like a credit card, mortgage, or car loan. They'll charge you more or less for the loan, depending on the score, which signifies how risky you are. But each lender also has its own scoring system, so different lenders might give you a higher score.

By law you can get your credit file for £2 from each of the three credit reference agencies; www.equifax.co.uk, www.experian.co.uk and www.callcredit.co.uk. You can get it for free by signing up to a trial of their pay-for services or free once a year (with no commitments) at www.annualcreditreport.co.uk. It includes basic information about all your accounts and payment history. Be careful to type that URL correctly, not the one that first comes to mind when you think "free credit report."

You can get an indication of your credit *score* for free at www.checkmyfile.com or you can pay for one from one of the credit reference agencies. Just pick any one—it doesn't really matter.

Why are your credit report and credit score important? Because a good credit score can save you hundreds of thousands of pounds in interest charges. How? Well, if you have good credit, it makes you less risky to lenders, meaning they can offer you a better interest rate on loans. "But Ramit," you might say naively, "I don't care about this. I don't need to borrow money." Maybe you don't today. But in three or four years, you might need to start thinking about a wedding or a house. What about cars? Vacations? Those ridiculous baby cribs that cost £7,000? And it goes on and on.

So please don't scoff or dismiss what you just read. One of the key differences between rich people and everyone else is that rich people plan before they need to plan.

If you doubt that a loan's interest rate really makes that much of a difference, check out the following table. Assuming you borrowed £200,000 on a 25-year interest-only mortgage, look at the differences in what you'd pay based on your credit score.

HOW CREDIT SCORES AFFECT WHAT YOU PAY

On a £200,000 25-year interest-only mortgage, if your credit score is . . .	. . . your APR (interest rate) might be . . .	. . . which means you'd pay interest . . .
851–1000 (best range)	2.5%	£125,000
781–850	2.75%	£137,000
620–780	3.0%	£150,000
450–699	4.5%	£225,000
0–499 (worst range)	You probably wouldn't get a mortgage	

Source: checkmyfile.com, based on a base interest rate of 0.5%

As you can see, a high credit score can save you hundreds of thousands of pounds over your lifetime—and that's just on a mortgage. While other people spend many hours cutting coupons, growing food in their gardens to save on grocery bills, or being frugal with lattes, they're failing to see the bigger picture. It's fine to be frugal, but you should focus on spending time on the things that matter, the *big wins*. So, let's dig into tactics for improving your credit, which is quantifiably worth much more than any advice about frugality.

Building Credit with Credit Cards

Credit comes in many forms (car loans, mortgages, and so on), but we're going to start with credit cards because almost all of us have one, and most important, they're the fastest and most concrete way to optimize your credit. Most people are making at least one or two major mistakes with their credit cards. The good news is that it's incredibly easy to fix this by learning a little bit about how credit cards work.

GUESS HOW MUCH AN iPOD COSTS IF YOU FINANCE IT WITH A CREDIT CARD?

One of the biggest problems with credit cards is the hidden cost of using them. It may be incredibly convenient to swipe your card at every retailer, but if you don't pay your bill the same month, you'll end up owing way more than you realize. Take, for instance, an iPod. If it looks like it costs £250, and you buy it using a credit card with the average 16% APR and a 2.5% minimum payment, and then only pay the minimum each month, you'll be out almost 20 percent more in total.

Let's say you buy this . . .	Paying minimum payments, it will take this long to pay it off . . .	You'll pay this much in interest . . .
£250 iPod	6 years 3 months	£136.38
£1,500 computer	18 years 8 months	£1,492.48
£10,000 furniture	31 years 11 months	£10,713.78

If you paid only the minimum monthly balance on your £10,000 purchase, it would take you more than 31 years and cost you more than £10,700 in interest alone. Remember, this doesn't even factor in your "opportunity cost": if you'd invested the same amount and earned 7%, it would've turned into about £81,451! Try calculating how much your own purchases really cost at www. whatsthecost.com/creditcard.aspx

From one perspective, credit cards are like a delightful gift from heaven. If you pay your bill on time, they're actually a free short-term loan. They help you keep track of your spending much more easily than cash, and online card providers let you download your transaction history for free. All credit cards offer free consumer protection (unless they're business cards) and some may have extra benefits too. But unfortunately, there's more to them than that.

Credit cards are also convenient enemies. Almost everyone has a bad story about late fees, unauthorized charges, or overspending. Not surprisingly, many pundits (and parents) have a knee-jerk reaction to credit cards: "Using credit cards is the worst financial decision you can make," they shout. "Cut them all up!" What an easy battle cry for people who want simple solutions and don't realize the benefits of multiple sources of credit.

The truth about credit cards lies somewhere between these two extremes. As long as you manage them well, they're worth having. But if you don't completely pay off your bill at the end of the month, you'll owe an enormous amount of interest on the remainder, usually about 16 percent. This is what's known as the annual percentage rate, or APR. Credit card companies also tack on a whopping fee every time you miss a payment—usually around £12. And don't forget the fees for making a payment even just a day or two late. It's also easy to overuse credit cards and find yourself in debt, as so many credit card users have done.

Most of us don't think about these fees. We just charge away and then make our monthly payments, right? Unfortunately, although they're not obvious, credit card charges are some of the largest unnecessary fees you'll ever pay—much more than the costs of eating out once a week or buying that nice outfit you've been eyeing.

This isn't meant to scare you away from using credit cards. In fact, I encourage you to use credit cards *responsibly*. If you can avoid the unreasonable fees and tricks, credit cards offer exceptional benefits (more on this later). To get the most out of using credit, you need to optimize your credit card(s) and use them as a spearhead to improve your overall credit. This is all the more important in the wake of the credit crisis; if you don't have good credit, it may be difficult to get an affordable home loan—even if you have a high income. By the end of this chapter, you'll know how to squeeze the credit card companies for everything they're worth—without paying unnecessary fees or late charges—and you'll know how to use your cards to boost your all-important credit score. Let's do it.

Getting a New Card

Whether you've never had a credit card before or you're thinking about getting an additional card, there are a few things to think about.

Avoid those credit card offers you receive in the mail. Let's cut to the chase: If you hate those credit card offers in the mail as much as I do, visit www.mpsonline.org.uk to get off their lists. The average American receives twenty credit card offers every year, and four out of every thousand people accept them. The numbers are markedly different for students. Out of every thousand students who are mailed offers, 150 accept them, an astonishingly high number. Students—and young people in general—are especially susceptible to these offers because they don't know any better. Let's get real. Taking a credit card offer you get in the mail is like marrying the first person who touches your arm—99 percent of the time it's the easy decision, not the right one. Most people know better and go out and find what's best for them; they don't just settle for the horrible offers that fall in their lap. For something as important as your credit, make the effort and pick a good card.

Avoid cash-back cards, which don't actually pay you much cash. People get really mad at me when I say this, but cash-back cards are worthless. "Get 1 percent back on all your spending!" Wow, if I spend £2,000 per

Getting a Credit Card When You Have No Income

A while ago, one of my friends called me and asked if she could borrow my credit card to buy something online. "How come? Don't you have a credit card?" I asked. Given all the benefits of having a card (assuming you use it wisely), you can imagine how angry I was when I learned that she didn't have a card of her own. In my mind, this was the equivalent of one of Dr. Koop's friends being morbidly obese because of eating only butter.

Anyway, I told her to get a credit card and start building her credit. Her response: "I can't get approved for a credit card because I have no income."

Okay, fair enough. Getting your first credit card can be tricky, especially if you're young. But there's an easy solution: Get a credit building card. These cards can have hefty interest rates of 30% or more, but if you pay off whatever you owe in full, it won't matter. After a year or so, assuming you've behaved responsibly, you can graduate to a lower rate card or get a regular one if your income level justifies it. To get one, call your bank and ask about it.

month on my credit card, I'll get back £20. "But Ramit," you might say, "twenty pounds is better than nothing." Sure, but what if you could save more by getting a free £500 flight? It wouldn't be as obvious as receiving money each month, but in the long term, you'd save more with a travel rewards card.

Compare cards online. The best way to find a card that is right for you is by researching different offers online (try www.moneyfacts.co.uk). In most cases, the simplest credit cards are offered by your bank, so this is often a good place to look. They'll connect with your bank account and you can choose from a variety of options, including credit limit, rewards, and more. On the plus side, they're easy to get without much research. The downside is that the rewards are usually fairly mediocre.

Rewards are important. You're going to be using this card a fair amount, so make sure the rewards it offers are something you'll actually want. I travel a lot, so I got an airline card that gives me free companion tickets, free flights, and points for every dollar I spend and every mile I fly. I get multiple free flights per year, and each one saves me about $350. But if you hardly ever travel, this card wouldn't make sense for you. Bottom line: If you're getting a rewards card, find one that gives you something you value.

Don't go card crazy. Now that you're in the market, you might be tempted by any number of card offers. But don't overdo it. There's no magic number of cards you should have. But each additional card you get means added complexity for your personal-finance system. Two or three is a good rule of thumb. (The average American has four credit cards.) Your credit score is based on overall sources of credit. Remember, there are other sources of credit besides credit cards. These include installment loans (such as auto loans), personal lines of credit, home equity lines of credit, and service credit (such as utilities). "Take it slow," Craig Watts of Fair Isaac Corporation says, cautioning against prescribing a specific number of credit sources. "It depends on how long you've been managing credit. The less information in your credit report, the higher the prominence of each new report. For example, if you're in college and you only have one credit card in your name, when you open another account, the weight of that action is more than it would be ten years down the line. If you limit yourself to opening one card a year, you'll be doing yourself a favor."

The Six Commandments of Credit Cards

Now it's time to take full advantage of your cards as a means to improving your credit. Optimizing your credit is a multi-step process. One of the most important factors is getting out of debt, which we'll tackle at the end of the chapter. But first, we'll set up automatic credit card payments so you never miss a payment again. Then, we'll see how to cut fees, get better rewards, and take everything you can from the credit card companies. (Hey, it's business, and they're in it to get your money, too.)

1. Pay off your credit card regularly.

Yeah, we've all heard it, but what you may not know is that your debt payment history represents 35 percent of your credit score—the largest

Awful Consequences

If you miss even one payment on your credit card, here are four terrible, horrible, no good, very bad results you may face:

1. Your credit score can drop. The amount will vary from lender to lender and future borrowing could be more difficult and expensive.

2. Your credit card provider may raise your interest rate or lower your limit.

3. You'll be charged a late fee, usually around £12.

4. Your late payment can trigger rate increases on your other credit cards as well, even if you've never been late on them because many lenders monitor existing customers' credit reports. (I find this fact amazing.)

Don't get too freaked out: You can recover from the hit to your credit score, usually within a few months. In fact, if you're just a few days late with your payment, you may incur a fee, but it won't always be reported to the credit reference agencies. Turn the page to find out what to do if you miss a payment.

chunk. In fact, the single most important thing you can do to improve your credit is to pay your bills on time. Whether you're paying the full amount of your credit card bill or risking my wrath by paying just part of it, *pay it on time*. Lenders like prompt payers, so don't give your credit card company the opportunity to raise your rates and lower your credit score by being a few days late with your payment. This is a great example of focusing on what will get you rich, not on what's sexy. Think about your friends who catalog every single website to get the best deals on travel or clothes. They might be thrilled after saving £10—and they can brag to everyone about all the special deals they get—but you'll quietly save thousands by understanding the invisible importance of credit, paying your bills on time, and having a better credit score.

"Paying your bills on time is absolutely critical," says FICO's Craig Watts. "It's by far the most important thing you can do to improve your credit rating." If you miss a credit card payment, you might as well just get a shovel and repeatedly beat yourself in the face. The credit card companies are going to get you—and the worst part is, you earned it.

Many people pay their credit card bills online or by phone. If you haven't set up a direct debit yet, log on to your bank's website to set it up now. Note: Don't worry if you don't always have enough money in your current account to pay off the full amount you owe on your credit card. You'll get an e-mail from your card company each month before the payment goes through so that you can adjust your payment as needed.

I just totally forgot the due date for my credit card. So not only did they charge me a late fee, but they charged me interest on that month's and the previous month's purchases. I called up the customer service line of my credit card and told them that I had been a good customer in the past, and asked if they could do anything for me with the fees. The representative removed the late fee and refunded $20 of the interest charge back to my account. They returned a total of $59 to me with one phone call.

—**ERIC HENRY**, 25

---

2. Get all fees waived on your card.

This is a great, easy way to optimize your credit cards because your credit card company will do all the work for you. Call them using the phone

What to Do If You Miss a Payment

Nobody's perfect. Despite my warnings, I understand that accidents happen and you might miss a payment at some point. When this happens, I use my Indian heritage to beat the companies by negotiating with them, and you can, too:

YOU: Hi, I noticed I missed a payment, and I wanted to confirm that this won't affect my credit score.

CREDIT CARD REP: *Let me check on that. No, the late fee will be applied, but it won't affect your credit score.*

(Note: If you pay within a few days of your missed bill, it usually won't be reported to the credit agencies. Call them to be sure.)

YOU: Thank you! I'm really happy to hear that. Now, about that fee ... I understand I was late, but I'd like to have it waived.

CREDIT CARD REP: *Why?*

YOU: It was a mistake and it won't happen again, so I'd like to have the fee removed.

(Note: Always end your sentence with strength. Don't say, "Can you remove this?" Say, "I'd like to have this removed.") At this point, you have a better-than-50-percent chance of getting the fee credited to your account. But just in case you get an especially tough rep, here's what to say.

CREDIT CARD REP: *I'm very sorry, but we can't refund that fee. I can try to get you our latest blah blah marketing pitch blah blah....*

YOU: I'm sorry, but I've been a customer for four years and I'd hate for this one fee to drive me away from your service. What can you do to remove the late fee?

CREDIT CARD REP: *Hmm ... Let me check on that.... Yes, I was able to remove the fee this time. It's been credited to your account.*

You don't believe me that it can be so simple? It is. Anyone can do it.

number on the back of the card and ask if you're paying any fees, including annual fees or service charges. Luckily very few credit cards in the UK charge annual fees, but if they do, try this:

YOU: Hi, I'd like to confirm that I'm not paying any fees on my credit card.

CREDIT CARD REP: *Well, it looks like you have an annual fee of £35. That's actually one of our better rates.*

YOU: I'd rather pay no fees. Which card can you switch me to that doesn't charge fees? I'd like to make sure my credit score isn't affected by closing this account, too. Can you confirm?

Yes, I really talk like that.

The vast majority of people don't need to pay any annual fees on their credit cards, and because free credit cards are so competitive now, you rarely need to pay for the privilege of using your card. The only exception is if you spend enough to justify the extra rewards a fee-charging account offers. (If you do pay an annual fee, use the break-even calculator on my website to see if it's worth it.)

Most people should switch from a for-fee card to a free card, so ask your credit card company what they'll do for you. If they waive your fees, great! If not, switch to a no-fee credit card. I suggest you do this at the same credit card company to simplify your life—and so you don't have to close one account and open another, which will affect your credit score. If you decide to close the account and get a new credit card, look for one with no fees and good rewards (read more about those on page 29).

3. Negotiate a lower APR.

Your APR, or annual percentage rate, is the interest rate your credit card company charges you. The average APR is 16 percent, which makes it extremely expensive if you carry a balance on your card. Put another way, since you can make an average of about 8 percent in the stock market, your credit card is getting a great deal by lending you money. If you could get a 16 percent return, you'd be thrilled—you want to avoid the black hole of credit card interest payments so *you* can earn money, not give it to the credit card companies.

So, call your credit card company and ask them to lower your APR. If they ask why, tell them you've been paying the full amount of your bill on time for the last few months, and you know there are a number of credit cards offering better rates than you're currently getting. In my experience, this works about half the time. It's important to note that your APR doesn't technically matter if you're paying your bills in full every month—you could have a 2 percent APR or 80 percent APR and it would be irrelevant, since you don't pay interest if you pay your total bill each month. But this is a quick and easy way to pick the low-hanging fruit with one phone call.

4. Keep your cards for a long time and keep them active.
Lenders like to see a long history of credit, which means that the longer you hold an account, the more valuable it is for your credit score. Don't get suckered by introductory offers and low APRs. If you're happy with your card, keep it. And if you're getting a new credit card, don't close the account on your old one. Having more than one 'active' card can improve your credit score. As long as there are no fees, keep it open and use it occasionally, because some credit card companies will cancel your account after a certain period of inactivity or will start to charge you an annual fee. To avoid paying these or having your account shut down, set up a direct debit on any card that is not your primary card. For example, I set it up so that one of my credit cards pays a $12.95 monthly subscription through my checking account each month, which requires zero intervention on my part. But my credit report reflects that I've had the card for more than five years, which improves my credit score. Play it safe: If you have a credit card, keep it active using an automatic payment at least once every three months.

5. Get more credit. (Warning! Do this only if you have no debt.)
This one is counterintuitive, and to explain it, I had to reach into personal-finance lessons of yore. Many people don't realize this, but in the classic '80s Salt 'N Pepa song "Push It," when they say that the dance isn't for everybody—*"Only the sexy people"*—they are actually detailing a sound personal-finance strategy:

Before I explain, I want to first acknowledge that yes, I did just quote Salt 'N Pepa in an actual, published book. Anyway, when Salt 'N Pepa talk about "only the sexy people," what they really mean is "this tip is only for the financially responsible people." I'm serious about this warning: This tip is only for people who have no credit card debt and pay their bills in full each month. It's not for anyone else.

If lenders can see that their competitors have given you credit and you haven't fully used your card up to its limit, they will feel more comfortable about extending more credit to you. If one lender can displace a competitor's card, it's a double whammy (its own business goes up at

Always Track Your Calls to Financial Companies

Unfortunately for you, credit card companies are very good at using B.S. late fees to increase their revenues. Unfortunately for them, I'm giving you lots of tactics for getting these fees reversed. One of the best ways to improve your chances of getting fees waived is by keeping track of every time you call your financial institutions. This is especially true of credit card companies, whom you should treat just slightly better than you would an armed militia coming after your younger sister. It's tempting, when calling, to be really nasty, but because I was raised right, I don't scream or threaten violence. Instead, when I call to dispute anything, I open a spreadsheet that details the last time I called them, whom I spoke with, and what was resolved. If only all criminals were as diligent as I am. (Unfortunately, in the UK it can be more difficult to get fees waived, but it's always worth trying.)

The Pocket Tracker for Tracking Credit Card Calls

Call Date	Time	Name of Rep	Rep's ID#	Comments

Download this spreadsheet from www.iwillteachyoutoberich.com.

Whenever you make a call regarding a dispute on your credit card, you wouldn't believe how powerful it is to refer back to the last time you called—citing the rep's name, date of conversation, and your call notes. Most credit card reps you talk to will simply give in because they know you came to play in the big leagues.

When you use this to confront a credit card company or bank with data from your last calls, you'll be more prepared than 99 percent of other people—and chances are, you'll get what you want.

The Cards I Use

I have two credit cards. My primary credit card is a Citibank Premier Pass Elite. Citibank offers no-fee and for-fee versions of this card (the no-fee card offers half the rewards). I ran the calculations and decided to pay the $75 annual fee because I spend enough to justify the cost. With this card, I earn one point for every dollar I spend and one point for every mile I fly, plus free companion fares for domestic flights over $379. You can check this card out, along with the free version, at www.citicards.com.

I also have a United Airlines student card that I got many years ago. I use this card only to maintain my credit history, so I've set up an automatic charge of $12.95/month for a music subscription site (see page 26 for why this is important). You can learn more details about this card at www.united.com.

the cost of its competitor). These are the daily joys that the credit card companies enjoy. Most lenders don't take your credit utilisation rate into account (that's the amount of money you owe divided by the amount you could borrow, multiplied by 100). However, for those that do, it is true to say that if you had two credit cards and owed £500 on each (with a £1,000 credit limit), you would be seen as a better risk than someone who had one credit card with a £1,000 limit, on which they owed £1,000.

For anyone who has a lot of credit cards (especially if they have not used them for some time) the advice would be to close one or two of the accounts down, to bring down their available credit. If you only have one or two cards, you might be better off increasing your credit limit.

Here's how: Call up your card company and ask for a credit increase.

YOU: Hi, I'd like to request a credit increase. I currently have five hundred pounds available and I'd like a thousand.

CREDIT CARD REP: *Why are you requesting a credit increase?*

YOU: I've been paying my bill in full for the last eighteen months and I have some upcoming purchases. I'd like a credit limit of one thousand pounds. Can you approve my request?

REP: *Sure. I've put in a request for this increase. It should be activated in about seven days.*

I request a credit-limit increase every six to twelve months. Remember, some lenders take your credit utilization rate into account when calculating your credit score. To improve it, the first thing you should do is pay off your debt. If you've already paid off your debt, *only then* should you try to increase your available credit. Sorry to repeat myself, but this is important!

When my husband and I were in college, we got a free T-shirt or something and got credit cards with reasonable limits ($500). Sure, I had no income, but that didn't seem important at the time. Wouldn't you know it, I was responsible enough to have my limit raised to $2,000 after a very short period of time! Except that I wasn't actually responsible, and I paid thousands of dollars in interest and late fees and wrecked my credit rating for several years. It took many years for us to clear up this debt. I can't name one purchase that was truly necessary either.

—MICHELE MILLER, 38

---

6. Use your rewards!

Before I get into rewards programs, let me say this: Just like with car insurance, you can get great deals on your credit when you're a responsible customer. In fact, there are lots of tips for people who have *very good* credit. If you fall in this category, you should call your credit cards and lenders once per year to ask them what advantages you're eligible for. Often, they can waive fees, extend credit, and give you private promotions that others don't have access to. Call them up and use this line:

"Hi there. I just checked my credit and noticed that I have a 900 credit score, which is pretty good. I've been a customer of yours for the last four years, so I'm wondering what special promotions and offers you have for me . . . I'm thinking of special offers that you use for customer retention."

Credit cards also offer rewards programs that give you cash back, airline tickets, and other benefits, but most people don't take advantage of all the free stuff they can get. For example, when I had to fly to a wedding in an obscure town in Wisconsin, I redeemed my credit card's travel reward to save more than $600 on the flight. That's an easy one, but there's better: Did you know that credit cards automatically give you

Disputing a Charge: How to Mobilize Your Credit Card's Army for You

Once, when I canceled my Sprint cell phone service, they told me my account had a $160 charge. For what? I asked. Wait for it. . . . "An early cancellation fee."

Yeah, right. I knew I didn't have a contract, and I had negotiated out of an early cancellation fee a long time before that. (Mobile phone companies make a lot of money from trying these shady moves, hoping customers will get frustrated, give up, and just pay.) Unfortunately for them, ever since Sprint had started trying to rip me off three years before, I had kept records of every phone conversation I'd had with them. The customer-service rep was very polite, but insisted she couldn't do anything to erase the charge.

Really? I've heard this tune before, so I pulled out the notes I had taken the previous year and politely read them aloud to her.

As soon as I read them, I experienced a miraculous change in her ability to waive the fee. Within two minutes, my account was cleared and I was off the phone. Amazing!!!!! Thank you, madam!!!

Wouldn't it be great if that were the end of the story? Although they told me they wouldn't charge me, they did it anyway. By this point, I was so fed up that I called in the big guns.

Many people don't know that credit cards offer excellent consumer protection. This is one reason I encourage everyone to make major purchases on their credit card (and not use cash or a debit card).

I called my credit card company and told them I wanted to dispute a charge. They said, "Sure; what's your address and what's the amount?" When I told them about my experience with Sprint, they instantly gave me a temporary credit for the amount and told me to mail in a form with my complaint, which I did.

Two weeks later, the complaint was totally resolved in my favor.

In the UK, it seems that credit card companies don't have a set way of dealing with disputes (unless they're covered by the Consumer Credit Act, which I talk about on the next page).

amazing consumer protection? Here are a few examples you might not know about:

- Under section 75 of the Consumer Credit Act, you are protected if you buy goods costing between £100 and £30,000. If the goods don't arrive, aren't of suitable quality or the supplier goes bust, you can make a claim against the credit card company.

- Some credit card providers offer an extended warranty if you buy electrical goods and gadgets on your card. You normally have to register them within a specified time limit.

- You may get free travel insurance if you pay for your holiday with your card. But check the excess levels, how much medical cover you have and whether winter sports are included.

- A number of exclusive credit cards (generally those that charge a hefty annual fee) come with a concierge service. They can track down hard-to-find concert or sports tickets, classic cars or plan your holiday for you.

Most important, your credit card makes it easy for you to track your spending. For these reasons I put almost all my purchases on a credit card—especially the large ones. Call your credit card company and ask them to send you a full list of all their rewards. Then use them!

I used to have a credit card that gave me cash back, which I thought was a great idea at the time, but when I looked at the paltry amount I realised it wasn't worth the virtual ink my online statement was printed with. So I switched to a credit card tied in with an airline that already gives me frequent flyer benefits. I love travelling so this was the most logical way for me to get a great benefit. Now I'm watching the air miles stack up with every purchase and planning a free get-away!

—HEATHER CONNELL, 31

LET'S LOOK AT SOME OTHER THINGS YOU NEED TO BEAR IN MIND . . .

Plan how you use your credit cards. Closing accounts doesn't harm your credit score negatively and some lenders may prefer to see that you don't have a large line of unused credit. The idea being that if you were to make use of all the credit, you could move from 'coping well' to 'in serious debt' pretty quickly. On the other hand, it's better not to have just one card and to max out on it. If you have two cards that you've not borrowed up to the limit on, that will be better. Of course, you should pay it off in full each month anyway, otherwise you're just adding to the credit card company's profits and they're normally quite good at making money without help.

Make sure all bills have been paid in good time. Your credit record shows your payment history over the last 12 months. Lenders will want to see you've managed all your accounts well, particularly in the last six months.

Register on the electoral roll. It's the easiest step to take, but it could make all the difference to your ability to get credit. It may not technically harm your score, but lenders check the electoral roll to make sure that you are who you say you are. Check out www.aboutmyvote.co.uk to find out how to register.

Don't play the zero percent transfer game. Some people have started playing the 0 percent transfer game to profit off of credit cards by making balance transfers or taking cash advances. They take the introductory zero percent APR that you get when you open many credit cards (which usually only lasts for six months). Then they borrow money from the card at this low rate and stick it in a high-interest savings account, which allows them to profit off the interest. Some actually invest the money in short-term bonds or even stocks. At the end, they plan to return the money and keep the interest. I find these 0 percent credit card games so moronic. Sure, you can make a few quid a year, or maybe even a few hundred, but the waste of time, risk of mismanaging the process, and possibility of screwing up your credit score just aren't worth it. Most important, this is a distraction that gets you only short-term results. You're much better off building a personal-finance infrastructure that focuses on long-term growth, not on getting a few quid here or there. Dave Ramsey, a popular personal-finance author and radio host, specializes in helping people get out of debt. He says, "I have met with thousands of millionaires in my years as a financial counselor, and I have never met one who said he made it all with Discover Card bonus points.

Oh No!
My Credit Score Just Dropped

Some of my Type-A readers worry too much about their credit scores. If your credit score suddenly drops, first you should figure out why by getting a copy of your credit report and score (see page 15). Then what's important is how you deal with it going forward. Your credit score can start recovering immediately as more positive information is reported, like paying your bills on time. So work to manage your credit wisely and consistently. As FICO's Craig Watts notes, "The natural movement of these scores is to slowly grow. How do you think people end up with scores above 900? It's through years and years of consistently boring credit management."

They all lived on less than they made and spent only when they had cash." Focus on the big wins if you want bigger results.

Avoid getting sucked in by "Apply Now and Save 10 Percent in Just Five Minutes!" offers. Stay away from the cards issued by every single retail store. These cards might as well have "You Are a Dumbass" written on them in thirty-six-point type. I can't count the number of times I've seen someone standing in front of me at The Gap or Bloomingdale's who gets suckered into these cards. "If you sign up today, you'll get 10 percent off your purchase!" the clerks say. They forget to mention that these cards, with an average APR of 20–25 percent and low credit limits, are issued to people with little regard for how credit-worthy they are. And, predictably, they contain some of the most onerous terms of any cards, including tremendous rate increases if your payment is late even once. And for what? Twenty pounds off a single purchase? Ask yourself if it's worth it. Here, I'll just tell you: It's not. Stay away from store cards.

Don't make the mistake of paying for your friends with your credit card and keeping the cash—and then spending it all. Finally, please don't do the same dumb thing I keep doing. The last few times I've gone out to dinner, the bill has come, everyone has plopped down cash, and I've

Rate Chasers: Wasting Time Earning $25/Month

One of my blog readers, a guy named Mike, wrote in to tell me about his rate chasing. In this case, it was savings accounts, not credit cards, but they're very similar: It's just moving money around from one account to another to eke out a few additional percentage points.

Mike admitted, "I'm one of those rate-chasers, so [with $40k in emergency savings], I've consistently been earning anywhere between 0.65 and 0.85 percent higher than my operating money market account. . . . That's an extra $300/year in interest, which is definitely worth changing banks every four to six months for me."

MY RESPONSE: "Mike, if you were smart enough to sock away $40k in an emergency fund (which is really impressive, by the way), I bet you're smart enough to spend your time doing something better than earning $300/year—something that will let you earn much more sustainably. You're only earning $0.82/day doing that! How about spending the same time optimizing your asset allocation? (see page 170) That step alone is probably worth thousands per year. Or starting a side business? Or even spending those few hours with your family? I don't know what you value, but in my eyes, any of those things would produce more value than $300/year . . . especially for someone who's so far ahead of everyone else, like you are. This is just my two cents . . . about 1/40th of what you earned today (sorry, couldn't resist)."

Focus on the big wins to get the big results. They may not be as obvious or sexy as jumping from account to account and getting a few extra bucks, but the big wins will make you rich over the long term.

realized I can just pay on my credit card and earn some miles. Here's where things go horribly wrong. Don't wake up the next day and say, "Wow! I have £100 extra cash in my wallet!" NO!!! Put it in the bank!! I forget to do this all the time and end up regretting it. Last time, I checked my statement and had shared-meal charges of $50, $64, $25, and so on. Then, my mouth agape, I opened my wallet and saw . . . one $1 bill. Great.

Debt, Debt, Debt

Statistically speaking, being in debt is normal. And yet, think about it: Is it really normal to owe more than you have? Maybe for certain things, like a house or education, but what about for random purchases on a credit card?

Some people differentiate debts by calling them "good debt" and "bad debt," depending on if the debt appreciates (education) or depreciates (car) over time. Others despise debt altogether. Whatever the case, most of us have a lot of it. And it doesn't feel good.

I want to talk about student loans and credit card debt, the two largest types of debt facing most twentysomethings and thirtysomethings. They get in the way of your getting rich, so I want to help you knock these barriers down with a simple plan.

THE BURDEN OF STUDENT LOANS

I'm not going to lie to you: Getting rid of student loan debt is hard. The average student graduates with about £16,000 of debts, but those on longer courses (doctors, etc.) could have more than £30,000 of loans to pay off. Unfortunately, it's not like you can just wave a magic wand and make it disappear. In fact, even if you declare bankruptcy, you'll still have to pay your student loans. However, even if you have huge student debt, I want you to pay attention to how much money you're putting toward the monthly payments. Because the loan amounts are so large, even an extra £100/month can save you years of payments.

Let's look at an example. "Tony" owes £8,100 to the Student Loans Company (which is the amount the average student owed the SLC in 2009) and pays 9% of his salary above £15,000. He earns £22,000 so his payment is £52.50 a month. He's currently paying 0 per cent interest (this may look great for now, but watch out because interest rates alter every year). If you can afford to, increase your student loan payments. But only do this once you've cleared your other—more expensive—debts.

Most of us accept our student debt as is. We get a bill each month, we pay it, and we shrug, frustrated about the burden of our loans but not really sure if we can do anything. Guess what: *You can change your student loan payments*.

First, to inspire you to take action on paying off your student debt,

play with the financial calculators at http://www.moneymadeclear.fsa.
gov.uk/tools.aspx?Tool=loan_calculator. You'll be able to see how paying
different amounts changes the total amount you'll owe.

Second, I want to encourage you to put at least £50 more each month
toward any debt you have. Not only is it a psychological victory to know
that you're consciously working to pay off your debt, but you'll also be
able to focus on investing sooner. Make sure this is automatic, drawing
right out of your checking account, so you don't even see the money.
(I describe automatic payments in Chapter 5.)

Finally, if you're having problems paying off the student overdraft you
graduated with (which may be interest-free for a couple of years after
you graduate) it's time to call your bank. Look at the phone number on
that monthly bill you keep ignoring. Call them up and ask them for their
advice. I can't emphasize this enough: *Call them.* Your lenders have heard
it all, from "I can't pay this month" to "I have five different loans and want
to consolidate them." You'll want to ask them the following:

- *What would happen if I paid £100 more per month? (Substitute in
  the right amount for you.)*

- *What would happen if I took longer to bring my overdraft or loan
  down?*

- *If you're looking for a job, you might ask, What if I'm looking for a
  job and can't afford to pay for the next three months?*

Your lender has answers to all these questions—and chances are they
can help you find a better way to structure your payment. Typically, they'll
help you by changing the monthly payment or the time line. Just think:
With that one call you could save hundreds of pounds.

WHEN CREDIT CARDS GO BAD

Just like with gaining weight, most people don't get into serious credit
card debt overnight. Instead, things go wrong little by little until they
realize they've got a serious problem. If you've ended up in credit card
debt, it can seem overwhelming. When you watch Dr. Phil, you wonder
why those people can't figure out how to solve their problems when the
answers are so clear: "Yes, you should leave him! He hasn't had a job for
the last eight years! And he looks like a rat. Are you blind?" But when
we have our own problems, the answers don't seem so simple. What

should you do? How do you manage your day-to-day finances? And why do things keep getting worse? The good news is that credit card debt is almost always manageable if you have a plan and take disciplined steps to reduce it. Yes, it's hard, but you *can* get out of debt.

Now, almost nothing makes people feel guiltier than having credit card debt. Seventy-five percent of Americans claim they don't make major purchases on their credit card unless they can pay it off immediately. Yet from looking at actual spending behaviors, 70 percent of Americans carry a balance and fewer than half are willing to reveal their credit card debt to a friend. Those numbers are an indication that American consumers are ashamed of their debt levels, says Greg McBride, a senior financial analyst from www.bankrate.com, which commissioned the study. Referring to a recent study on consumer behavior, he told me, "They [are] more willing to give their name, age, and even details of their sex life than provid[e] the amount of their credit card debt." Really? Their sex lives? I would like to talk to these people . . . alone.

When I was engaged, I asked my credit union to raise my Visa limit of $500 to $1,500. This was a horrible mistake. My wedding dress budget of $500 suddenly became $1,200 when I "fell in love" with a dress in a boutique. I've paid only the minimum balance on my Visa each month, since emergency expenses seem to be keeping our budget stretched paper-thin, so I'm throwing away $30 or more per month in interest for a credit card balance from just one day in my life. My husband and I will most likely be paying for the wedding for years to come.

—CLAIRE STUBBLEFIELD, 24

This shame means that those in debt often don't educate themselves on how to stop the madness. Instead, they fall victim to the credit card companies' nefarious practices, which prey on the uninformed—and the undisciplined. These companies have become very good at extracting more money from us, and we've become very bad at knowing enough to say no.

For instance, the number one mistake people make with their credit cards is carrying a balance, or not paying it off every month. Astonishingly, of the 115 million Americans who carry a monthly credit card balance, half of them pay only their minimum monthly payments.

Sure, it's tempting to think that you can buy something and pay it off little by little, but because of credit cards' insanely high interest rates, that's a critical mistake.

Let's say it again: The key to using credit cards effectively is to pay off your credit card in full every month. I know I said that prosaically, in the same way someone would ask you to pass the salt, but it is REALLY IMPORTANT. Ask your friend with £12,000 in credit card debt how it happened. Chances are he'll shrug and tell you he decided to "just pay the minimum" every month.

I'm not going to belabor the point, but you would be *shocked* by how many people I talk to who charge purchases without knowing how much they'll actually end up paying once interest is figured in. Paying the minimum amount on your credit card is the grown-up equivalent of a little boy letting the school bully take his lunch money on the first day of school, then coming back with his pockets jingling every single day afterward. Not only are you going to get your ass kicked, but it's going to happen again and again. But by learning how the system works, you can figure out how to avoid the card companies' traps and get out of debt more quickly.

PAY YOUR DEBT OFF AGGRESSIVELY

If you've found yourself in credit card debt—whether it's a lot or a little— you have a triple whammy working against you:

- First, you're paying tons of high interest on the balance you're carrying.

- Second, your credit score may suffer. Some lenders will mark you down and they won't like it if it looks like you are up to your limit on all your lines of credit.

- Third, and potentially most damaging, debt can affect you emotionally. It can overwhelm you, leading you to avoid opening your bills, causing more late payments and more debt, in a downward spiral of doom.

It's time to make sacrifices to pay off your debt quickly. Otherwise, you're costing yourself more and more every day. Don't put it off, because there's not going to be a magic day when you win a million pounds or "have enough time" to figure out your finances. You said that three years ago! Managing your money has to be a priority if you ever want to be in a better situation than you are today.

Think about it: The average interest rate on credit cards is a hefty 16 percent, which means you're likely paying a tremendous amount of interest on any balance you're carrying. To see how this plays out, let's assume someone has £5,000 in debt on a card with 16 percent APR. If Dumb Dan pays the monthly minimum payment of 2.5%, it will take him over twenty-seven years to pay off this debt—assuming he doesn't rack up more debt, which you know he will. Over the entire process, he'll pay nearly £5,300 *in interest alone.* Smart Sally, by contrast, decides to pay £250 each month, which is double the minimum payment. It takes her just two years to pay off the full debt, and she pays less than £900 in interest. Plus, since it's automatically withdrawn from her current account each month, she doesn't even notice the extra money she's paying.

That's just from paying £250 every single month. Don't have £250 extra? How about £50? Or even £20? Any increase over the minimum helps.

If you set up automatic payments (which I discuss on page 131) and work your debt down, you won't pay fees anymore. You won't pay finance charges. You'll be free to grow your money by looking

DUMB DAN VS. SMART SALLY: PAYING OFF £5,000 CREDIT CARD DEBT AT 16% APR

Dumb Dan pays the minimum monthly payment		
His first payment is . . .	Paying minimum payments, it will take this long to pay off . . .	Total amount of interest he pays is . . .
£125	27 years, 3 months	£5,289.48
Smart Sally pays twice the minimum monthly payment		
Her monthly payment is . . .	Paying twice the minimum payments, it will take this long to pay off . . .	Total amount of interest she pays is . . .
£250	24 months	£854.46

ahead. In the credit card companies' eyes you'll be a "deadbeat," a curious name American card firms use for customers who pay on time every month and therefore produce virtually no revenue. You'll be worthless in their eyes, which is perfect in mine. But to beat them, you have to prioritize paying off whatever you already owe.

The day I paid off my last credit card bill was surreal. I had spent four years in college racking up debt that I was certain I'd pay off so easily once I started working. I Spring Break-ed in Las Vegas, Mexico, and Miami. I bought Manolo Blahnik shoes. I went out several nights a week. I had no idea then that I'd spend five post-college years paying that debt off—five years in which I could not vacation, could not buy fancy shoes, and could not go out very much at all. So on the day when I sent my final payment to my credit card company, I decided that that payment would be my last. I promised myself that I would never go back into debt again.

—JULIE NGUYEN, 25

Five Steps to Ridding Yourself of Credit Card Debt

Now that you see the benefits of climbing out of debt as quickly as possible, let's look at some concrete steps you can take to get started. *I Will Teach You to Be Rich* is a six-week program, but obviously paying off your loans will take longer than that. Even if you're carrying debt, you should still read the rest of the book now, because there are important lessons on automating your finances and getting conscious about your spending. Just keep in mind that you won't be able to invest as aggressively as I recommend until you pay off your debt. Yeah, it sucks, but that's a reasonable cost to pay for incurring your debt. Now, here's what to do.

1. Figure out how much debt you have.

You wouldn't believe how many people don't do this and continue blindly paying off any bills that come in with no strategic plan. This is exactly what the credit card companies want, because you're essentially just dumping money into their mouths. You can't make a plan to pay off your debt until you know exactly how much you owe. It might be painful to learn the truth, but you have to bite the bullet. Then you'll see that it's not hard to end this bad habit. In fact, you can get the credit card companies to help you: Look at the back of your credit cards for their numbers, call them, and let them tell you the answers to fill in this spreadsheet.

Congratulations! The first step is the hardest. Now you have a definitive list of exactly how much you owe.

HOW MUCH DO YOU OWE?

Name of credit card	Total amount of debt	APR	Monthly minimum payment

Download this spreadsheet from www.iwillteachyoutoberich.com.

2. Decide what to pay off first.

Not all debts are created equal. Different cards charge you different interest rates, which can affect what you decide to pay off first. There are two schools of thought on how to go about this. In the standard method, you pay the minimum on all cards, but pay more money to the card with the *highest APR*, because it's costing you the most. In the Dave Ramsey Snowball method, you pay the minimum on all cards, but pay more money to the card with the *lowest balance* first—the one that will allow you to pay it off first.

This is a source of fierce debate in credit card circles. Technically, the Snowball method isn't necessarily the most efficient approach, because

PRIORITIZING YOUR DEBT

	Snowball method: lowest balance first	Standard method: highest APR first
How it works	Pay the minimum on all cards, but pay more on the card with the lowest balance. Once you pay off the first card, repeat with the next-lowest balance.	Pay the minimum on all cards, but pay more on the card with the highest interest. Once you pay off the first card, repeat with the next-highest-APR card.
Why it works	This is all about psychology and small wins. Once you pay off the first card, you're more motivated to pay off the next one.	Mathematically, you want to pay off the credit card that's costing you the most first.

the card with the lowest balance doesn't necessarily have the highest APR. But on a psychological level, it's enormously rewarding to see one credit card paid off, which in turn can motivate you to pay off others more quickly. Bottom line: Don't spend more than five minutes deciding. Just pick one method and do it. The goal is not to optimize your payoff method, but to get started paying off your debt.

3. Negotiate down the APR.

I'm a huge fan of taking 50/50 odds if the upside is big and it takes only five minutes of my time. Accordingly, try negotiating down your APR. It works surprisingly often and if it doesn't, so what? Just call your card companies and follow this script:

YOU: Hi, I'm going to be paying off my credit card debt more aggressively beginning next week and I'd like a lower APR.

CREDIT CARD REP: *Uh, why?*

YOU: I've decided to be more aggressive about paying off my debt, and that's why I'd like a lower APR. Other cards are offering me rates at half what you're offering. Can you lower my rate by 50 percent or only 40 percent?

CREDIT CARD REP: *Hmm . . . After reviewing your account, I'm afraid we can't offer you a lower APR. We can offer you a credit limit increase, however.*

YOU: No, that won't work for me. Like I mentioned, other credit cards are offering me zero percent introductory rates for twelve months, as well as APRs of half what you're offering. I've been a customer for X years, and I'd prefer not to switch my balance over to a low-interest card. Can you match the other credit card rates, or can you go lower?

CREDIT CARD REP: *I see . . . Hmm, let me pull something up here. Fortunately, the system is suddenly letting me offer you a reduced APR. That is effective immediately.*

It doesn't work every time, but when it does, you can save a significant amount of money with a five-minute conversation. Make the call, and if you're successful, don't forget to recalculate the figures in your debt spreadsheet.

I fell behind in my payments to my Sears Gold MasterCard. I racked up $3,400 in debt, so I called and told them I was having difficulties paying my bill. They offered me 0 percent financing on my balance for twelve months to help me get back on track.

—CHRIS MANCINI, 25

---

4. Decide where the money to pay off your credit cards will come from.

One common barrier to paying off debt is wondering where the money should come from. Balance transfers? Should you use your ISA money or your savings account? How much should you be paying off every month? These questions can be daunting, but don't let them stop you.

■ **BALANCE TRANSFERS.** Many people begin by considering a balance transfer to a card with a lower APR. I'm not a fan of these. Yes, it can help for a few months and save you some money, particularly on large balances. But this is just a Band-Aid for a larger problem (usually your spending behavior, when it comes to credit card debt), so changing the interest rate isn't going to address that. Plus, balance transfers are a confusing process fraught with tricks by credit card companies to trap you into paying more, and the people I've known who do this end up spending more time researching the best balance transfers than actually paying their debt off. As we just discussed, a better option is to call and negotiate the APR down on your current accounts.

(continued on page 46)

I asked some of the bloggers I trust and admire to add their two cents to the book. Look for their contributions scattered throughout.

— Ramit

ADVICE FROM THE BLOGOSPHERE

SO, YOU'VE DECIDED TO GET OUT OF CREDIT CARD DEBT

Here's How to Do It Right

By Flexo of www.consumerismcommentary.com

I t's fine to use credit cards as tools for convenient spending and to rack up "bonus points," as long as you're aware of the possibility you are subtly spending more due to the ease of use. I would even understand it if you use a credit card in an emergency situation when no other options are available. But when you use that same card to buy products or experiences you cannot afford, it's time to admit your behavior is damaging and get a grip on your situation.

You're reading this book because you want to improve your money situation— perhaps even get rich—and the only way to tread that path is to get out of credit card debt. Here's how.

FIRST, YOU NEED THE CASH FLOW. *To eradicate debt, you need to have enough income every month to meet your regular obligations like groceries, utilities, your mortgage, and the minimum payments on your credit cards, plus enough to throw toward putting that debt away for good. If you do not have enough income to cover more than your minimum payments, you have to clear that hurdle by earning more money, negotiating with your credit card issuers to lower your minimum payments, or working with a legitimate, nonprofit debt consolidation organization that negotiates with creditors on your behalf, not one that provides you with a loan. Try the National Foundation for Credit Counseling at www.nfcc.org. [Ramit says: 'UK equivalents are the Consumer Credit Counselling Service (www.cccs. co.uk) and National Debtline (www.nationaldebtline.co.uk).]*

NEXT, PRIORITIZE YOUR CREDIT CARDS. *The best way to do this is to list your debts from highest interest rate to lowest. If you do a little research, you may find some people—vocal professionals with motivational seminars and radio talk* shows—who disagree with this premise. They want you to list your credit cards with the lowest balances as the most important, the ones to fully pay off first. They claim that the emotional "quick win" of paying off the first card as quickly as possible will motivate you to continue paying off debt. (This sounds more like a "quick win" for the credit card industry because they will get more of your money from interest.) You're already motivated—and it could well be your emotions that got you into this mess of debt in the first place. Leave your emotions at the door and get out of debt the quickest, cheapest, and most efficient way possible.

PAY THE MINIMUM ON EVERYTHING EXCEPT THE TOP CARD.
Once your credit cards are ranked properly, pay the minimum amount due listed on the statement for every card except the one at the top of the list. Dedicate all the extra funds you have to paying it off. Do this every month until that first credit card balance disappears. Then move to the second card on the list.

STOP USING YOUR CARDS. When you're paying off debt, you don't want to be adding more at the same time. Eliminating debt is more than just paying off your balances, it's also about resisting consumerist temptations. Don't cancel your cards, but stop using them. Some people have found resisting the temptation to spend to be easier when the credit cards are out of sight. One creative method is to literally "freeze your credit": Freeze your plastic into a block of ice as described at www.calculatorweb.com/calculators/creditcardcalc.shtml.

Repeat this monthly payment process until the credit card debt is gone. This method will get you there quickly as long as you stick to it diligently. Don't believe me? Check out the "snowball calculator" at www.whatsthecost.com/snowball .aspx?country=uk.

Additional resources that might help you eliminate credit card debt:

- How much will that £350 jacket really cost on a credit card? Find out by entering the price paid for a product as the "current account balance." www.whatsthecost.com/creditcard.aspx.

- Use the "social" financial management application Mint to analyze your credit cards and provide you with suggestions for lowering your interest rates. www.mint.com.

- Eliminating your credit card debt should have a positive effect on your credit score. Get an indicative credit score for free from Check My File and simulate scenarios to see how your future score might change with improved money habits. www.checkmyfile.com.

Flexo blogs about personal finance, the economy, and current financial events at www.consumerismcommentary.com.

Websites altered for Ramit's British friends

- **TAKING OUT A SECURED LOAN OR REMORTGAGING.** I don't recommend the first option because you're converting unsecured debt into a loan that is secured on your home. You'll be adding to your monthly payments and possibly even jeopardising your home if you can't keep up the repayments. Remortgaging to a lower rate and adding your credit card debt to your loan means you've reduced the amount of equity you have. That might mean you miss out on the best mortgage deals or even—if prices fall—that you're in negative equity.

- **REDUCING SPENDING AND PRIORITIZING DEBT.** Not sexy, but it works. The most sustainable way to pay off credit card debt is also the least sexy. Unlike balance transfers or remortgaging, which you can brag to your friends about, it's not very exciting to tell people you decided to spend less on other things so you could pay off your debt. But it works.

Let me ask you a question. Right now, for every £100 you earn, how much of it goes to debt? Two pounds? Maybe £5? What if you paid £10 toward your debt? You'd be surprised that many people don't even have to cut much spending to pay off debt quickly. They just have to stop spending on random items, get conscious about making debt a priority, and set up aggressive automatic transfers to pay off their credit card debt. I don't want to make this sound easy, because paying off your credit card debt is extremely difficult. But millions of others have done it.

As you read the rest of this book, think of yourself as being on a little treasure hunt to figure out where to get the money to pay off your credit card debt. Pay special attention to these discussions:

- "The Next £100" Principle on page 128.

- Figuring out how much you can afford to put toward your debt using the Conscious Spending Plan on page 103.

- The "Save $1,000 in 30 Days" Challenge on page 115.

- Setting up automatic payments on page 23.

You'll notice that I haven't offered you a simple secret or cute sound bite about how to pay off your debt with no work. That's because there isn't one. If there were, I would be the first to tell you. But truthfully, paying off debt just takes hard work and a plan. It may seem like pure agony for the first few weeks, but imagine the relief you'll feel when you see your debt growing smaller and smaller with each passing month. And sometime after that, you'll be debt-free! Then you can focus all your energy on getting ahead, investing, and living your life. It may not happen overnight, but if you pay off your credit card debt as aggressively as possible, you'll soon be on the road to getting rich and staying rich.

5. Get started.

Within the coming week, you should start paying more money toward your debt. If you find yourself taking more time than that to get started, you're overthinking it. Remember the philosophy behind the 85 Percent Solution: The goal is not to research every last corner to decide where the money will come from, it's action. Figure out how much debt you have, decide how you want to pay it down, negotiate your rates, and get started. You can always fine-tune your plan and amount later.

My biggest mistake was not thinking about the future, and using credit cards to live beyond my means. I got myself into debt in my mid-twenties by spending, spending, spending—and on stupid things like clothes, eating out, DVDs, etc. Once I allowed myself to carry a balance that first time, it got easier to let it build up. I learned my lesson, and am now living within my means on a strict budget that will allow me to be debt-free in two years. Being in debt means giving up choices, means staying at a job you hate because it pays good money, means not being able to build a decent savings account. On a happier note, all of my debt is now on cards with APRs between 0 and 4.99 percent. I have a small but growing savings account, a pension, and a plan to achieve financial freedom.

—MELISSA BROWN, 28

ACTION STEPS

WEEK ONE

1 **Get your credit report and credit score (one hour).** Check them to make sure there are no errors and to get familiar with your credit. You can pay £2 to any of the three credit reference agencies (Experian, Equifax and Call Credit) or a free copy of your credit report once a year from www.annualcreditreport.co.uk. You can also get an indicative score for free from www.checkmyfile.com.

---

2 **Set up your credit card (two hours).** If you already have one, call and make sure it's a no-fee card. If you want to get a new credit card, check out www.moneyfacts.co.uk.

---

3 **Make sure you're handling your credit cards effectively (three hours).** Set up an automatic payment so your credit card bill is paid off in full every month. (Even if you're in debt, set up an automatic payment for the largest amount you can afford.) Get your fees waived. Apply for more credit if you're debt-free. Make sure you're getting the most out of your cards.

---

4 **If you have debt, start paying it off (one week to plan, then start paying more).** Not tomorrow, not next week, today: Give yourself one week to figure out how much you owe, call the lender to negotiate down the APR or restructure your payments (in the case of student loans), and set up your automatic payment with more money than you're paying now. Getting out of debt quickly will be the best financial decision you ever make.

That's it! You've mastered improving your credit by using your credit card. You've waived your card fees, negotiated your rates down, and even set up automatic payments. And if you have debt, you've taken the first steps toward paying it all off. Congratulations! In the next chapter, we're going to optimize your bank accounts. You'll earn more interest, pay no fees, and upgrade to better accounts than the worthless current and savings accounts we grew up with. Once you've tackled your credit card and bank accounts, you'll be ready to start investing—and growing your money significantly.

CHAPTER 2

BEAT THE BANKS

Open high-interest, low-hassle accounts and negotiate fees like an Indian

L ast week, you got your credit cards organized, and now in Week 2 we're going to get your bank accounts set up right. Since they're the backbone of your personal-finance infrastructure, we're going to spend a little time picking the right ones, optimizing them, and making sure you're not paying unnecessary fees. The good news is that this can be done in just a few hours over the next week, and once you do it, your accounts will basically run themselves. The bad news is that the bank account you have—probably from your high street bank—is most likely a big fat rip-off with high overdraft fees and charges, and low interest rates if you're in credit. See, banks love young people because we're new to banking, and they think we don't know any better about things like payment protection insurance. With this chapter, that's going to change. I'll show you how to pick the best bank and the best accounts so you can earn the maximum amount of interest.

How Banks Rake It In

Fundamentally, banks earn money by lending the money you deposit to other people. For example, if you deposit £1,000, a Big Bank will pay you 0.5 percent to hold on to that money, and then they'll turn around and lend it out at 7 percent for a home loan. Assuming that everyone repays the full amount they're loaned, the bank makes a fourteen-times return on their money for simple arbitrage. (To be fair, banks don't get 100 percent of their principal plus interest back, so they do incur some risk and should be compensated accordingly. But fourteen times is a lot of money.) To me, this is a lot like a lazy Godzilla outsourcing a city's destruction to the Stay Puft Marshmallow Man while he sits around and eats a big old pizza, then takes a nap.

FEES, FEES, FEES. Banks also make money from fees—a lot of money. In 2006, banks made more than $10 billion from overdraft fees alone. For example, if you're using a debit card and accidentally buy something for more money than you have in your current account, you could end up paying a lot in charges. Your bank may charge you £30 if it lets the sale go through (because now you're overdrawn) or a similar fee if it rejects the transaction. You could be hit by several charges plus a monthly overdraft fee (which varies). But there are some positives! Bank of America is nice enough to charge you only $20 for the first overdraft (but $35 for each subsequent overdraft). What a great deal! Check out Bank of America's ridiculous "fees and processes" site, which offers FULL-SCREEN VIDEO and thousands of words but, crucially, does not actually tell you the amount they charge.

NO MORE OVERDRAFTS. One overdraft fee at your crappy neighborhood bank wipes out your interest for the entire year and makes you hate your bank even more than you already do, if that's even possible. More than half the people I've spoken to during my personal-finance talks have had at least one overdraft. One night back in college, I was out for dinner and my friend "Elizabeth" started asking me questions about overdrafts. They got increasingly complex, which weirded me out because I wondered how she knew so much about them. (I thought I was the only nerd who read up on overdraft fees for fun.) Then I asked her a simple question: "How many overdrafts have you had?" She suddenly got quiet, which forced me to interrogate her like Mike Wallace. I ended up learning that she'd incurred more than $400 in overdraft fees over four years of college by simply not paying attention to how much money she had in her account. I screamed at her so much. The sad thing is that she could have negotiated her way out of the first few and then set up a system so that it never happened again. For more on negotiating bank fees, see page 65.

Remember, your bank's fees are often more important than the interest rate it offers: If you have £1,000 and another bank has a 1 percent higher interest rate, that's a difference of £10 per year. *Just one overdraft fee equals three times that amount. Costs matter.*

The UK current account market is a very competitive one. It means you should be able to track down an account that won't insist that you pay in hundreds of pounds each month and that won't charge you a monthly fee, but will pay you interest on your current account balance and give you a low or fee-free overdraft. The overdraft is normally limited to a couple of hundred pounds (and you shouldn't need to use it) but it's good to know you won't be whacked with fees if you do go into the red.

The banks are constantly dreaming up new offers. My advice is to look for an account that consistently pays a reasonable interest rate on credit balances and where the bank gets a high rating for its customer service. Check the interest rates on the bank's easy access savings accounts as well. If you bank online, you can easily transfer money from your current to your savings account (and vice versa).

Steer clear of packaged accounts (that charge a monthly fee of £8-£12 in return for extras such as travel insurance) unless you're absolutely sure you'll save money by taking one. Generally, the banks have a tendency to exaggerate how much the benefits are worth.

When interest rates are so low, it may be hard to get excited about how much your savings will earn, but if you put a bit of effort into choosing your bank at the outset, you'll have done the hard work.

If you're worried about security, remember that the first £50,000 of your savings (per individual, not per account) is covered by the Financial Services Compensation Scheme. It's an independent safety net if a bank or building society fails. Be aware that currently, the £50,000 limit applies to each banking licence. Some banks that are members of the same group (such as Halifax, Birmingham Midshires and Bank of Scotland), share a banking licence; others don't. The financial regulator, the FSA, is looking to simplify the compensation rules, but as I write this, it hasn't changed them.

Banks that are based in Europe (strictly, it's the European Economic Area, not just the EU), may be covered by the country's own compensation scheme. In some cases, the limits are lower, in others, they're higher. Check out the details at the FSCS website (www.fscs.org.uk).

The Nuts and Bolts

Now that I've got my bank rants out of the way, let's go over a few account basics. You may think you know all this stuff (and a lot of it you probably do), but bear with me.

CURRENT ACCOUNTS

As you know, current accounts let you deposit money and withdraw money using debit cards, checks, and online transfers. I think of my current account like an e-mail inbox: All my money goes in my current account, and then I regularly filter it out to appropriate accounts, like savings and investing, using automatic transfers. I pay most of my bills through my credit card, but occasionally there are bills that I can't pay with my card—like rent or my car payment—that I pay directly from my current account using automatic transfers. (In Chapter 5, I'll show you how to make these transfers and bill paying work automatically.) Traditionally, banks paid no interest on current accounts, but this is changing. Most online banks now offer current accounts with interest, blurring the line between current and savings accounts. Current accounts are the number one place where unnecessary fees are levied, which we're going to fix (see p.65).

HOW MUCH YOU EARN AT
ONLINE BANKS VS. BIG BANKS

If you saved ...	Online high-interest banks: At 3% interest, you'd earn ...	Big useless banks: At 0.5% interest, you'd earn ...
£1,000	£30 per year	£5 per year
£5,000	£150 per year	£25 per year
£10,000	£300 per year	£50 per year
£25,000	£750 per year	£125 per year
£50,000	£1,500 per year	£250 per year

SAVINGS ACCOUNTS

Think of savings accounts as places for short-term (one month) to mid-term savings (five years). You want to use your savings account to save up for things like a vacation, Christmas gifts, or even longer-term items like a wedding or down payment on a house. The key difference between current accounts and savings accounts is this: Savings accounts pay interest (although, as we saw, the lines are being blurred with new interest-bearing current accounts). Some high street banks pay 0 percent interest on savings accounts, meaning that if you put £1,000 in a savings account, you'd earn £0.08 in monthly interest, or £1 per year. I'd expect to find more than that on the pavement each morning, so I'm not very impressed by that kind of return. Interestingly, if your money were sitting in one of those accounts, you'd actually be losing money every day because inflation is over 2 percent. That's right: You may be earning 0.1 percent interest on your savings account, but you're losing 2.4 percent every year in terms of real purchasing power.

The most important practical difference between current accounts and savings accounts is that you withdraw money regularly from your current account—but you rarely withdraw from your savings account (or at least that's the way it should be). Current accounts are built for frequent withdrawals: They have debit cards and ATMs for your convenience. But your savings account is really a "goals" account, where every pound is assigned to a specific item you're saving up for.

Most people keep their savings account and current account at the same bank, although this is increasingly changing as electronic transfers become the industry standard. In fact, with electronic transfers and online banks, options have gotten considerably better for consumers. Banks generally pay a higher interest rate for online savings accounts—currently 2 to 3 percent, which would produce £20 to £30 interest per year on that £1,000, compared with as little as £1 per year on a branch-based savings account. And as with any savings account, your money just keeps growing and compounding, meaning it is working for you by just sitting there.

There is one downside to having an online savings account: It can take a few business days to access your money. Typically, if you want to withdraw your money, you'll log in to your online savings account, initiate a free transfer to your current account, and then wait three to five days for it to happen. If you need your money immediately, this could cause a problem—but then again, you shouldn't be withdrawing very frequently from your savings account, so most likely this won't be a big issue.

To see how much you'd make from an online account versus a branch-based one, plug in your own numbers using the online spreadsheet at my website, iwillteachyoutoberich.com.

WHY YOU NEED BOTH A SAVINGS ACCOUNT AND A CURRENT ACCOUNT

Having your money in two separate accounts makes money management easy. One basic way of looking at it is that your savings account is where you deposit money, whereas your current account is where you withdraw money. Yet there's something profoundly different about having two accounts: If your friends want to go out on Friday night, you're not going to say, "Hold on, guys, I need three business days to transfer money to my current account." If you don't have the money available in your discretionary (current) account because you've spent your "going out" money, you're staying in that night. Having a separate savings account forces you to keep your long-term goals in mind instead of just blowing them off to have a few rounds of drinks.

Right now, you might be saying to yourself, "Why should I bother with a savings account? I only have £300." I hear this all the time. It's true, the interest you'll be earning on that kind of money isn't really that much.

How My Bank Accounts Work

It's not easy being me. Just as the paparazzi follow Paris Hilton and Lindsay Lohan, wanting to know what they're wearing and which clubs they're going to, people are always dying to know about my personal-finance infrastructure.

MY ACCOUNTS. All of my money goes through my interest-bearing Schwab online checking account. Deposits happen through direct deposit and by mailing checks in preaddressed, prestamped Schwab envelopes. I have a brick-and-mortar Wells Fargo checking account because it was required to open my savings account and I haven't gotten around to closing it. But in general, once you've opened the online account, you can close your brick-and-mortar account any time.

MY SYSTEM. My finances work on a monthly cycle, and my system automatically disburses money where it needs to go. I've set up accounts to draw from my checking account. For example, my ING Direct savings account automatically withdraws a certain amount every month from my checking account, as does my investment account (more about these in Chapter 3). For consumer protection, I pay my bills using my credit card. The credit card is automatically paid in full every month by my online checking account. For cash expenses, I use the Schwab ATM card to withdraw money at any ATM nationwide. All ATM charges are fully reimbursed at the end of the month. Generally, I use my ING Direct account as a receiver, not a sender: I rarely transfer money out of there unless I need to cover a temporary shortage in my checking account or want to spend savings money on something important, like a vacation or birthday gift.

And that's how I do it.

But it's not just about your immediate earnings—being young is about developing the right habits. We're cutting our teeth with small amounts of money, but as our savings accounts increase from £5,000 and £10,000 to £100,000 to £1 million, the habits really start to matter. Start small now so that when you *do* have a lot of money, you'll know what to do with it.

FINDING THE PERFECT ACCOUNT SETUP

I wish I could suggest the one best current and savings account for everyone, but each person is different. (That doesn't mean I'm going to cop out and hold back my bank recommendations. I'll give you my favorite accounts in a few pages.) Before you go about finding the specific banks and accounts you want to use, take a minute to consider the bigger picture of how you want to organize your accounts. I'll take you through simple and advanced setups for your current and savings accounts, but pick the one that works well with your personality. You have to know yourself: Do you value simplicity? Or are you the kind of person who wants to spend your time building a complicated system for a slightly larger payout? For most people, the second option—"basic option + small optimization"—is perfect.

Most basic option (good for lazy people). This is the bare minimum. All you need is a current account and a savings account at any local bank. Even if you already have these accounts, it's worth talking to your bank to be sure you're not paying fees.

Basic option + small optimization (recommended for most people). This option means opening accounts at two separate institutions. Go for a current account that doesn't charge a fee (avoid packaged accounts) and a high-yield online savings account. Whether it's a branch-based current account, one that offers telephone banking or an online account, the main thing is that you don't pay unnecessary fees. With the current account, you'll have immediate access to your money and the ability to transfer cash to your high-interest online savings account for free. If you already have this, great! Just call to make sure you're not paying unnecessary fees.

Advanced setup + full optimization (perfect for people who read things like lifehacker.com and The 4-Hour Workweek*).* This setup consists of several current accounts and savings accounts at different banks, usually to eke out the most interest and services that various banks have to offer. For example, I have a basic checking account at a brick-and-mortar bank, an interest-bearing checking account at an online bank, and a savings account at yet another online bank. Although you can set up automatic online transfers, having multiple banks means multiple websites, multiple customer-service numbers, and multiple passwords. Some people find this overly complicated—if you're one of them, stick to one of the more basic setups, unless it's very important to you to fully optimize your bank accounts.

SO MANY CHOICES, SO LITTLE TIME

Depending on what accounts you already have and what setup you've opted to go with, getting this part of your financial infrastructure squared away may be as easy as making small changes to accounts you've had for a while. Or you may need to open new accounts, which can be pretty overwhelming. Imagine walking into a strip club in Vegas where you can see everyone lined up and take your pick. I am really hesitant to go further into this analogy because my mom is going to read this book, but suffice it to say that both strippers and banks want your money. Also, there are a lot of choices. That's all, Mom!!!

As usual with financial decisions, we have too many options, leading most of us to make less-than-ideal choices—like opening a bank account in college and then staying with that bank forever. There are some good accounts out there, but of course banks don't always make these deals easy to find.

Why Use a Building Society Over a Bank?

If you prefer, you could look at accounts offered by building societies. Unlike banks, they're owned by their members. They don't have shareholders to answer to or to take a slice of the profits. As a result they can provide better rates and a more personalised service than other high street banks. But don't assume all building societies are the same or that they'll automatically give you the best rate. Do your own research first.

If you're looking to save or borrow a small amount of money, you could find out if there's a credit union near you (or your place of work). I'm a big fan of credit unions, which are small not-for-profit community saving and lending institutions. They don't normally offer bank accounts, but will let you build up savings and can be a lifeline to people with a bad credit history who need a loan.

Most traditional banks offer different current and savings accounts to serve customers with different needs and amounts of money. They start with basic accounts, for those who have a bad credit record. These accounts don't let you go overdrawn. Next come student accounts, which normally offer an interest-free overdraft and sometimes a low-limit credit card. Standard current accounts should let you bank free of charge; let you pay bills by direct debit or standing order, withdraw money from cash machines and—depending on the bank—will let you bank online or by phone as well. Packaged accounts—which charge a monthly fee—are aimed at the higher end market and impose a minimum earning threshold (which can be £50,000 a year plus) or insist you deposit a certain amount each month. They offer benefits ranging from lower loan, overdraft rates and free travel insurance to discounted will-writing, reduced price concert tickets etc. These accounts are worthless. Avoid them. If you have that much money lying around, I'll show you how to put it to work in Chapter 7 and earn more than any bank could give you.

You should research the options at a few different banks. I suggest calling (or even going in) and asking them if they can help you find a no-fee, no-minimum account. Ideally they'll be able to offer you a few options. Remember, even if the accounts have fees or minimums, ask about ways (like direct deposit) to get them waived. Here are some websites to get you started:

HSBC: .... www.hsbc.co.uk

NatWest: .... www.natwest.com

Lloyds TSB: .... www.lloydstsb.com

Barclays: .... www.barclays.co.uk

Co-operative: .... www.co-operativebank.co.uk

Halifax: .... www.halifax.co.uk

Royal Bank of Scotland: .... www.rbs.co.uk

Santander: .... www.santander.co.uk
(will replace Abby, Alliance & Leicester and Bradford and Bingley by end of 2010)

Beyond just the type of accounts offered, there's more to consider when choosing your bank(s). I look for three things: trust, convenience, and features.

Five Shiny Marketing Tactics Banks Use to Trick You

1. Teaser rates ("6 percent for the first two months!"). Your first two months don't matter. You want to pick a good bank that you can stick with for years—one that offers overall great service, not a promo rate that will earn you only £25 (or, more likely, £3). Banks that offer teaser rates are, by definition, to be avoided.

2. Requiring minimum balances to get better interest rates on credit balances and fee-free overdrafts.

3. Up-sells to expensive accounts ("Expedited customer service! Wow!"). Most of these "value-added accounts" are designed to charge you for worthless services.

4. Offering you a packaged account at an introductory rate. The current account market is a competitive one. Banks will try and entice you into a fee charging account with a 'fee free' offer for the first few months. Avoid this. You don't want to change current accounts every few months as it will damage your credit score.

5. Bundling a credit card with your bank account. If you didn't walk in specifically wanting the bank credit card, don't get it.

Trust. For years, I've had a Wells Fargo account because their ATMs are convenient, but I don't trust American Big Banks anymore. I'm not the only one. At the moment, Big Banks are looking around wildly, wondering why young people like me are moving to high-interest accounts online. Perhaps it's because Big Banks pay a meager 0.5 percent interest, and they try to nickel-and-dime us for every small service. Perhaps it's because they secretly insert fees, like the charges for using another ATM, then count on our inaction to make money off us. There are still some good banks out there, though. The best way to find one is to ask friends if they have a bank they love. You should also browse the major bank websites. Within about five minutes, you should be able to tell which banks are trustworthy and which are not by seeing how straightforward they are with their accounts and fees. Your bank shouldn't nickel-and-dime you through minimums and fees. It should have a website with clear descriptions of different services, an easy setup process, and 24/7 customer service available by phone. Another thing: Ask them if they send you promotional material every damn week. I don't want more junk mail! Stop sending crap! A couple of years ago, I switched my car insurance because they would not stop sending me mail three times a week.

Convenience. If your bank isn't convenient, it doesn't matter how much interest you're earning—you're not going to use it. Since a bank is the first line of defense in managing your money, it needs to be easy to put money in, get money out, and transfer money around. This means its website has to work, and you need to be able to get help when you need it—whether by e-mail or phone.

Don't Be a Rate Chaser

Do me a favor: If your bank account offers 3 percent and another bank starts offering 3.1 percent, don't change accounts. Half the time, those rates are simply introductory teaser rates that will drop after six months. I'd rather take a slightly lower interest rate if it's at a bank I can trust to give me great service over the long term. But there are a lot of dorks who spend every waking hour online digging up the best interest rate and switching to it immediately. "OMG!!!!" they say. "Emigrant Direct increased its rate from 2.25 percent to 2.75 percent!! Now it's 0.02 percent higher than ING Direct! I must switch accounts right away!! Onward!!!" If you do this, you are a moron. Do you really want to spend each month figuring out which bank is offering a slightly better rate? That's a colossal waste of time for most of us, since a 0.5 percent difference equals just a few pounds per month more in interest. Plus, interest rates change over time, so rate chasing doesn't even make sense. I plan on sticking with my bank for the next few *decades,* and I'm sure you have better things to do with your time. So focus on the big problems, not on rate jumping.

My bank's website is TERRIBLE. It's horrible—most of it isn't in plain English, and they seem to think that everyone should speak like a stock trader. Even worse, it obfuscates how much you actually have versus how much you owe, and doesn't give you streamlined access to moving things around. For example, on a recent charge I made, I can see it online but I can't pay it. I will have to call them and authorize them to pay it. How messed up is that?

—ELEANOR P., 25,

Features. The bank's interest rate should be competitive. If it's an online account, the bank's website should be customer friendly, so it's easy to navigate and doesn't crash all the time. You should be able to transfer money between your accounts (whether they're with the same bank or not) quickly and easily. It's nice if the bank lets you categorize your spending and get images of canceled checks, but these aren't necessary.

The Best Accounts

As we've seen, there's a lot that goes into finding the right accounts. Here are a few specific options that I've found work well for many people:

CURRENT ACCOUNTS

Your local bank or building society's current account with no fees and no minimums. As I explained earlier, you can get a fee-free account that doesn't require a minimum amount to be paid in. You should be able to pay all your bills by direct debit or standing order, free of charge. You can also transfer money and take cash out of ATMs without paying a penny (although some cash machines do charge). These accounts pay little or no interest, but because you won't be storing much money here, that's no big deal. Using the criteria I laid out on the last few pages, you should be able to find a bank or building society that you'll be happy with.

SAVINGS ACCOUNTS

I would not encourage anyone to use a standard branch-based savings account. Online savings accounts let you earn dramatically more interest with lower hassle. And because you'll primarily be sending money there, not withdrawing it, what does it matter if it takes a few days to get your money?

However, even though online accounts are generally a much better deal, there's still quite a difference between the best and the worst. While there's no point spending hours chasing every penny, a bit of time researching what's on offer before you open your account is well worth it.

My tip? Go for an account that's consistently paying a competitive rate of interest. Lots of savings accounts (whether they're offered by the high street banks or by online providers) have sneaky terms and conditions which mean the headline-grabbing rate they offer to entice customers in, disappears after a few months.

Others come up with an account offering a great rate of interest (long enough for it to get in the 'best buy' tables in the papers and online) and then drop the rate without warning. The money information service Moneyfacts (www.moneyfacts.co.uk) regularly looks into which accounts consistently pay a decent rate of interest and which are flash in the pan (look for the tab 'consistent savings' onsite). This is what it found in April 09: Over 18 months ICICI Bank's HiSave account was the most consistent, followed by two building societies (Yorkshire and Principality) and Sainsbury's bank Internet Saver account also made it into the top five. Over a longer period of time (three years), Sainsbury's bank Internet Saver account was the most consistent, while Nationwide building society's e-Savings account was number two.

CASH ISAS

If you don't already have a cash ISA, it's worth opening one. Cash ISAs are simply tax-free savings accounts, which means that if you have an ordinary savings account instead of an ISA, you're paying tax on the interest. It's not often the taxman gives you an easy way to pay less tax, so you should take it.

The really great thing about cash ISAs is that – not only is all the interest completely tax-free, but you don't have to lock your money away. You can get hold of it any time you want. OK, maybe not last thing at night if the bank's closed, but, unlike pensions (which I'll talk about later), with a cash ISA you save tax and can get access to your money when it suits you.

Before you rush to pay every last penny you own into a cash ISA, you should know that there are limits on how much you can save in one every year (that's the tax year, running from April 6th to April 5th the following year). These limits change from time to time so it's worth keeping a check on them.

Don't use your cash ISA account for regular expenses (such as holiday, car repair and so on). The reason is that once you've paid in the maximum allowed into your cash ISA, you can't top it up if you take money out of it.

Optimizing Your Bank Accounts

Whether they're accounts you just opened or already had, you need to optimize your current and savings accounts. This means you shouldn't be paying fees or minimums. The key to optimizing an account is talking to an actual customer-service rep, either in person or on the phone. Yes, nerds, you have to get out of your chair and either go over to the bank or pick up the telephone. For some reason, half my friends are afraid of talking to people on the phone and it ends up costing them lots of money. I have a friend who recently lost his bank password and, for security reasons, had to call the bank to prove who he was. He turned into a Stockholm Syndrome victim in front of my eyes, muttering, "It's not that important. I'll just wait until I go into the bank" over and over. He didn't get his password for four months! What the hell is wrong with people? You may not like to talk on the phone, but most of the special deals I'll show you how to get require talking to someone in person or on the phone. So suck it up.

AVOIDING MONTHLY FEES

Maybe I'm too demanding, but if I'm lending a bank my money to re-lend out, I don't believe I should have to pay them additional fees. Think about it: If your Big Bank charges you a £5 monthly fee, that basically wipes

Alert to Students

If you're a student, there's no reason you shouldn't have an account with no fees and no minimums. If you decide to stick with a Big Bank account, make sure you're in a student account with no annual fees. Here's how the conversation will probably go:

YOU: Hi, I'm a student and I'd like to get a savings account and a current account with no annual fees. I'd like free checking and no minimum balance, please.

BANKER: *I'm really sorry, but we don't offer those anymore.*

YOU: Really? That's interesting because [HSBC/NatWest/other competitor] is offering me that exact deal right now. Could you check again and tell me which comparable accounts you offer?

(Eighty percent of the time, you'll get a great account at this point. If not, ask for a supervisor.)

SUPERVISOR: *Hi, how can I help you?*

YOU: (Repeat argument from the beginning. If the supervisor doesn't give you an option, add this:) Look, I've been a customer for X years and I want to find a way to make this work. Plus, I know that your customer-acquisition cost is more than two hundred dollars. What can you do to help me stay a customer?

SUPERVISOR: *What an astounding coincidence. My computer is suddenly allowing me to offer the exact account you asked for!*

YOU: Why, thank you, kind sir. (Sip Darjeeling tea.)

You're in a customer group that's very profitable for banks: ING Direct and the American Bankers Association put the cost of acquiring a new customer between $100 and $3,500—including all of their advertising, personnel, and technology costs. They don't want to lose you over something as small as a $5 monthly fee. Use this knowledge as leverage whenever you contact any financial company.

out any interest you earn. This is why I'm fanatical about my savings and checking accounts having no fees of any kind, including monthly fees, overdraft fees, or setup fees. If you already have an account at a bank you like, but they're charging a monthly fee, try to get them to waive it. They will often do this if you set up direct deposit, which lets your employer deposit your paycheck directly into your account every month.

Banks will also try to trick you by demanding "minimums," which refer to minimum amounts you must have in your account to avoid fees or to get "free" services like bill pay. These are B.S. Imagine if a bank required you to keep £1,000 sitting in its low-interest account. You could be earning twenty times that much by investing it.

If you can't do direct deposit because your job doesn't offer it or if you can't get the bank to waive a "minimum," I strongly recommend that you switch to an online high-interest account, which has no fees and no minimums.

Note: Certain charges are okay for services like money orders and reordering checks. Please don't run into your bank screaming, "BUT RAMIT TOLD ME NO FEES!!!!" when you're trying to order more checks. That would be cool, though.

ALMOST ALL BANK FEES ARE NEGOTIABLE

The most painful and expensive fees are usually overdraft fees— which is the fee your bank charges you if you don't have enough money in your current account to cover a purchase. Of course, the best way to avoid overdraft fees is to not let them happen in the first place. Set up automatic transfers and keep a cash cushion in your account (I keep about $1,000 in my checking at all times). But mistakes do happen. Most banks understand that people are occasionally forgetful and they'll waive a first-time fee if you ask. After the first time, it gets harder but can still be done if you have a good excuse. Remember: They want to keep you as their customer. A well-executed phone call can often make a difference. But when calling, keep in mind that you should have a clear goal (to get your fee erased) and should not make it easy for companies to say no to you.

Here's how I negotiated my way out of a $20 overdraft fee and a $27.10 finance charge from Wells Fargo.

I had transferred money from my savings account to my

checking account to cover a temporary shortage, and the transfer arrived one day late. I saw the overdraft fee, sighed, and called the bank to get it waived.

RAMIT: Hi, I just saw this bank charge for overdrafting and I'd like to have it waived.

BANK REP: *I see that fee . . . hmm . . . Let me just see here. Unfortunately, sir, we're not able to waive that fee. It was [some B.S. excuse about how it's not waiveable].*

Bad Things to Say Here:

"Are you sure?"
> Don't make it easy for the rep to say no to your request.

"Is there anything else I can do?"
> Again, imagine if you were a customer-service rep and someone said this. It would make your life easier to just say no. As a customer, don't make it easy for companies to say no.

"Well, this Indian blogger dude told me I could."
> Nobody cares. But it would be cool if a thousand customers called their banks and said this.

"Okay."
> Don't give up here. Despite what you learned in sex ed, "no" does not mean "no" when it comes from a bank.

Try this instead:

RAMIT: Well, I see the fee here and I'd really like to get it waived. What else can you do to help me? (Repeat your complaint and ask them how to constructively fix it.)
> At this point, about 85 percent of people will get their fees refunded. I have hundreds of comments from people on my blog who have taken this advice and saved thousands of dollars in fees. But in case the rep is obstinate, here's what you can do.

BANK REP: *I'm sorry, sir, we can't refund that fee.*

RAMIT: I understand it's difficult, but take a look at my history. I've been a customer for more than three years, and I'd like to keep the relationship going. Now, I'd like to get this waived—it was a mistake and it won't happen again. What can you do to help?

BANK REP: *Hmm, one second, please. I see that you're a really good customer. . . . I'm going to check with my supervisor. Can you hold for a second?*

(Being a long-term customer increases your value to them, which is one reason you want to pick a bank you can stick with for the long term. And the fact that you didn't back down at the first "no" makes you different from 99 percent of other customers.)

BANK REP: *Sir, I was able to check with my supervisor and waive the fee. Is there anything else I can help you with today?*

That's all I had to do! This doesn't just work for overdraft fees—it can also work for certain processing fees, late fees, and even ATM fees. I learned this lesson the hard way. I lived in New York for a summer when I was doing an internship. I decided not to open a bank account while I was there because it would take time and I was lazy. So I just used those ATMs left and right and ate the $3 charges ($1.50 from my bank, $1.50 from the ATM) each time. Now I feel dumb because I just talked to a friend who recently moved to New York for a few months. She didn't want to open a bank account for such a short time either, but instead of just shrugging and saying "Oh, well," she actually called her bank. She just asked them if they would waive the ATM fees while she was there. "No problem," they said. She saved more than $250 just by making a phone call! Remember, with a customer-acquisition cost of more than $200, banks want to keep you as their customer. So use this information to your advantage, and next time you see any fees levied on your account, make the call.

While many bank fees are ridiculous, I find that they are quite willing to wipe them for a good customer. I had a bounced-check fee wiped because I stupidly wrote a check out of the wrong account. I simply walked into the bank and asked, and they did it right there on the spot. I didn't have to do any convincing or anything. Plus, I'd been a customer for about five years.

—ADAM FERGUSON, 22

ACTION STEPS

WEEK TWO

1 Open a current account or assess the one you already have (one hour). Find an account that works for you, call the bank (or go in), and open the account. If you've already got one, make *absolutely sure* it is a no-fee, no-minimum account. How? Review your last bank statement or, if you don't have that, call your bank and say, "I'd like to confirm that my bank account has no fees and no minimums whatsoever. Can you confirm that?" If you discover you've been paying fees, use the negotiating tactic on page 64 to get your account switched to a no-fee, no-minimum account. Be aggressive in threatening to leave if they don't switch you. If you decide to switch, your new bank should move all your payments for you.

2 Open an online high-interest savings account (three hours). You'll earn more in interest and pay less in fees. Plus, it's psychologically powerful to have your savings account separate from your current: You're much less likely to dip into your savings if it's not immediately reachable through your normal banking. Spend a couple of hours researching accounts; make sure you check the rate and how consistent the rates offered by accounts have been in the past. To see a more comprehensive list, go to www.which.co.uk.

2a Optional: Open an online current account (two hours). This isn't absolutely necessary—but if you're ready to be more advanced and earn a higher interest rate, go ahead and do it. Remember, the main benefits of an online current account are a high interest rate and fewer tricky fees.

3 Fund your online savings account (one hour). Leave one and a half months of living expenses in your current account, or as close to it as you can manage. (This prevents overdrafts as you're getting used to transferring money between accounts. Transfers may be same day or could take several days, depending on the sending and receiving bank.) Transfer the rest to your savings account—even if it's only £20.

Congratulations! Now that you've got the backbone of your personal financial infrastructure up and running, we're going to open your investment account.

CHAPTER 3

GET READY TO INVEST

*Open your pension account and stocks and shares ISA—
even with just £50*

There's something special about Indian parents. To understand what I mean, ask any Indian kid you know what happened when he excitedly brought home his straight-A report card. His parents probably gleamed with pride, gave him a huge hug, and then immediately frowned. "Vijay, this is very good! But why did you get this A minus? What happened?" they said. As you can imagine, this approach tends to promote a slightly warped view of the world for Indian children. I can't wait to do this to my future kids someday.

Perhaps the fact that I grew up with this worldview explains why, when people finally start thinking about their finances, I congratulate them for approximately six seconds before I secretly judge them because I know they're not doing enough. In the last chapter we talked about saving, and I'm happy you've opened up a high-interest savings account. I really am. But it's not enough! Saving a little money here and there is not enough, despite what you read in the myriad books and blogs filled with tips and tales of frugality. "Buy 200 cases of orange juice," these fantastic articles say, "and you can save 6 percent! Amazing!"

Get a life. The sad fact is, if you do only the bare minimum—for example, if you get frugal and save £100 a month in an online savings account—the results will not be especially impressive. Even if you're earning a competitive 3 percent or higher from a high-interest online savings account, it will take you a long, long time to get a substantial return. You need a way to put that money to work for you so it earns more than even the highest-yielding savings account, and investing is the first and best way to do it. "Compounding," Albert Einstein said, "is mankind's greatest invention because it allows for the reliable, systematic accumulation of wealth."

Rather than earning 0.5 percent interest like most people do in their savings account, or even six times that amount with a high-interest savings account (like the one you now have, right?), you can earn around 5 percent per year over the long term by investing: Between 1899 and 2008 the average annual stock market return was 4.9 percent (with inflation taken off). To put that in perspective, if you invested £1,000 at age twenty-five and didn't touch it until age sixty-five, it would be worth about £3,000 in your 3 percent high-interest savings account, but if you put it in an investment account that earned 5 percent, you'd have more than £7,000.

Investing may seem intimidating, especially considering the volatility of the markets during the global financial crisis. But it's actually quite painless. I'll walk you through it, and by the end of this chapter, you'll have opened an investment account. You don't actually have to worry about choosing where to invest yet—that comes in Chapter 7. For now, we'll set up the right accounts so that when you're ready, you can simply set up automatic transfers to funnel cash there each month.

There must be something about turning 40 that causes you to evaluate where you've been and where you are going. My husband was offered a new position with better pay, but even with a $15,000 increase in salary our debt load has been so high we have continued to struggle. The turning point was when we received a fairly sizable inheritance and used it to pay down our debt, but even that wasn't enough to pay it off.

—ANN BERG, 40

Why Your Friends Probably Haven't Invested a Penny Yet

Before we go any further, let's take a minute to understand why young people are not investing. Then you can secretly scorn them once you've opened your own investment accounts.

Ask any of your friends how much they've invested and they'll say things like, "Huh?" or "I don't earn enough to invest." Most of them will say, "I don't know how to pick stocks," which is ironic because INVESTING ISN'T ABOUT PICKING STOCKS. Although it's true that some of them might participate in a pension, through work or privately, that's probably the extent of their investments. And yet these are the most important investing years of our lives!

Another reason young people don't invest is that they're scared. You can hear the media scream "Global financial crisis!" only so many times before you decide to opt out altogether. And yet, a drop in the stock market is a *good* thing for young people. It means investments are essentially on sale, so we can buy stocks for less now and then let our

Three Startling Stats About Young People and Pensions

Remember, a pension is just a type of investment account—one that offers huge benefits that I'll cover on page 78. Here's what's stunning: Of employees age twenty-five and under in America,

- Less than one-third participate in a pension;

- Less than 4 percent max out their contributions;

- And, astonishingly, only 16 percent contribute enough to get the full company match. The company match is literally free money, so 84 percent of young employees are losing thousands of dollars per year because they haven't spent a few hours to learn how this stuff works.

OLDER PEOPLE REGRET NOT INVESTING

I'm not a crotchety old man yet, but when I see these numbers, it's tempting to run around with a cane and a vodka tonic in hand, screaming at young people. Not only do we fail to invest our money, but we don't even know why it's important!

Age of employee	Percentage who participate in a pension	Percentage of pay they Contribute	Median balance of their pension	My comment
18–25	31.3%	5.6%	$1,280	Too busy watching *The Hills.*
26–41 computer	63.1%	7.2%	$14,730	These people have realized that perhaps saving money is important.
42 and up	72.0%	8.3%	$44,330	These older folks are wishing they could go back in time and beat themselves for not saving more, like Biff in *Back to the Future II.*

Source: Hewitt and Associates (http://articles.moneycentral.msn.com/CollegeAndFamily/MoneyInYour20s/YoungAdultsAllButIgnore401ksIRAs.aspx)

money grow for decades. When people say "buy low, sell high," this is what they're talking about.

Remember, knowing how to invest isn't obvious. And that's the problem. When it comes to money, it's actually very easy to end up like most other people: You just . . . do nothing. After years of talking to young people about money, I have come to a couple of conclusions: First, I pretty much hate everyone. Second, I believe there are three categories of people: the As, the Bs, and the Cs. The As are already managing their money and want to optimize what they're doing. The Bs, the largest group of people, are not doing anything but could be persuaded to change that if you figure out what motivates them. The Cs are an unwashed mass of people who are a lost cause. Theoretically, they *could* be motivated,

---

I have a friend who loves cycling and movies. He never liked to "dress up," preferring dirty jeans and T-shirts, and didn't want a boring office job. I don't think he's ever received more than $9 an hour in his life. He has spent all of his money on lighter bike parts and VHS movies. When DVDs came out, he started rebuying the same movies on DVD because they were "better quality." Meanwhile, he filed for bankruptcy to get out from under credit card debt and now lives in a trailer behind his parents' house, with his sister paying most of his bills.

—**RONALD WAGNER, 25**

---

but it's impossibly hard to get through their knuckleheaded reasons and excuses for putting money management so far down their list of priorities.

Sadly, although some people are limited by circumstances, most people will never get rich simply because they have poor attitudes and behaviors about money. In fact, most people in their twenties are Bs: not great, but not bad. There's a lot of time left for them to set aggressive investment goals, but if they don't take any action, they end up inevitably drifting toward being a C. Don't let this happen to you!

Why do so many of us have such poor attitudes toward money? You could make a convincing case for a lack of education, too much information, confusing messages from the media, or simply a lack of interest. Whatever the reason, we *know* young people aren't investing enough.

Financial institutions have noticed an interesting phenomenon: When people enter their forties, they suddenly realize that they should have been saving money all along. As a result, the number one financial concern Americans have is not having enough money for retirement. "Even a majority of Americans in upper-income households say they are 'very' or 'moderately' worried about their retirement income," says Lydia Saad of the Gallup News Service. To bring this close to home, ask your parents what they worry about most. I'll bet you their answer is, simply, "money." Yet we're not paying much more attention to our finances than our parents did.

Although it's easy to "plan" on winning the lottery to get rich, the real way to do it is actually much simpler: Of America's millionaires, 80 percent are first-generation affluent, meaning their parents weren't rich. They collected their significant wealth through controlling their spending,

A FIFTH OF YOUNG PEOPLE THINK THEY'LL GET RICH THROUGH THE LOTTERY

Percentage of young people . . .	. . . Who believe they'll get rich . . .	My comment
21%	By winning the lottery	I hate you.
11%	Through an inheritance	I hate you.
3%	Via an insurance settlement	How about the insurance of doing some actual work to learn about your money?

regular investing, and in some cases, entrepreneurship. Not as sexy as winning the lottery, but much more realistic.

On average, millionaires invest 20 percent of their household income each year. Their wealth isn't measured by the amount they make each year, but by how much they've saved and invested over time. In other words, a project manager could earn £50,000 per year and be richer than a doctor earning £250,000 per year—*if* the project manager has a higher net worth by saving and investing more over time.

American culture doesn't help us think about investing our money. We see shows like *My Super Sweet 16* that show us the *results* of being rich, not *how to get there*. Not surprisingly, as such TV shows have become more popular, our attitudes have changed. According to a Roper Center study in 1975, a lot of Americans thought "the good life" meant a happy marriage, one or more children, an interesting job, and a home. By 1999, the responses were more materialistic: "a lot of money," a second car," "a second TV," "a vacation home," "a swimming pool," and "really nice clothes."

Despite this preoccupation with material goods and a dizzying array of information sources—including 24/7 financial-news channels and dozens of personal-finance magazines—most of us don't seem to be concerned with managing our financial situation. Even high-income earners don't handle their money well: 34 percent of those who earned $250,000 or more said the need to pay everyday bills was the top reason why they weren't saving more. One in ten said they weren't making enough to make ends meet, according to an HSBC Bank report in 2007.

Even though lots of young people have naive and often delusional ideas about money, you don't need to be one of them. I'm going to help you confront reality and take a few simple steps to get rich. Ten years from now—hell, maybe even three months from now—you'll see an investment account full of money that is automatically added to each month. You'll be earning while you sleep. And instead of waiting for a magical lottery win, you'll consciously use your investment account to get rich.

INVESTING IS THE SINGLE MOST EFFECTIVE WAY TO GET RICH

By opening an investment account, you give yourself access to the biggest moneymaking vehicle in the history of the world: the stock market. Setting up an account is an excellent first step toward actually investing, and you don't have to be rich to open one. Many account providers will reduce minimum investment levels (depending on the investment you take out) to as little as £20 if you make regular monthly payments (more on this in Chapter 5).

INVEST NOW...
YOU'RE NOT GETTING ANY YOUNGER

What if you had started investing £10 per week five years ago, receiving a 5 percent return (if it was a pension, you'd get more because of tax efficiency)? Guess how much you'd have? It turns out that by now, you'd have thousands of pounds—all from investing a little more than £1 per day. Think about that £10 a week—where did it go, anyway? If you're like most people, it probably slipped through your fingers on random things like cab rides and lunches. Despite wild rides in the stock market, with a long term perspective, the best thing you can do is start investing early.

If you invest this much per week ...	After 1 year, you'll have ...	After 5 years, you'll have ...	After 10 years, you'll have ...
£10	£532	£2,947	£6,728
£20	£1,064	£5,893	£13,457
£50	£2,660	£14,734	£33,643

I didn't open an investment account until I was twenty-three, because I simply didn't know I should. And once I learned I should, I wasn't sure I had enough money to. Investing is for rich people, right? Not people going to college and earning less than $10 an hour, right? My other issue was that I didn't know what to do with the money even if I opened an account. I had no idea where to start, and as a (now recovering) perfectionist, the number of choices freaked me out.

—**SHANNON HULSEY, 26**

The Ladder of Personal Finance

hese are the five systematic steps you should take to invest. Each step builds on the previous one, so when you finish the first, go on to the second. If you can't get to number 5, don't worry. You can still feel great, since most people never even get to the first step. In Chapter 5, I'll show you how to make this automatic, so your system runs itself with just a few hours of work *per year*—but remember, opening these accounts and getting started is the most important step.

Rung 1: If your employer offers a pension scheme where they will match your contributions, invest to take full advantage of it. If it's a final salary scheme (sometimes called defined benefit), your employer will pay in a lot more than your own contributions. If not, find out how much you should contribute to get the maximum contribution from your employer. If you earn £40,000 and your employer offers a 100 percent match up to 5 percent of your salary, if you pay in £150 a month, your company will match it. This is free money and there is, quite simply, no better deal.

Rung 2: Pay off your credit card and any other debt. The average credit card APR is 16 percent, and many APRs are higher. Whatever your card company charges, paying off your debt will give you a significant instant return. For the best ways to do this, see page 40 in Chapter 1.

Rung 3: Open up a stocks and shares ISA account and contribute as much money as possible to it. ISA limits are increasing to £10,200 a year—including up to £5,100 in a cash ISA.

Rung 4: If you have money left over, go back to your pension and contribute more (as much as your employer will allow). The current limit is 100% of your salary or £245,000 (unless you're not earning, in which case you can pay £3,600 into a stakeholder pension) although employer-based schemes may have much lower limits.

Rung 5: If you still have money left over pay extra on any mortgage debt you have, and consider investing in yourself: Whether it's starting a company or getting an additional degree, there's often no better investment than your own career.

Remember, this ladder of personal finance only shows you *where* to invest your money. In Chapter 7, I'll show you *what* to invest in.

Mastering Your Pension

I t is a universally acknowledged truth that girls named Nancy are never hot. But imagine that you met the hottest Nancy of your life on spring break in Cabo. Would you be willing to challenge your deep-seated worldview and hang out with her?

That's the trade-off you make with a pension: uncool name, kinda boring, but huge . . . benefits. Here's how they work:

If you're employed, you'll normally be offered the chance to join a work-based pension. Different employers have different schemes and some have more than one type. The main thing to find out is whether the employer is going to pay into it or not. If they do, it's generally a no-brainer. It's not often your boss gives you something for free, so why would you turn this down?

Whatever type of pension your employer offers (and I'll talk about these in more detail later), what you need to understand is that it's simply a retirement account that gives you large tax advantages if you agree not to withdraw money until you reach retirement age (the earliest age you can withdraw money is 50, rising to 55 in April 2010). Depending on the type of pension you're paying into, you may not have to take any money out of it until you're 75. (But don't worry about that now. By the time you're 75, we'll all have flying jet packs and robots to handle all our finances.) To set up your pension, you fill out a form authorizing part of

(continued on page 79)

These tables show the percentage of employees who sign up to work-based pension schemes, based on the type of scheme and the amount employers contribute

PERCENTAGES OF EMPLOYEES WHO JOIN FINAL SALARY PENSIONS

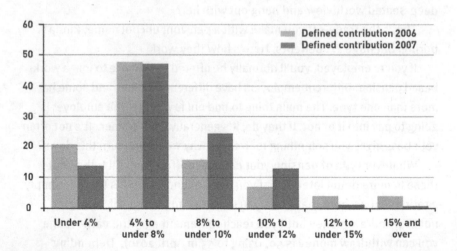

Excludes schemes with fewer than 12 members. Excludes non-contributory arrangements and contributions paid as fixed amounts only. Percentages are Source: Occupational Pension Scheme Survey, Office for National Statistics.

Defined-benefit plans are useful if your employer matches above 15%.

your paycheck—you decide how much—to be sent to your account each month. The money goes straight from your employer to your pension, so you never see it in your paycheck. When you set the account up, you choose among some simple investment options, then let your money accumulate over time.

Let's dig deeper into the benefits of your pension.

Pension Benefit 1: Using Pretax Money Means an Instant 25 Percent Accelerator: Retirement accounts offer you a deal: You promise to invest your money for the long term, and in exchange they give you huge tax advantages. Because the money you're contributing isn't taxed until you withdraw it many years later (this is called "pretax money"), you have much more money to invest for compound growth—usually 25 to 40 percent more (although this could change for some higher earners in 2010).

Let's look at a regular investment account first (we'll ignore stocks and shares ISAs for now). If you open one of these at any investment firm, you don't get many tax advantages: For every £100 you make, you'll be able to invest only about £75 of it because, depending on your tax rate, about 25 percent goes to pay income taxes.

A pension is different. It's "tax-deferred," meaning you can invest the entire £100 and let it grow for about thirty-plus years. Sure, you'll pay taxes when you withdraw your money later, but that extra 25 percent turns out to make a huge difference as it gets compounded more and more.

Pension Benefit 2: Your Employer Match Means Free Money: In many cases, your employer will match part of your contribution, meaning you get automatic free money for investing—a win-win situation. To find out if your company offers a pension match, just ask your HR rep what the matching policy is.

How exactly does matching work? Here's an example: Again say your company offers a 100% match up to 4 percent. This means your company will match every pound you invest up to 4 percent of your salary. For easy math, let's pretend you make £50,000 per year. You contribute £2,000 (4 percent of your salary) each year. Your employer then matches the £2,000, so your actual investment is £4,000 per year.

If you start at age twenty-five and earn 7 percent on your money, you'll have more than £638,000 with a company pension with a 100% match. And each year you invest, the difference grows larger.

RETIREMENT VS. NONRETIREMENT ACCOUNT EARNINGS OVER TIME	Your Contributions Over 40 years	Tax Relief	Employer Contributi
Regular Taxable Investment Account	£80,000	NIL	NIL
Pension Scheme by Yourself	£80,000	£20,000	NIL
Pension Scheme with Employer Contributions	£80,000	£20,000	£100,000

Pension Benefit 3: Automatic Investing: With a pension, your money is sent into your investment account *without you having to do anything.* If you don't see the money in your paycheck because it's automatically sent to your pension, you'll learn to live without it. This is an excellent example of using psychology to trick yourself into investing. In fact, there's an emerging body of literature on how powerful these effects are.

Research for the Department for Work and Pensions showed that, whereas only 41 percent joined a scheme on an "opt-in" basis, that rose to 60 percent when employees were automatically enrolled. Sure, you're given the freedom to opt out, but automatic enrolment takes advantage of the fact that most people don't do anything active with their money. That's why a new pension, which is due to be introduced in 2012, called the personal account, would—for the first time—use automatic (or auto) enrolment to encourage people to save for their retirement.

COMMON CONCERNS ABOUT PENSIONS

What happens if I really need my money? A company pension is a retirement account for long-term investments, not a current or savings account that you can dip in and out of it as you wish. Your company scheme may not allow you to take your pension early (before the normal retirement age of the scheme, which may be 60 or older). In any case, you cannot access your pension before the age of 50 (55 from April 2010) although you may be able to cash it in and take it as a lump sum if you are seriously ill and have less than a year to live. The punishments are intentional: this is money for your retirement, not to go out drinking on Saturday. Remember, the biggest problem most people have is not saving and investing at all, so don't let worrying about

butions	Investment Growth Rate	Fund at Retirement	Tax Payable	What You Would Receive
00	6%	£248,000	NIL	£248,000
00	7%	£319,000	£48,000	£271,000
000	7%	£638,000	£96,000	£542,000

how you'll get your money out stop you. Once you've saved and invested money, you can always figure out a way to withdraw it if you really need to.

Will I have to pay taxes when I withdraw my money? Yes. Although your pension is tax-deferred, it's not tax-free: When you start withdrawing after age 50 (55 from 2010), you'll have to pay taxes. But don't feel bad about paying these taxes, since your money will have been compounding at an accelerated rate for the last thirty to forty years. Because you agreed to invest your money in a pension, you were able to put in about 25 percent more money to grow for you.

What if I switch jobs? The money in your pension is yours, so if you move to another company, don't worry. You have a few options:

1. LEAVE IT AT YOUR CURRENT COMPANY. This may be a good option if the benefits offered by the scheme are generous (for example if it's a final salary pension and you're moving to an employer who doesn't offer this). The disadvantage is that you could end up with several pension pots and forget about them. Some defined contribution schemes have higher charges once you leave the company and you certainly won't stay up to date on the investment options and changes offered through the plan.

2. TRANSFER IT INTO YOUR NEW COMPANY'S PENSION SCHEME. Depending on the type of pension you were paying into at your old employer and the type of pension that's being offered by your new employer, you may be able to transfer your old pension to your new employer's scheme. But that doesn't necessarily mean it will be the best course of action. For example, if your old employer had a final salary pension scheme, it's probably a bad idea. You should take advice before you make the switch; if the pension scheme you're moving to has less generous benefits than the one you're leaving or is a different type of pension scheme, you may be better off leaving your pension where it is.

3. TRANSFER IT INTO A PERSONAL OR STAKEHOLDER PENSION. This can be a good option if, for example, your current scheme has high charges or doesn't offer you the investment flexibility you'd like, or if you have a final salary scheme and you're worried that your employer may cease trading and may not be able to pay out the pension they've promised. Although there's a protection scheme in place to compensate people who've signed up to occupational pensions where the pension scheme fails, there are limits on how much compensation you would receive. However, you should still take independent, professional advice. It's certainly not always a good idea to transfer your pension from a company scheme into a personal or stakeholder pension (if you have a long enough memory, you might be able to think back to the pensions mis-selling scandal of the 1980s when thousands were advised to transfer out of company schemes into private pensions that gave them a fraction of the pension they would have otherwise received). Take independent advice before you go down this route.

SUMMARY OF EMPLOYER PENSION BENEFITS

We've covered this, but it bears repeating: employer pensions are great because with virtually no effort on your part you get to put pretax money to work. What this means is that since you haven't paid taxes on the money yet, there's more of it to compound over time. On top of this, your company might offer a very lucrative pension match, which amounts to free money that you'd be insane not to take. If it's a final salary scheme, you don't even have to worry about how well the stock market performs— your pension will be based on your salary, not investment perfomance.

DO IT NOW: SETTING UP YOUR COMPANY PENSION

How you become a member of your company pension will depend on the type of scheme it is. If it's a final salary (sometimes called 'defined benefit') pension scheme, you just need to call your HR administrator and get the paperwork so that you can join the scheme. You won't be given a choice of funds or contribution levels – so the only decision you have to make is whether or not to join in the first place.

If your employer offers a defined contribution pension scheme, find out how much your employer will contribute and how much you need to pay into the scheme in order for them to match you at maximum levels,

If your employer has a group personal pension (GPP) or stakeholder scheme and contributes on your behalf, it's normally worth joining. Money will be deducted from your paycheck every month, so you shouldn't even notice it's gone.

PERSONAL AND STAKEHOLDER PENSIONS

If you don't have access to a pension scheme through your employer (or your employer has set up a group personal pension or stakeholder plan but doesn't pay a penny into it) you can pay into your own pension plan. Don't get too hung up on the jargon; stakeholders and personal pension plans are very similar, except that stakeholders have strict limits on how much the pension company can take every year in management fees and charges, they have to let you stop and start contributions or transfer to another scheme without charging any penalty and you can pay in as little as £20 a month.

You don't even have to be working or earning a salary to take out a stakeholder (you can pay up to £3,600 year into one if you don't have any earnings). As with company and employer-based pensions, you get tax relief on any money you pay into a personal or stakeholder pension.

SIPPS (AND WHY THEY'RE DIFFERENT)

There's another kind of personal pension that you might be interested in. SIPPs (the name stands for "self invested personal pensions") let you invest in all kinds of funds and investments that you wouldn't be able to put your money into if you had an ordinary personal or stakeholder pension. Some employers offer SIPPs to their workers (but normally only to senior staff), but most SIPPs are taken out by individuals who aren't happy simply to hand their money over to a pension company each month. They can be a good idea if you're someone who wants to take more control over your pension, but probably not worth it if you'd rather "invest it and forget it".

What SIPPs let you do—that ordinary pensions don't—is to get access to a very wide range of investments. If you're someone who would like to take an active interest in where your pension money is invested, you can do that easily with a SIPP. And if you'd rather put a lot of your pension money into low-risk investments, such as bonds, you're able to do that as well. The list of assets you can invest your pension contributions in through a SIPP

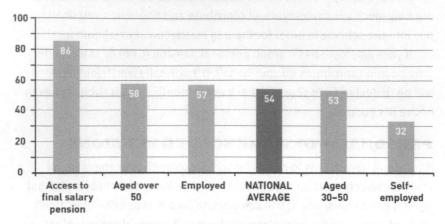

Scottish Widows Pension Index Score

Source: Scottish Widows' Pensions Report 2009/You Gov

includes: shares, investment trusts, commercial property and government bonds. But for many, it's the fact that SIPPs let them change their investment strategy that's one of the major attractions.

The other advantage is that if you're interested in particular investments (such as climate change or ethical funds), you may be better off with a SIPP, because of the choice they offer.

But—as with everything—there are downsides and they shouldn't be overlooked. The main disadvantage of SIPPs is that they can have higher charges; sometimes significantly higher and that's meant they've generally been bought by people who've already saved quite a lot of money into their pension fund (or those who plan to do so in the future).

WHY PEOPLE MISS OUT

As the chart above shows, people are far more likely to save if they are employed (which means they will normally be able to join their employer's pension scheme). And if your workplace has a final salary scheme you're almost three times more likely to sign up to it than to set up your own pension if you work for yourself. Don't miss out because you don't have a pension scheme ready and waiting for you to join, courtesy of your boss.

EMPLOYER-BASED VS PERSONAL STAKEHOLDER PLANS

Okay, so here's the confusing thing. You can take out a stakeholder pension directly with a pensions company or you can join one that's been organised through your work (assuming you're not self-employed). What's the difference and which is better?

If your employer has a stakeholder pension at work and pays into it, you should definitely join it rather than setting up one of your own. Not only will you get free money but all the hard work will be done for you. Money will be taken straight from your salary. But if they've just set up a stakeholder pension but don't pay a penny into it, it's a tougher call. Then it's down to you to do a bit of research into the stakeholder pension company your employer has chosen and whether you can find something better if you go it alone.

PENSION RESTRICTIONS

Unless you have a final salary pension, you've got to convert your pension fund into a regular monthly payment when you retire. For most people, that means buying an annuity.

Annuities (I prefer to think of them as a monthly retirement income) get quite a bad press because a) people who've paid into a pension want

Growth Vs. Access

Q: *I don't want to lock my money up in a retirement account—I might need it soon. What should I do?*

A: Saving in a pension (whether it's through your employer's scheme or your own private pension) does mean locking your money away until you're at least 50 (55 from 2010). That's why you get the generous tax breaks. If you're really worried about getting hold of your money, you could invest in a stocks and shares ISA instead (or split your money). They're also meant for long-term investing but have different tax breaks to pensions. The difference is you can cash them in at any time.

If you need your money in fewer than five years, put it in a high-interest savings account. But don't make the mistake of keeping your money in a savings account just because you're too lazy to take the time to learn how to invest it. If you'd invested ten years ago, wouldn't it feel good to have a lot more money right now? Well, the next best time to invest is today.

to be able to spend their money how they want to once they retire and b) because the money you get every month from your pension depends on the annuity rate and at the moment, they're pretty low.

That argument doesn't really stack up because you do have some flexibility about when you buy your annuity (although there are some exceptions, you have to do it by the time you hit 75).

All I'd add is that those who really struggle when they retire are people who've never bothered to start a pension, not those who've taken out a personal plan and had to buy an annuity when rates are low.

SETTING UP YOUR PERSONAL OR STAKEHOLDER PENSION

Don't put off opening a personal or stakeholder pension because you think it's complicated or that it will take hours to do. It's not and it won't. You can do it online in 20–30 minutes. Get off your ass!

If you're not sure whether you should take out a stakeholder pension you can look at the Financial Services Authority's website where it's got a 'decision tree' to help you make up your mind: http://www.moneymadeclear.fsa.gov.uk/tools/stakeholder_pensions/notes_index.html.

You can go to a financial adviser if you'd rather someone talked you through the options, but don't ignore this decision because you don't know which adviser to talk to or you don't think you can afford their advice. Just by putting off starting your pension by a year or two, you'll have to pay far more into it every month to get the same amount of money when you retire.

With a stakeholder pension, you can transfer money between funds without penalty so it doesn't matter if you decide to invest in one fund and then change your mind. The main thing is to get started.

STOCKS AND SHARES ISAS

I've talked about the different types of pensions, but you don't have to save in a pension to get money for your retirement. If you're really worried about having your money locked up, perhaps because you know you're going to take a break from work to have kids later on, you could invest in a stocks and shares ISA instead (but don't do this if you'll need the money in 5 years or less).

ISAs don't get the same tax break as pensions, but they're still pretty good if you're looking to save tax. Unlike pensions, ISAs don't give you a helping hand from tax relief on the money you pay in, but you don't pay any extra tax when you cash in your ISA. Not a penny. What you do get is the chance to cash in your ISA whenever you want to, without paying a penalty (although if the stock market has just fallen through the floor, you could lose a chunk of money).

TAKING OUT AN ISA

If you know what you want, you can avoid paying the upfront (or initial) charges, which can be as much as 5.5% of the money you pay in. If you use a discount broker, you'll be able to do that.

So how much can you put into your ISA? Well, because you get far more freedom about when you cash in your ISA (and there are no restrictions on what you spend the money on) they have much lower annual limits than pensions. At the moment, the maximum you can pay into a stocks and shares ISA is £7,200 a year (although that's due to rise to £10,200) and whatever you may have saved into a cash ISA comes off that limit.

DISCOUNT BROKERAGES AND ISAS

Discount broker	Costs and savings	Things to know
Hargreaves Lansdown www.h-l.co.uk	Discounts all initial charges on 80% of funds, most on the rest. An annual loyalty bonus of up to 0.5%.	The Vantage service offers investors access to over 2,220 funds as well as cash, shares, ETFs, investment trusts and Gilts.
Cavendish online www.cavendishonline.co.uk	£20 flat fee. £10 annual service fee. All initial charge and renewal commission is discounted.	Access to over 1100 funds (via Fidelity Fundsnetwork).
Bestinvest www.bedstinvest.co.uk	Save up to 5.5% on initial charges (not all initial charge is discounted on all funds).	Access to over 1500 funds and you can keep money in cash while you decide to invest. Ongoing advice included.

Keep Track of All Your Accounts

To help me manage all my accounts, I set up a free online workspace from PBworks (www.pbworks.com) to store my account numbers and passwords on a private page. It's like an online notepad that you can keep private or public, and you can access it from wherever you can get on the web. My own wiki has a page to store my passwords, another to store future blog posts, and an entirely separate section to collaborate on marketing ideas I'm working on.

Full disclosure: I know it works, is secure, and that there are no gimmicks behind PBworks because I co-founded the service.

Features. You should also investigate the features your account offers. Will you have customer service via phone toll-free, 24/7? Is the online interface easy to use? Will your account allow easy automatic investing? Most of them do, but it is important to find out beforehand.

And that's it. Yes, you could spend hundreds of hours doing a detailed comparison of the total number of funds offered, frequency of mailings, and alternative pension or ISA accounts available, but more is lost from indecision than bad decisions. As Benjamin Franklin said, "Don't put off until tomorrow what you can do today." And as Ramit Sethi said, "Let others debate minutiae—all you need to do is open a pension or ISA account at a discount brokerage. Sucka."

Signing up to a pension or stocks and shares ISA shouldn't take long. You may be able to do it online or you might have to send off some forms. Ideally you'll be able to increase your monthly payments – you'll learn exactly how much you're able to invest monthly after reading the next chapter.

I did not have much startup money since I am a graduate student. So saving even a thousand dollars to open an account would take a while, and those savings might be continually eaten up by general life emergencies like car repairs before I ever opened the account. I went with T. Rowe Price. It had no minimums with a fifty-dollar-a-month automatic contribution. Fifty dollars a month is easy to commit to, and from there raising my monthly contribution by ten bucks is easy to justify. No minimum meant I could open it immediately.

—**HANNAH FLATH, 24**

CHOOSING YOUR FUNDS

At the start of the chapter, I talked about company pension schemes and depending on the type of pension your employer offers, you may not have any choice about where your money is invested. If it's a final salary scheme, you have to invest your money alongside everybody else's. If you're taking out any other type of pension (stakeholder or defined contribution scheme) or an ISA, you should be able to put your money into a cash-based or money market account while you work out what you want to do with it.

Beware that pensions are normally set up so that if you don't actively choose an investment fund at the start your money is paid straight into a default account. Default accounts vary widely between different schemes (if it's an employer-sponsored plan) and different pension companies. To avoid going into the default fund, you should actively select to put your money in a cash-based fund (or in a cash account if it's a stocks and shares ISA) and switch to a different fund or funds when you're ready.

You don't want to leave your money in cash or cash-based funds if you're investing for your retirement (or at least for the long term), but if you're paying money into your pension or ISA every month, then in the first few months you'll won't have much money in the account, so keeping it in cash won't make much difference to your returns. We'll cover the different investment options in Chapter 7.

BEYOND RETIREMENT ACCOUNTS

If you've joined your employer's pension scheme (paying as much as you need to get matching contributions, where relevant) or started your own personal or stakeholder scheme (or a stocks and shares ISA if you're worried about being locked in), your next stage is to learn more about the choices to grow your money.

Congratulations!

You've started up the Ladder of Personal Finance. Take a moment to pat yourself on the back. You now have a system set up to grow your money. This is so important. Having investment accounts means you're starting to think about rapid growth and distinguishing between short-term savings and long-term investing. And that £50 you sent may seem like a small step, but I believe it's the most significant £50 you'll ever invest.

WEEK THREE

1 Join your employer's pension scheme (one to three hours). Get the paperwork from your HR manager and fill it out. Check to see if your employer offers a match. If it does, contribute enough to get the full match. If it's a final salary (defined benefit) scheme, contribute to the level set by your employer.

2 Come up with a plan to pay off your debt (three hours). Get serious about getting out of debt. Run a calculation from www.moneybasics. co.uk to see how much you could save by paying an extra £100 or £200 per month. Also revisit page 35 in Chapter 1 and see page 220 in Chapter 9 for details on how to pay off your credit card debt and student loans.

3 Open a personal or stakeholder pension and set up automatic payment (one hour). Send as much as you can, but even £50/month is fine. We'll dive into the details a little later.

Now that you've opened these accounts, let's figure out a way to get them as full as possible. In the next chapter, I'll show you how to get control of your spending to make your money go where you want it to go.

CHAPTER 4

CONSCIOUS SPENDING

*How to save hundreds per month
(and still buy what you love)*

I used to find it ridiculous when people said you could judge a person by their belt or shoes. Are you kidding me? Can I tell what kind of soup you like by the earrings you're wearing? Get the hell out of here.

Recently, however, I discovered I was wrong. It turns out there *is* one universal shortcut to discovering someone's true character: if they eat chicken wings like an immigrant.

Because I don't understand or care about sports, last Super Bowl Sunday I decided to go on a wing crawl. It's like a pub crawl, but with wings. I quickly realized that the most interesting part of eating wings with friends is seeing how much meat they leave on the bone. Some people leave half the chicken and move on to the next wing. These people are worthless, and I quickly distance myself from them. Then there are people who clean the bone so thoroughly, flawlessly ridding it of every last shred of meat and marrow, that you can conclude only two things: They will be stellar successes in all facets of life, and they must be from another country. You see, immigrants (like my parents) never leave a shred of meat on a chicken wing—we can all learn something from them.

I feel guilty about not having a budget. I have a hard time wrapping my brain around how to set a budget and then not actually spend more than the budget allows. I feel guilty that I'm a nerd in most other respects, but I just can't sit down and do the math about my spending.

—SARAH ROBESON, 28

That kind of economy is rare these days. (Although in the wake of the global financial crisis, frugality—or at least giving lip service to it—is becoming more common.) We spend more on our mobile phones than most people in other countries do on their mortgages. We buy shoes that cost more than our grandparents paid for their *cars*. Yet we don't really know how much these individual costs add up to. How many times have you opened your bills, winced, then shrugged and said, "I guess I spent that much"? How often do you feel guilty about buying something—but then do it anyway? In this chapter, the antidote to unconscious spending, we're going to gently create a new, simple way of spending. It's time to stop wondering where all your money goes each month. I'm going to help you redirect it to the places *you* choose, like investing, saving, and even spending *more* on the things you love (but less on the things you don't).

Wait! Before you run away thinking this is a chapter on creating a budget, hang on a second. This isn't about creating a fancy budget that you'll have to maintain every day for the rest of your life. I hate budgeting. *Budgeting* is the worst word in the history of the world. I could be sitting on a golden throne surrounded by forty-three scantily clad models, and if I accidentally uttered the word *budget,* I sincerely believe they would all instantaneously look up (from feeding me grapes and fanning me, duh), open their jaws in shock, and then flee in horror. Nobody wants to budget.

I'm not finished. "Create a budget!" is the sort of worthless advice that personal-finance pundits feel good prescribing, yet when real people read about making a budget, their eyes glaze over faster than John Goodman's lips at Krispy Kreme. Who wants to track their spending? The few people who actually try it find that their budgets completely fail after two days because tracking every penny is overwhelming. Amusingly, in a 2007 survey by bankrate.com, 75 percent of Americans said they have a budget—which is complete nonsense. "There's probably a lot of wishful thinking in this response," says Jared Bernstein, director of the Living Standards Program of the Economic Policy Institute. "It's probably more accurate to say that three-quarters *think* they should work on a monthly budget." My kind of man: exposing the delusions of people everywhere!

HOW MANY TIMES HAVE YOU OPENED YOUR BILLS, WINCED, THEN SHRUGGED AND SAID, "I GUESS I SPENT THAT MUCH"?

For the last fifty years, budgeting has been the battleground for snobby personal-finance writers who've tried to shove a daily tracking system down everyone's throats because it sounds logical: "Track your spending! It's so simple!" There's only one catch: NOBODY EVER DOES IT.

And I don't believe for a second that because times are tough, Americans are going to buckle down and stop consuming over the long term. Most people wouldn't know where to start if I told them to stop spending and start saving. I might as well try to convince an Ankylosaurus to dance a jig.

Many of my friends just throw up their hands when they have done something stupid with their money and don't learn from their mistakes. I see people get out of huge credit card debt and once their balances are wiped clean to zero, start the process of maxing out their cards again.

—FRANK WILES, 29

Because we know that budgets don't work, I'm not about to make the same mistake in recommending them to you.

Let's try something that actually works. Forget budgeting. Instead, let's create a Conscious Spending Plan. What if you could make sure you were saving and investing enough money each month, and then use the rest of your money guilt-free for whatever you want? Well, you can—with some work. The only catch is that you have to plan where you want your money to go *ahead of time* (even if it's on the back of a napkin). Would it be worth taking a couple of hours to get set up so you can spend on the things you love? It will automate your savings and investing, and make your spending decisions crystal clear. When your friends say, "I never have any money," you're going to wonder why they don't just spend a couple of hours to set things up right—like you did.

The Difference Between Cheap and Frugal

A while back, a couple of friends and I were talking about where we want to travel this year, and one of them said something that surprised me: "You probably wouldn't approve, but I want to go to the Caribbean."

Huh? Why wouldn't I approve?

I stared at him pensively for many moments, taking the form of Rodin's *Thinker* and wishing that I had a pipe and perhaps a tweed jacket. Then I figured it out. Apparently, he thought of me as a Finger-Wagging Money Judge, as if I silently disapproved of him for spending his money on something "frivolous." In other words, someone who writes about personal finance is automatically "the guy who tells me I can't do stuff because it costs too much money."

Nothing could be further from the truth. Now, I will call your ass out when you make mistakes (like one of my readers who wasn't worried about his cable bill increasing $5/month, yet complained every time the price of gas went up two cents a gallon). But I'm *not* the nagging parent who tells you not to spend money on lattes. I spend lots of money on eating out and traveling, but I never feel guilty. Instead of taking a simplistic "Don't spend money on expensive things!!!" view, I believe there's a more nuanced approach to spending.

Let's first dispense with the idea that saying no to spending on certain things means you're cheap. If you decide that spending £2.50 on Cokes when you eat out isn't worth it—and you'd rather save that £15 each week for a movie—that's not cheap. That's using frugality to drive conscious spending. Unfortunately, most Americans dismiss frugality because they confuse it with cheapness, thinking that frugality is all-or-nothing: "Frugal people don't spend money on anything! I'm never going to cut all my spending, so forget it." Furthermore, our parents never taught us how to be frugal, so not only have we confused frugality with cheapness, but we never really practiced it in the first place. As a country, we spend more than we make each year and virtually nothing seems to change our behavior. Even though we may tighten our wallets during a downturn, we soon return to our usual spending behaviors. And frankly, nobody's interested in changing the status quo: Consumer spending accounts for about 70 percent of the American economy.

Frugality isn't just about our own choices, though. There's also the social influence to spend. Call it the *Sex and the City* effect, where your friends' spending directly affects yours. Next time you go to the mall, check out any random group of friends. Chances are, they're dressed similarly—even though chances are good that they have wildly different incomes. Keeping up with friends is a full-time job. In fact, continuing the parallel between our attitudes toward money and food

TOO OFTEN, OUR FRIENDS INVISIBLY PUSH US AWAY FROM BEING FRUGAL AND CONSCIOUS SPENDERS.

that I mentioned in the introduction, researchers found in a landmark 2007 study published in the *New England Journal of Medicine* ("The Spread of Obesity in a Large Social Network over 32 Years") that friends had a direct influence on one's likelihood of gaining weight. When a friend became obese, a person increased his or her chances of becoming obese by 57 percent. How do you think your friends' spending influences yours?

Too often, our friends invisibly push us away from being frugal and conscious spenders. Right around the time when the 3G iPhone came out, for example, I went to dinner with two friends. One of them was considering getting the new iPhone, and she pulled out her old phone to show us why she was thinking about buying a new one. My other friend stared in disbelief: "You haven't gotten a new phone in four years? What's wrong with you?" she asked. "You need to get the iPhone *tomorrow*." Even though it was only three sentences, the message was clear: There's something wrong with you for not getting a new phone (regardless of whether or not you need it).

CHEAP PEOPLE VS. FRUGAL PEOPLE

Cheap	Frugal
Cheap people care about the cost of something.	Frugal people care about the value of something.
Cheap people try to get the lowest price on everything.	Frugal people try to get the lowest price on most things, but are willing to spend on items they really care about.
Cheap people's cheapness affects those around them.	Frugal people's frugality affects only them.
Cheap people are inconsiderate. For example, when getting a meal with other people, if their food costs £7.95, they'll put in £8, knowing very well that tax and tip mean it's closer to £11.	Frugal people know they have to pick and choose where they spend their money. If they can spend only £10 on lunch, they'll order water instead of Coke.
Cheap people make you uncomfortable because of the way they treat others.	Frugal people make you feel uncomfortable because you realize you could be doing better with your money.
Cheap people keep a running tally of how much their friends, family, and coworkers owe them.	Some frugal people do this, too, but certainly not all.
Because of the fear of even one person suggesting they spent too much on something, cheap people are not always honest about what they spend.	Neither are frugal people.
Cheap people are unreasonable and cannot understand why they can't get something for free. Sometimes this is an act, but sometimes it's not.	Frugal people will try as hard as cheap people to get a deal, but they understand that it's a dance, and in the end, they know they don't intrinsically *deserve* a special deal.
Cheap people think short term.	Frugal people think long term.

Spend on What You Love

Frugality isn't about cutting your spending on everything. That approach wouldn't last two days. Frugality, quite simply, is about choosing the things you love enough to spend extravagantly on—and then cutting costs mercilessly on the things you don't love.

The mind-set of frugal people is key to being rich. Indeed, as the researchers behind the landmark book *The Millionaire Next Door* discovered, 50 percent of the more than one thousand millionaires surveyed have never paid more than $400 for a suit, $140 for a pair of shoes, and $235 for a wristwatch. Again, frugality is not about simply cutting your spending on various things. It's about making your own decisions about what's important enough to spend a lot on, and what's not, rather than blindly spending on *everything*.

THE PROBLEM IS THAT HARDLY ANYONE IS DECIDING WHAT'S IMPORTANT AND WHAT'S NOT, DAMMIT! That's where the idea of conscious spending comes in.

How My Friend Spends $21,000 Per Year Going Out—Guilt-Free

I want you to consciously decide what you're going to spend on. No more "I guess I spent that much" when you see your credit card statements. No. Conscious spending means you decide exactly where you're going to spend your money—for going out, for saving, for investing, for rent—and you free yourself from feeling guilty about your spending. Along with making you feel comfortable with your spending, a plan keeps you moving toward your goals instead of just treading water.

The simple fact is that most young people are not spending consciously. We're spending on whatever, then reactively feeling good or bad about it. Every time I meet someone who has a Conscious Spending Plan ("I automatically send money to my investment and savings accounts, then just spend the rest"), I'm so enchanted that my love rivals Shah Jahan's for his wife, Mumtaz Mahal (look it up).

I'm going to tell you about three friends who are spending lots and lots of money on things you might consider frivolous—like shoes and going out—but whose actions are perfectly justified.

THE SHOE LOVER

My friend "Lisa" spends about $5,000/year on shoes. Because the kind of shoes she likes run more than $300, this translates to about fifteen pairs of shoes annually. "THAT'S RIDICULOUS!!!" you might be saying. And on the surface, that number is indeed large. But if you're reading this book, you can look a little deeper: This girl makes a very healthy six-figure salary, has a roommate, eats for free at work, and doesn't spend much on fancy electronics, gym membership, or fine dining. In fact, her job provides many of the amenities that other people pay for.

Lisa loves shoes. A lot. She's funded her company pension and maxed out on her tax-efficient investment account. She's putting away money each month for vacation and other savings goals, and giving some to charity. And she still has money left over. Now here's where it's interesting. "But Ramit," you might say, "it doesn't matter. Three-hundred-dollar shoes are ridiculous. Nobody needs to spend that much on shoes!"

Before you chastise her for her extravagance, ask yourself these questions: Have you funded your company pension and opened additional investment accounts? Are you fully aware of where your spending money is going? And have you made a strategic decision to spend on what you love? Very few people decide how they want to spend their money up front. Instead they end up spending it on random things here and there, eventually watching their money trickle away. Just as important, have you decided what you *don't* love? For example, Lisa doesn't care about living in a fancy place, so she has a tiny room in a tiny apartment. Her decision to live in a small place means she spends $400 less every month than many of her coworkers.

After planning for her long-term and short-term goals, she has money left over to spend on the things she loves. I think she's right on.

THE PARTYER

My friend "John" spends more than $21,000 a year going out. "OMG, THAT'S SO MUCH *#%#%#% MONEY!" you might say. Well, let's break it down. Say he goes out four times a week—to dinners and bars—and spend an average of $100/night. I'm being conservative with the numbers here, because a dinner can run $60/person and drinks could be $12 each.

So You Want to Judge Your Friends' Spending?

When it comes to judging our friends' spending, we look at surface characteristics and make snap judgments. "You spent $300 on jeans!" "Why do you shop at Whole Foods?" "Why did you decide to live in that expensive area?" I know we all wonder these things about our friends because I do, too.

And, in fact, most of our judgments are right: Because young people are not carefully considering their financial choices in the context of their long-term goals—we're not paying ourselves first and we're not developing an investment/savings plan—you're probably right when you think your friend can't afford those $300 jeans.

I've been trying to be less judgmental about this. I'm not always successful, but I now focus on the fact that the sticker price doesn't matter—it's the context around it. You want to buy a $1,000 bottle of wine? And you already saved $20,000 this year at age twenty-five? Great! But if your friends are going out four times a week on a $25,000 salary, I bet they're not consciously spending.

So although it's fun to judge your friends, keep in mind that the context matters.

(Warning: If you want to judge your significant other, tread lightly: Check page 225 for my breakup-prevention financial advice.)

I'm not including bottle service, which might cost $800 or $1,000. (He lives in a big city.) That's easily $400/week.

Now, John also makes a healthy six-figure salary, so he's been able to make a Conscious Spending Plan without much difficulty. But even he has to decide what he doesn't want to spend on. For example, when his coworkers took a weekend trip to Europe from the United States (I am not kidding), he politely passed. In fact, because he works so hard, he almost never takes vacations. Similarly, because he's always at work, he doesn't care about decorating his apartment at all, so he's skipped virtually all decoration costs: He still has wire hangers holding up the few bargain suits that he wears, and he doesn't even own a spatula.

(continued on page 102)

Use Psychology Against Yourself to Save

One of my readers makes $50,000/year and, after working through some of my suggestions, realized she's paying 30 percent of her after-tax income for subscriptions. That's a truly shocking figure, so I want to share a method to dramatically cut down on unneeded subscriptions that you currently pay for. Subscriptions can be anything from LOVEFiLM to mobile phone plans to your cable bill. They are a business's best friend: They let companies make a reliable, predictable income off of you—*with no action on your part.* There's a convenience to this, of course—but there's a significant cost: When was the last time you scrutinized your monthly subscriptions and canceled one? Probably never. Yet compare this with any recent time you went shopping. When was the last time you saw something you liked but decided not to buy it?

THE À LA CARTE METHOD (updated for my UK friends). The À La Carte Method takes advantage of psychology to cut our spending. Here's how it works: Cancel all the discretionary subscriptions you can: your magazines, Sky+, cable—even your gym. (It would be totally ridiculous to cancel your Internet, though. I'd cry like a little girl if I couldn't get online from my house.) Then, buy what you need à la carte:

- Instead of paying for a ton of channels you never watch on cable, buy only the episodes you watch for £1.89 each off iTunes.

- Buy a day pass for the gym each time you go (around £5–£10).

- Buy songs you want for £0.79 each from Amazon or iTunes.

The À La Carte Method works for three reasons:

1. You're probably overpaying already. Most of us dramatically overestimate how much value we get from subscriptions. For example, if I asked you how many times a week you go to the gym, chances are you'd say, "Oh . . . two or three times a week." That's B.S. In fact, one 2006 study showed that gym members overestimate how much they'll use their membership by more than 70 percent. Members who chose a monthly fee of about £70 attended an average of 4.3 times per month.

That comes out to more than £17/gym visit—when in reality they'd have been better off buying pay-as-you-go passes for £10 each.

2. You're forced to be conscious about your spending. It's one thing to passively look at your credit card bill and say, "Ah, yes, I remember that cable bill. Looks like a valid charge. Tallyho!" It's quite another to spend £1.89 each time you want to buy a TV show—and when you actively think about each charge, you *will* cut consumption.

3. You value what you pay for. You place a higher premium on the things you pay for out of your pocket than those that come via subscripton.

THE DOWNSIDE OF THE À LA CARTE METHOD. The big downside is that this method requires you to de-automate your life. This is the price you pay for saving money. Give it a shot for two months and see how it feels. If you don't like it, go back to your old subscriptions.

HOW TO IMPLEMENT THE À LA CARTE METHOD:

1. Calculate how much you've spent over the last month on any discretionary subscriptions you have (for example, music subscriptions, LOVEFiLM, and the gym).

2. Cancel those subscriptions and begin buying these things à la carte. (But don't let losing the gym membership be your excuse to become a fat ass.)

3. In exactly one month, check and calculate how much you spent on these items over the last month. That's the *descriptive* part.

4. Now, get *prescriptive*. If you spent £100, try to cut it down to £90. Then £75. Not too low—you want your spending to be sustainable, and you don't want to totally lose touch with what's going on in the world. But you can control exactly how many movies you rent or how many magazines you buy, because each one comes out of your pocket.

Remember, this isn't about depriving yourself. The ideal situation is that you realize you were spending £50/month in subscriptions for stuff you didn't really want—now you can consciously reallocate that money into something you love.

(continued from page 99)

For John, the limiting factor is *time*. He knows he'll never send money regularly anywhere, so he's set up his investment accounts to automatically withdraw money before he ever sees it. The key here is that John knows himself and has set up systems to support his weaknesses. In terms of spending, he works hard and plays hard, going out twice during the week and twice on the weekends, when he causes some real damage. Yet, despite spending ungodly amounts going out each week, in just a couple of years John has saved more than almost any of my friends. And although $21,000 sounds outrageous on the surface, you have to take the context of his salary and priorities into consideration. Whereas other friends might spend thousands decorating their apartments or taking vacations, John, after meeting his investment goals, chooses to spend that money going out.

The point here is that whether or not I agree with his choices, he's thought about it. He sat down, considered what he wanted to spend on, and is executing that plan. He's doing more than 99 percent of the young people I've talked to. If he had decided he wanted to spend $21,000/year on furry donkey costumes and Fabergé eggs, that would have been great, too. At least he has a plan.

THE NONPROFIT EMPLOYEE

You don't have to make a six-figure salary to be a conscious spender. My friend "Julie" works at a nonprofit firm in San Francisco, making about $40,000 per year, but she saves more than $6,000 per year—far more than most Americans.

She does this by being extremely disciplined: She cooks at home, shares rent in a small apartment, and is reimbursed for her driving by her office. When she's invited out to eat, she checks her envelope system (more on that on page 115) to see if she can afford it. If not, she politely declines. But when she *does* go out, she never feels guilty about spending because she *knows* she can afford it. Yet it's not enough to save money on just rent and food. She also chooses to save aggressively, maxing out her pension and putting aside extra money for traveling. Each month, that money is the first to be automatically transferred out.

From talking to Julie at a party or over dinner, you would never know that she saves more than most Americans. We glibly make snap decisions about people's spending using the most cursory data: Their job and their clothes give us most of what we think we need to know to understand someone's financial situation. But Julie proves that the surface data isn't always enough. Regardless of her situation, she's chosen to put her investing and saving priorities first.

WHAT THEY'RE DOING RIGHT

The friends I wrote about above are exceptions to most people our age.

They have a plan. Instead of getting caught on a spending treadmill of new phones, new cars, new vacations, and new everything, they plan what's important to them and save on the rest. My shoe friend lives in a microscopic room because she's hardly home, saving her hundreds per month. My partyer friend uses public transportation and has exactly zero décor in his apartment. And my nonprofit friend is extraordinarily detailed about every aspect of her spending.

Each of them pays themselves first, whether it's $500/month or $2,000/month. They've built an infrastructure to do this automatically so that by the time money ends up in their checking account, they know they can spend it guilt-free. They spend less time worrying about money than most people! They already know about online savings accounts and credit cards and basic asset allocation. They're not experts—they've just got a head start.

To me, this is an enviable position to be in, and it's a big part of what *I Will Teach You to Be Rich* is about: automatically enabling yourself to save, invest, and spend—enjoying it, not feeling guilty about those new jeans, because you're spending only what you have.

You can do it. It takes a plan. And it's really as simple as that.

The *I Will Teach You to Be Rich* Conscious Spending Plan

Clearly, budgeting sucks. But agreeing that conscious spending is good is like forming a group called "Americans for Babies and Lovable Koala Bears." Who would ever disagree with you? The real challenge, of course, is doing something about it.

Let's get on with the specifics of how you can make your own Conscious Spending Plan. I'm not going to lie to you: The most difficult thing in this book is not structuring your tax-deferred accounts or understanding the difference between APR and APY, it's this section right here. But I'll try to make it as painless as possible. Whatever you do, don't get overwhelmed by the idea that you need to create a massive budgeting system. All you need is to just get a simple version ready today and work to improve it over time.

Here's the idea: A Conscious Spending Plan involves four major buckets where your money will go: Fixed Costs, Investments, Savings, and Guilt-free Spending Money.

CATEGORIES OF SPENDING

Fixed costs Rent, utilities, debt, etc.	50–60% of take-home pay
Investments pension, ISA	10%
Savings Vacations, gifts, house down payment, unexpected expenses	5–10%
Guilt-free spending money Dining out, drinking, movies, clothes, shoes	20–35%

MONTHLY FIXED COSTS

Fixed costs are the amounts you must pay, like your rent/mortgage, utilities, mobile phone, and student loans. A good rule of thumb is that fixed costs should be 50–60 percent of your take-home pay. Before you can do anything else, you've got to figure out how much these add up to. You'd think it would be easy to figure this out, right?

Ha! It turns out this is one of the toughest questions in personal finance. Luckily, my way of answering this question is far faster and easier than most other methods.

Okay, let's walk through this step by step. Check out the chart on the next page with common basic expenses (the bare minimum that any ordinary person would use to live). If you see any glaring omissions for major spending categories, add them. Notice that I didn't include "eating out" or "entertainment," as those come out of the guilt-free spending category.

Category	Monthly Cost
Rent/mortgage	
Utilities	
Mobile phone, landline	
Insurance, bills	
Car payment	
Public transportation	
Loans	
Food	
Clothes	
Internet/cable	

Fill in the pound amounts you know offhand.

Now, to fill in the costs and categories you haven't yet accounted for, you're going to have to dive a little deeper. You'll need to look at your past spending to fill in all the pound amounts, and to make sure you've covered every category. Limit this to the past month to keep things simple. The easiest way to get an idea of what you've spent where is to look at your credit card and banking statements or, if you're old-fashioned, review your receipts. Sure, you may not capture every last expense doing it this way, but it's probably good enough.

Finally, once you've gotten all your expenses filled in, add 15 percent for expenditures you haven't counted yet. Yes, really. For example, you probably didn't capture "car repair," which can cost £400 each time (that's £33/month). Or dry cleaning or emergency vet care or charitable donations. A flat 15 percent will cover you for things you haven't figured in, and you can get more accurate as time goes on.

(I actually have a "Stupid Mistakes" category in my money system. When I first started this, I saved $20/month for unexpected expenses. Then, within two months, I had to go to the doctor for $600 and I got a traffic ticket for more than $100. That changed things quickly, and I currently save $150/month for unexpected expenses.)

Once you've got a fairly accurate number here, subtract it from your take-home pay. Now you'll know how much you'll have left over to spend in other categories like investing, saving, and guilt-free spending. Plus, you'll have an idea of a few targeted expense areas that you can cut down on to give yourself more money to save and invest.

LONG-TERM INVESTMENTS

This bucket includes the amount you'll send to your pension and ISA each month. A good rule of thumb is to invest 10 percent of your take-home pay (after taxes, or the amount on your monthly paycheck) for the long term. Your pension contributions count toward the 10 percent, so if you already participate in a pension, you'll need to add that amount to your take-home money to get a total monthly salary.

If you're not sure how much to allot to your investing bucket, open up an investment calculator from www.thismoney.co.uk/calculators and enter some numbers. Experiment with contributing £100/month, £200/month, £500/month, or even £1,000/month. Assume an 8 percent return. You'll see dramatic differences over forty years.

Because most of your investments will be in tax-advantaged retirement accounts, which we'll cover in Chapter 7, remove the taxes to get a back-of-the-napkin calculation. Just understand that taxes ultimately will take a chunk out of your pension returns. Remember, the more aggressively you save now, the more you'll have later.

SAVINGS GOALS

This bucket includes short-term savings goals (like Christmas gifts and vacation), midterm savings goals (a wedding in a few years), and larger, longer-term goals (like a down payment on a house).

To determine how much you should be putting away each month, check out these examples. They'll shock you:

GIFTS FOR FRIENDS AND FAMILY. In 2007 Americans spent around $900 on Christmas gifts, according to the American Research Group. In 2008 it was about half of that. If you're an average consumer and want to

The 60 Percent Solution

You've heard me talk about the 85 Percent Solution, which focuses on getting most of the way there rather than 100 percent and ending up doing nothing at all. Well, Richard Jenkins, the editor-in-chief of MSN Money, wrote an article called "The 60 Percent Solution," which suggested that you split your money into simple buckets, with the largest being basic expenses (food, bills, taxes) making up 60 percent of your gross income. The remaining 40 percent would be split four ways:

1. Retirement savings (10 percent)

2. Long-term savings (10 percent)

3. Short-term savings for irregular expenses (10 percent)

4. Fun money (10 percent)

The article has been widely distributed, although curiously, none of my friends had heard of it. My Conscious Spending Plan relates to Jenkins's 60 percent solution, but it's more focused toward young people. We spend a huge amount on eating out and going out, whereas our housing costs are lower because we can share apartments and rent more comfortably than older people with families.

pay for your gifts without going into debt, that means you need to save £75/month for your Christmas gifts. (And what about birthday gifts?) Check out my site nochristmasgiftsthisyear.com.

YOUR WEDDING (WHETHER YOU'RE ENGAGED OR NOT). The average wedding costs about £20,000. Because we know the average wedding age is thirty-two for men and thirty for women, you can figure out exactly how much you need to be saving, assuming you want to pay for it without help or debt: If you're twenty-seven years old, you need to be saving more than £300/month for your wedding. If you're thirty, you should be saving more than £800/month. (I cover financing weddings in detail on page 229.)

BUYING A HOUSE. If you're thinking about buying a house in a few years, log on to www.mouseprice.com and check home prices in your area. Let's just say the average house in your neighborhood costs £300,000 and you want to do a traditional 20 percent down payment. That's £60,000, so if you want to buy a house in five years, you should be saving £1,000/month.

Crazy, right? Nobody thinks like this, but it's truly eye-opening when you plot out your future spending for the next few years. It can almost seem overwhelming, but there's good news: First, the longer you have to save for these things, the less you have to save each month. (For example, if you're a man saving for an average wedding at age twenty-four, you would have to save about £208/month. By age thirty-one, however, you'd have to save £1,666/month.) Second, we often get help: Our spouse or parents may be able to chip in a little, but you can't count on someone else coming to rescue you. Third, theoretically you could use some of your investment money from Step 2 to pay for these savings goals. It's not ideal, but you can do it.

Regardless of exactly what you're saving for, a good rule of thumb is to save 5 to 10 percent of your take-home pay to meet your goals.

GUILT-FREE SPENDING MONEY

After all that spending, investing, and saving, this bucket contains the fun money—the stuff you can use for anything you want, guilt-free. Money here covers things like going out to restaurants and bars, taxis, movies, and vacations.

Depending on how you've structured your other buckets, a good rule of thumb here is to use 20 percent to 35 percent of your take-home income for guilt-free spending money.

Optimizing Your Conscious Spending Plan

Now that you've worked out the basics of your Conscious Spending Plan, you can make some targeted improvements to tweak your spending and make your money go where you want it to go. Instead of having this dull, throbbing cloud of worry over your head—"I know I'm spending too much"—your plan will serve as a living, breathing

Tools of the Trade

Q: *What can I use to manage my finances?*

A: For budgeting, use a combination of Kublax (www.kublax.com), Excel, and plain paper. Enter expenses into your system within two days. Otherwise, you'll forget.

For investing, use Instant X-Ray (www.morningstar.co.uk/instantxray/default.aspx?lang=en-GB) to make sure asset allocations makes sense.

For other money management, opt out of credit card offers at www.msponline.org.uk. Get an indicative credit score for free from www.checkmyfile.com (you can also get your credit card file free once a year from www.annualcreditreport.co.uk). Sign up with www.tpsonline.org.uk to stop unwanted sales calls to your home or mobile. Try www.moneybasics.co.uk for online calculators.

system that signals you when something's broken. If the alarm bells aren't going off, you don't need to waste time worrying.

GO FOR BIG WINS

Optimizing your spending can seem overwhelming, but it doesn't have to be. You can do an 80/20 analysis, which often reveals that 80 percent of what you overspend is used toward only 20 percent of your expenditures. That's why I prefer to focus on one or two big problem areas and solve those instead of trying to cut 5 percent out of a bunch of smaller areas. To run an 80/20 analysis yourself, do a Google search for "conducting a Pareto analysis."

Let's take an example: Brian takes home $48,000 per year after taxes, or $4,000/month. According to his Conscious Spending Plan, here's how his spending *should* look:

- *Monthly fixed costs (60 percent): $2,400*
- *Long-term investments (10 percent): $400/month*
- *Savings goals (10 percent): $400/month*
- *Guilt-free spending money (20 percent): $800/month*

Big Win: No More Fees

I recently had breakfast with someone who told me the most interesting story. He'd been dating his girlfriend for two years before they talked about finances. "It took me that long to gain her trust," he said. She was a public school teacher, so she didn't make much money. When he looked at her finances, he noticed that she had a lot of overdraft fees. He asked her to estimate how much she had spent in overdraft fees. "About $100 or $200?" she guessed.

It turns out that her overdraft fees totaled $1,300 in the last year.

Did he freak out or start yelling about how to negotiate out of bank fees? No, he simply pointed out something very gently: "What if you focused on your overdrafts? If you eliminated *just* that category of fee, you'd be so much better off." Simply avoiding overdraft fees was a big win for her.

Brian's problem is that $800 isn't enough for his spending money—this plan leaves him $250 short each month. What should he do?

Bad answer: The superficial answer is that Brian can decrease his contributions to his long-term investments and savings goals. Sure, he could do that, but it will cost him down the line.

A better way is to tackle the two most problematic areas on his monthly spending: *monthly fixed costs* and *guilt-free spending money.*

Good answer: Brian decides to pick his three biggest expenses and optimize them. First, he looks at his *monthly fixed costs* and realizes that because he's been consistently paying the minimum monthly payment on his credit card debt at 18 percent, he has $3,000 of debt left. Under his current plan, it will take him about twenty-two years and cost him $4,115 in interest to pay off his debt. But he can call his credit card to request a lower interest rate (see page 42 for details). With his new lower credit card APR of 15 percent, it will take him eighteen years and he'll pay $2,758 in interest. He saves fifty-three months and $1,357 of payments. That's only $6/month, but over eighteen years it adds up to a lot.

Next, he checks his subscriptions and realizes he's been paying for a DVD rental account and a Star Wars membership site, both of which he rarely uses. He cancels them, saving $60/month and increasing his chances of getting a girlfriend.

Finally, he logs in to his money-management account at www.kublax.com and realizes that he's spending $350 eating out each month, plus $250 at bars, or $600 in total. He decides that over the next three months, he'll slowly ratchet that amount down to $400/month, saving him $200/month.

Total amount saved: $266/month. By adjusting his spending, Brian is able to create a Conscious Spending Plan that works for him.

Brian was smart to focus on changing the things that mattered. Instead of promising that he'd stop spending money on Cokes every time he ate out, he picked the big wins that would really make an impact on his total dollar amount. You'll see this a lot: People will get really inspired to budget and decide to stop spending on things like appetizers with dinner. Or they'll buy generic cookies. That's nice—and I definitely encourage you to do that—but those small changes will have very little effect on your total spending. They serve more to make people feel good about themselves, which lasts only a few weeks once they realize they still don't have any more money.

Try focusing on big wins that will make a large, measurable change. In fact, I focus on only one or two big wins each month: eating out, and buying books because I am a huge, huge dork. You probably know what your big wins are. They're the expenses you cringe at, the ones you shrug and roll your eyes at, and say, "Yeah, I probably spend too much on ____." For most of my friends, these big wins are eating out and drinking.

SET REALISTIC GOALS

Last year, a friend of mine started getting really into fitness. I think it was because of his laudable goal of "getting some girls." Kudos, sir. Anyway, he started working out a lot: going to the gym in the morning, running during the day, then hitting the gym *again* at night. Needless to say, this fitness program didn't last long. Do you know people who get so into their idea du jour that they go completely overboard and burn out? I would rather do less but make it sustainable. The problem is that that's rarely sexy.

This idea of sustainable change is core to personal finance. Sometimes I get e-mails from people who say things like, "Ramit! I started managing my money! Before, I was spending $500 a week! Now I'm saving $495 of it and

(continued on page 114)

ADVICE
FROM THE
BLOGOSPHERE

DON'T JUST SAVE—
SAVE FOR A GOAL

It's Hard to Save Unless There's a Reason

by Jim Wang of www.pfblueprint.com

My friend and I are the same age, make roughly the same amount, and have similar lifestyles. So, over five years, why was I able to save $20,000 for a down payment and buy a house . . . and he ended up with hardly anything? He came to talk to me about it one day.

We soon sorted out that the key difference was that we had a different approach to saving money. In his mind, he was simply "saving." I, on the other hand, was "saving for a down payment." Though it might not seem like a big deal, that small distinction makes all the difference in the world. I brought in a bag lunch because I was saving toward a house, he brought in a bag lunch because he was simply saving. When it came time for lunch, his was merely a decision between whether he wanted his sandwich or something different. For me, it was whether I was willing to sacrifice that $5 or $10 that could be going toward a house on something more interesting to eat that day. Saving with a goal—whether it's tangible like a house or intangible like your kid's education—puts all your decisions into focus.

MAKE THE TRADEOFFS WORTHWHILE. Having a goal means that you are working toward something concrete. It gives you a reason to make those tradeoffs. You don't just think of that $5 saved as $5—instead it is something that gets you closer to your goal of having $20,000 for a down payment on a home. It changes the entire motivation for saving.

Spending less isn't always easy, but with this newfound motivation, it's much easier to make and justify your decisions. For a while, I was only going out with my friends one night a week, rather than the two or three times we normally did. This still gave me a chance to hang out with my buddies, but I was spending one-third less than I used to! When my friends asked, I told them I couldn't go out because I *was saving up for a down payment. They accepted this as a pretty good reason not to go out all the time. My friends might give me grief if I was simply being lazy, or lame, but because I had a concrete goal—and one that they could identify with— they became supporters of my cause rather than unwitting detractors.*

SET UP A SPECIFIC ACCOUNT. *Another key difference was how I was saving. I opened up an ING Direct savings account and named it "Down Payment," regularly transferring in the amount I had determined I wanted to save. As the months passed, the amount in that account grew larger and larger, and I felt as though I was making progress toward my goal. My friend never set aside an account, so his regular checking account was one big pot of money mentally "earmarked" for various things. His account balance grew but he had no pride of achievement or sense of closing in on his goal (because he didn't have a goal). It's possible that he could have saved as much as I had and just not have known it!*

Saving with a goal— whether it's tangible like a house or intangible like your kid's education—puts all your decisions into focus.

That second difference was psychological. Rather than being motivated to save, he developed a feeling of despair about it. Trying to save $20,000 sounds daunting until you spread it out over three years—then it's $555 a month. Spread it out over five years and it's only $333 a month (not including interest earned). That's certainly doable if you make sacrifices and track your progress. After my friend opened a separate account, he told me that this step alone changed his whole perspective about saving money for his down payment (once he accomplished that goal, he planned to use the account to save for his annual vacations and his emergency fund).

ENJOY LUNCH! *Don't listen to experts telling you that you should stop buying CDs or how you should brown bag a lunch. Think about your goals. Ask yourself if you'd rather spend $10 on lunch or save $10 toward a house or a car. If you would rather spend the money on lunch, by all means enjoy lunch! You save money so that you can spend it later on the things that make you happy. You don't save money just to watch your account balance grow. Once you list your goals and start making those trade-offs, you'll realize that saving money becomes far easier.*

Jim Wang writes about personal finance and money management at www.pfblueprint.com.

(continued from page 111)

putting it into a bank account!" I read this and just sigh. Although you might expect me to get really excited about someone contributing $495/month to their savings, I've come to realize that when a person goes from one extreme to another, the behavioral change rarely lasts.

When I make a change, I almost always make it bite-sized in an area that matters (see my previous discussion of big wins) and work in increments from there. This is why I just shake my head when I see personal-finance pundits giving families advice to go from a zero percent savings rate to a 25 percent savings rate ("You can do it!!!"). Giving that kind of advice is not useful. Habits don't change overnight, and if they do, chances are it won't be sustainable.

For example, if I started keeping track of my expenses and discovered I was short $1,000/month (this happens more than you think), I'd pick the two big wins—two items that I spend a lot on, but know I could cut down with some effort—and focus my efforts on them. Say I was spending about $500/month eating out, here's how it would look:

Month 1: .... $475 on eating out

Month 2: .... $450 on eating out

Month 3: .... $400 on eating out

Month 4: .... $350 on eating out

Month 5: .... $300 on eating out

Month 6: .... $250 on eating out

It's not a race, but within six months, I'd have cut my eating out budget *in half*. And it'd be much more likely to be sustainable.

The other way to do it is to look at your current spending, freak out, and cut half your total spending. Then you're suddenly forced to spend in a completely different way, without the means to cope. How long do you think your ambitious spending goal will last?

How many times have you heard friends say something like, "I'm not going to drink for a month"? I don't understand the point of short-term whims like that. A month from now, okay, you spent only 50 percent of what you normally do. And . . . then what? If you can't keep it up and you bounce right back to your normal spending habits, what did you really

Join the "Save $1,000 in 30 Days" Challenge

Last year, I got sick of reading the same old frugality tips, so I launched this challenge to help people save $1,000 in thirty days. I wrote thirty tips, including how to negotiate your car insurance, save $2,000/a year eating out, and how to optimize your mobile-phone bill. Tens of thousands of people joined and they saved over $500,000 in thirty days. Check it out at www.iwillteachyoutoberich .com/30daychallenge.

accomplish? I'd rather have people cut their spending by 10 percent and sustain it for thirty years than cut 50 percent for just a month.

Whether you're implementing a change in your personal finances, eating habits, exercise plan, or whatever . . . try making the smallest change today. Something you won't even notice. And follow your own plan for gradually increasing it. In this way, time is your friend because each month gets better than the one before it, and it adds up to a lot in the end.

USE THE ENVELOPE SYSTEM TO TARGET YOUR BIG WINS

All this conscious spending and optimizing sounds nice in theory, but how do you do it? I recommend the envelope system, in which you allocate money for certain categories like eating out, shopping, rent, and so on. Once you spend the money for that month, that's it: You can't spend more. If it's really an emergency, you can dip into other envelopes at the cost of spending in *that* category. These "envelopes" can be figurative (like in Kublax or Excel) or literally envelopes that you put cash in. This is the best system I've found for keeping spending simple and sustainable.

One of my friends, for example, has been carefully watching her spending for the last few months. When she started tracking her spending, she noticed that she was spending an unbelievable amount going out every week. So she came up with a clever solution to control her discretionary spending. She set up a separate bank account with a debit card. At the beginning of each month, she transfers, let's say, $200, into it. When she goes out, she spends that money. And when it's gone, it's gone.

The Envelope System

1. Decide how much you want to spend in major categories each month. (Not sure? Start with one: Eating out.)

2. Put money in each envelope (category):

£200	£150	£60
Groceries	Eating out	Entertainment

3. You can transfer from one envelope to another . . .

£100

£100	£250
Groceries	Eating out

. . . but when the envelopes are empty, that's it for the month.

Tip: If you want to make sure you don't go overdrawn, ask your bank if you can sign up for text alerts that tell you when you're near your limit. Not all banks offer them and some will charge a fee for you to receive them. Most banks can't block transactions to stop you from going overdrawn, but they can normally warn you that your funds are getting low. If you don't do this, you'll likely run up tons of overdraft fees.

Whatever system you want to use to divvy up the money is fine. Just decide how much you want to spend in major categories each month. (Pick your big wins to start.) Put the allotted money in each "envelope." When the envelopes are empty, that's it for the month. You can transfer from one envelope to another . . . but that money is coming out of another category, so your total spending doesn't actually increase.

Some of my nerdier friends even get more detailed with their system. One of my readers created this table:

	Eating out	Taxis	Books
Times per month	12	8	5
Amount per event	£23	£9	£17

"Each month, I try to cut the quantity and amount I spend on something," he told me. I looked at him in shock, but how can I argue? In less than eight months, he cut his spending by 43 percent (he knew the exact figure, of course). In my opinion, that level of analysis is overkill for most people, but it shows how detailed you can get once you set up a Conscious Spending Plan.

What If You Don't Make Enough Money?

Depending on your financial situation, setting up a workable Conscious Spending Plan may seem out of reach for you. Some people have already cut their spending to the bone and still don't have any extra money. For me to suggest that they put away 10 percent for retirement is, frankly, insulting. How can they be expected to contribute 10 percent toward long-term savings when they don't have enough to fill the car with gas?

Sometimes this is reality, and sometimes it's perception. Many of the people who've written me saying they live paycheck to paycheck actually have more wiggle room in their budgets than they think (cooking instead of eating out, for example, or not buying a new mobile phone every year). They just don't *want* to change their spending.

However, it's true that many people really cannot afford to cut more spending and really are living check to check. If you simply can't cut more out of your budget, this spending plan may be a useful theoretical guide, but you have more important concerns: making more money. Once you increase your earnings, you can use the Conscious Spending Plan as your guide. Until then, here are three strategies you can use to earn more.

NEGOTIATE A RAISE

If you already have a job, it's worth trying to negotiate a raise even in the current climate. A recent study by NACE, the National Association of Colleges and Employers, showed that companies pay more than $5,000 to hire the average college graduate. If you've been out of school for a few years, it's even more expensive. If they've already spent $5,000 recruiting you, and thousands more training you, would they really want to lose you?

Asking for a raise takes careful planning. Don't do what my friend "Jamie" did. When he realized he was being drastically underpaid for his contributions, he seethed without taking any action for more than two months. When he finally got up the courage to ask his boss for a raise, he said it in the most timid way: "Do you think I might possibly ask you about a raise?" If you're a manager, the first thing you'd think is, "Oh God, not another thing in my day." My friend's boss brushed him off, leaving Jamie, who's still at the company, frustrated and underpaid.

REMEMBER THAT GETTING A RAISE IS NOT ABOUT YOU. IT'S ABOUT YOU DEMONSTRATING YOUR VALUE TO YOUR EMPLOYER.

Remember that getting a raise is not about you. It's about you demonstrating your value to your employer. You can't tell them you need more money because your expenses are higher. Nobody cares. You *can,* however, show how your work has been clearly contributing to the company's success, and ask to be compensated fairly. Here's what you need to do:

Three months before you ask for a raise, start tracking everything you do at work *and the results you get.* If you were on a team that sold 25,000 widgets, figure out what you did to help make that happen and, as much as possible, quantify it. If you can't figure out the exact results you're causing, ask someone at work who's more experienced. This is a classic question that new employees have, and many experienced coworkers would be happy to help you.

At the same time, ask your boss if you can sit down and discuss ways you can excel at work. Make it clear you want to exceed expectations, and ask what that would entail. If you're really clever, you can hint about discussing compensation in the future.

Two months before you ask for a raise, meet with your boss again and show him your tracking from the previous month. Ask what you could do better. You want to know if you're on the right track with your work and, more important, the way you're communicating it.

One month before the big event, mention to your boss that because you've been doing so well, you'd like to discuss compensation at a meeting the next month. Ask what you'll need to bring to make it a fruitful discussion. Listen very carefully to what he says.

Around this time, it wouldn't hurt to ask your fellow coworkers to put in a good word with the boss. This assumes, of course, that you've been exceeding expectations and driving concrete results.

Two weeks before you ask for a raise, ask a couple of friends to role-play your job negotiation. This seems really weird, but negotiating is *not* a natural behavior. It will feel extremely odd and uncomfortable the first couple of times you do it. Better to do it with friends than your boss. And pick good friends, people who have business experience and will give you feedback on how you performed.

On the day you negotiate, come in with your salary, a couple of competitive salaries from www.salaryexpert.com and www.mysalary.co.uk, and your list of accomplishments, and be ready to discuss fair compensation. Remember, you're not asking your mommy for lemonade, you're a professional who's asking to be compensated fairly. You want to proceed as partners, as in "How do we make this work?"

If you get the raise you were looking for, congratulations! That was a huge first step toward increasing your income. If you don't, ask your boss

Cool Trick: Quickly Discover How Much You Make

To find your annual salary, just take your hourly rate, double it, and add three zeros to the end. If you make £20/hour, you make approximately £40,000/year. If you make £30/hour, you make approximately £60,000/year.

This also works in reverse. To find your hourly rate, divide your salary by two and drop the three zeros. So £50,000/year becomes approximately £25/hour.

This is based on a general forty-hour workweek and doesn't include taxes, but it's a good general back-of-the-napkin trick. And it's most useful when you're deciding whether to buy something or not. If that pair of pants is going to cost you eight hours of work, is it worth it?

When I was in college, I used to measure those decisions by the number of quarters I'd have to trade away from my laundry stash. Those may have been the most intellectually rigorous years of my life.

what you can do to excel in your career, or consider leaving to find another company that will give you greater room to grow.

GET A HIGHER-PAYING JOB

This takes us to the second way to increase your income. If you find that your existing company doesn't offer you growth potential, or you're in the process of getting a new job, negotiating your salary will never be easier. During the job-hiring process, you have more leverage than you'll ever have.

I cover negotiating a new salary in detail on page 234.

DO SOME FREELANCE WORK

Freelancing can be a relatively easy way to earn some extra money. Think about what skills or interests you have that others could use. You don't necessarily have to have a technical skill. Babysitting is freelancing (and it pays very well). If you have free time, you can pitch for work at www.peopleperhour.com. Tutoring is also a simple, profitable way to make some extra side cash: You might be able to moonlight at a company like

> **YOU DON'T NECESSARILY HAVE TO HAVE A TECHNICAL SKILL TO FREELANCE. BABYSITTING IS FREELANCING (AND IT PAYS VERY WELL).**

Kaplan and help kids with test prep, or you can post a notice at your neighborhood library and offer to teach English, math, or anything. What about dog walking? Remember, busy people want others to help them with their lives. A great place to start is www.gumtree.com.

If you have expertise in something, reach out to companies who'd need someone like you. For example, when I was in high school, I e-mailed fifty websites from all different industries that looked interesting but had poor marketing and copywriting. I offered to help them rewrite their websites. About fifteen responded, and I ended up editing copy for one company that eventually promoted me to run their sales department.

Later, during college, I consulted for venture capitalists, teaching them about Web 2.0 technologies, like YouTube, Facebook, and Flickr. This is stuff you and I know like the back of our hand, but it was new to these VCs—and valuable enough that they paid a great consulting fee.

Maintaining Your Spending Plan

O nce you've done what you can to design and implement a Conscious Spending Plan that you're comfortable with, give yourself some time to settle into a rhythm with it. Sure, eventually you can spend your time on strategic money decisions—"Should I be contributing 10 percent or 12 percent to my monthly savings goals?"—but first, you've got to get the basics down. As you go along from month to month with this new system, you'll discover some surprises you hadn't anticipated.

You'll always have unexpected cash expenses like cabs or an umbrella when you forgot yours. And don't flip out if you miss tracking a few pounds here or there—the minute your system becomes too oppressive for you to use is the minute you stop using it. I try to make as many purchases on my credit card as possible, so my software can automatically download my transactions. For cash spending, try to get the receipts and enter them into your system within seven days. After that, I tend to lose receipts or let them build up so much that I forget what some of the receipts were for. Make tracking your spending a weekly priority. For example, set aside thirty minutes every Sunday afternoon.

HOW TO HANDLE UNEXPECTED AND IRREGULAR EXPENSES

It can be frustrating to have a spending plan that keeps getting disrupted by surprise expenses like wedding gifts, car repairs, and late fees. So another key to having a plan you'll use is to account for the unexpected and build in a bit of flexibility.

Known irregular events (vehicle registration fees, Christmas gifts, vacations). There's an easy way to account for this type of irregular event. In fact, this is already built into your spending plan: Under *Savings Goals,* you allocate money toward goals where you have a general idea of how much it will cost. It doesn't have to be exact, but try to get a rough ballpark figure and then save every month toward that goal. For example, if you know you'll have to spend about £500 on Christmas gifts, start saving £42/month (that's £500 divided by twelve months) in January. By the time December rolls around, you won't have to take a huge hit on your spending.

Unknown irregular events (surprise vet expenses, late fees for your library card, or £50 flowers to make up to your girlfriend for something stupid you did last night). These types of surprises fall under your *Monthly Fixed Expenses* because no matter how hard you try to avoid them, there will always be unexpected expenses. Earlier, I suggested that you add about 15 percent to your estimate of your fixed costs to accommodate these surprises. In addition, I recommend starting by allocating £50/month for unexpected expenses. You'll soon realize that this cartoonishly low figure is not enough. But with some time, you'll have a better idea of what the figure should actually be and can change the amount accordingly.

> ADD ABOUT 15 PERCENT TO YOUR ESTIMATE OF YOUR FIXED COSTS TO ACCOMMODATE SURPRISE EXPENSES.

Fortunately, with each month that goes by, you'll get a more accurate picture of your spending. After about a year or two (remember, think long term), you'll have a very accurate understanding of how to project. The beginning is the hard part, but it only gets easier.

THE "PROBLEM" OF EXTRA INCOME

Just as there are surprise expenses, there is also surprise income. It's tempting to take a windfall and blow it all on something fun, but I urge you not to follow that instinct. Instead, work within your Conscious Spending Plan.

Unexpected onetime income. Sometimes money unexpectedly falls in your lap, like a birthday gift or from selling something on eBay. Believe it or not, I don't encourage you to save all this money. Instead, whenever I make money I didn't expect, I use 50 percent of it for fun—usually buying something I've been eyeing for a long time. Always! This way, I keep motivating myself to pursue weird, offbeat ideas that may result in some kind of reward. The other half goes to my investing account. Compare this with not having a plan and letting your money "just sort of" get spent.

Raises. A raise is different from onetime income because you'll get it consistently, and it's therefore much more important to do the right thing financially. There's one important thing to remember when you get a raise:

Maintain your current standard of living. Too many people get a raise at work and say, "Great! I'll go on that vacation!" Sure, you can do that. Then, "I'll buy that new sofa I've been wanting!" Uh oh. And then, "I think I need those new shoes. What? I've been working hard!" And then you want to kill yourself because you're swirling into a downward spiral of spending.

If you get a raise, be realistic: You earned it, and you should enjoy the results of your hard work. Buy yourself something nice that you've been wanting for a long time, and make it something you'll remember. After that, however, I strongly encourage you to save and invest as much of it as possible, because once you start getting accustomed to a certain lifestyle, you can never go back. After buying a Mercedes, can you ever drive a Toyota Corolla again?

I was really struggling to come up with a reason why, at the end of the month I came in slightly more overdrawn when I was curbing virtually all my guilt-free spending. Having completed the conscious spending grid I found that 80% of my income goes on fixed costs—it wasn't the guilt-free spending that needed to be cut but my subscriptions and bills. Realising that it's not essential for me to have the latest mobile phone technology just so that I can send text messages and make calls I have grasped a big win in cutting my phone bill in half.

—BEN GUTCHER, 29

The best part about setting up a strategic budget is that *it* guides your decisions, letting you say no much more easily—"Sorry, it's not in my plan this month"—and freeing you up to enjoy what you do spend on. This is guilt-free spending at its best. Sure, there will be tough decisions. Deciding to change the way you spend is the most difficult part of this book. It involves making choices and saying no to certain things. Your system, however, makes this much less painful. If a friend asks you out to dinner and you don't have enough spending money left, it will be easier to politely pass. After all, it's not personal—it's just your *system*. Remember that most people are, by definition, ordinary. They go through their twenties and thirties feeling a gnawing sense that they "should" do something about their money— tomorrow. They don't think about saving until their mid-forties. And yet, you are now extraordinary, because you see that setting up a simple system will let you make the tough decisions up front and spend your money guilt-free.

WEEK FOUR

1 Get your paycheck, determine what you've been spending, and figure out what your Conscious Spending Plan should look like (thirty minutes). Do this now and don't overthink it. Just break your take-home income into chunks of fixed costs (50–60 percent), long-term investments (10 percent), savings goals (5–10 percent), and guilt-free spending money (20–35 percent). How does it fit?

---

2 Optimize your spending (two hours). Dig in deeper to your savings goals and monthly fixed costs. Try the À La Carte Method. How much does your insurance actually cost—can you improve on that? How much will you spend for Christmas gifts and vacation this year? Break these expenses down into monthly chunks, then recalculate your plan.

---

3 Pick your big wins (five hours). Open an account at Kublax or Personal Account. Assuming you want to cut your spending by £100/month, what one or two big wins will you target? Start using the envelope system.

---

4 Maintain your Conscious Spending Plan (one hour per week). Enter any cash receipts into your system each week. Tweak the percentages you send to each part of your spending plan (we'll cover this in detail in the next chapter). And most important, make sure your system is realistic enough that you'll stick with it for the long term.

All right, deep breath. You did it. You made it through the most difficult part of the book! Now you've got a strategic spending plan. You no longer have to constantly worry about how much money you're spending. Phrases like "Can I afford this?" and "I know I'm going to worry about this later, but for now . . ." will be erased from your vocabulary. Now we're going to automate this system so each new pound that comes into your system gets instantly sent to the right area, whether it's investments, savings, fixed costs, or guilt-free spending.

CHAPTER 5

SAVE WHILE SLEEPING

Making your accounts work together—automatically

I want to be clear about something: I plan to do less and less work as I go through my life. When I meet people on a career path that will have them working *more,* not less, I'm always puzzled. That's like being a real-life Mario Brother, where every level you beat means your life gets progressively more difficult. Why would you want that?

Managing money is no different: By investing a little now, we don't have to invest *a lot* later. Of course, that's easier said than done. Somehow we just never get around to consistently managing our money—and let's be honest: That will never change. Because who really cares about managing money? It's about as appealing as cleaning the garage . . . every week for the rest of your life. We dream of having an automated system that handles most of the work for us, something that *just works*.

In the last chapter, you set up a Conscious Spending Plan to determine how much you want to spend in each category (fixed costs, investments, savings goals, and guilt-free spending money). You didn't think you'd have to manually transfer money each month, did you? Not a chance. In this chapter, we'll create an Automatic Money Flow to manage your money for you. It will take the accounts you've set up—your credit cards, current, savings, and investment accounts—and create automatic transfers so your money goes where it needs to go.

I'm saving money for a house deposit, but I hate spending time looking for good interest rates and finding the best places to save. The least painful way of saving effectively seems to be signing up for an online high interest savings account – the bank takes my money automatically each month, so I don't have to do anything. My interest rate is fixed, so I know what I'll get at the end and best of all their interest rates are usually quite a lot higher than your average savings account.

—**HELEN HALL, 27**

DO MORE BEFORE DOING LESS

Some people just seem to have a magical ability to manage money. They enrolled in their pension years ago, they always know how much money they have, and they seem to relish tweaking their system to optimize it. Usually, these people are extremely annoying and unattractive. But that doesn't mean we can't learn something from them. You see, they don't spend more time on day-to-day money management than most average people. In fact, they spend *less* time thinking about their money because they've set up an automated system that frees them from having to worry. These people don't work harder, they just work smarter.

You can become one of these people (only you'll be very attractive and not at all annoying) if you follow my advice about automating. This is all driven by a principle I'll call The Curve of Doing More Before Doing Less:

This is as much about where to invest your time as it is about where

The Next Few Weeks

to put your money. Sure, setting up an Automatic Money Flow will take you a few hours. It would be easier to do nothing—but that would mean you'll have to manage your money constantly for the rest of your life. By spending a few hours up front, you'll end up saving huge amounts of time over the long term. Your money flow will be automatic, and each pound that comes in will be routed to the right account in your Conscious Spending Plan from Chapter 4 without you really having to think about it.

The payoff for these few hours is huge because this automatic system will let you focus on the fun parts of life. No more worrying about whether you paid that bill or if you're going to overdraft again. You'll start to see money as a tool for getting what you want without the manual drudgery of tracking categories and transferring money from one account to another each week.

I spend an hour per month managing my money, perhaps. Paying bills, checking the balance on my credit card and my bank accounts, and watching a few holdings in my portfolio (but I'm not an active trader—just maintaining situational awareness). Once a month, I might evaluate my savings plan to see if I can plan a vacation or make a larger purchase.

—JENNIFER CHANG, 32

THE POWER OF DEFAULTS

We know people are incredibly lazy and will do whatever requires no work—often at their own financial expense. Think about how many people lose thousands of pounds per year by not taking advantage of employer pension contributions matches alone. How much more money do we lose from inaction overall?

The key to taking action is, quite simply, making your decisions automatic. You think you'll actually do the work each week? No, you won't. You don't care. Sure, you might care right now, but in two weeks it'll be back to Twitter and Perez Hilton. Nobody really cares about managing their money. Hell, I don't even care. Get away from me, endless mailings from banks and investment accounts. (That's the line I will use as a bedtime story to soothe my future children. I know, I know. My future wife is a lucky woman.)

Your money management must happen by default. We've already talked about it in reference to pensions, but now we're going to apply that to every pound you make. You'll be making your contributions to your savings and investing accounts grow passively—with no action required. In fact, by setting up an automatic payment plan you actually make it difficult to *stop* the contributions to your retirement account! Not because you can't—you can adjust your system any time—but because you're lazy and you won't. Hey, I'm lazy, too. You just have to know how to take advantage of it. Once it's set up, this system is so hands-off that if you got eaten alive by a Komodo dragon, your money system would continue transferring money from account to account by default, a ghostlike reminder of your financial prescience. Haunting, but cool.

If you want to build wealth over your lifetime, the only sure way to do it is to get your plan on autopilot and make everything that's financially important in your life automatic. . . . I recommend that people automate a handful of things in their financial lives. You can set it up once in less than an hour and then go back to your life.

—**DAVID BACH, AUTHOR OF** *THE AUTOMATIC MILLIONAIRE*

How to Spend Only Three Hours a Month Managing Your Money

I hope I've convinced you by now that automation is the way to go. In Chapter 4, you set up a basic system—the Conscious Spending Plan—that gave you an idea of where you're going to distribute your money. As a refresher, check out the rough percentages to assign to the four categories (or buckets) in the table on the next page.

Now, let's take your Conscious Spending Plan and make it automatic. To do this, I use a concept called "The Next £100." This means, simply, where will the next £100 you make go? Will it all go to your investment account? Will you allocate 10 percent to your savings account? Most people just shrug and don't take any time to think about how their money

CATEGORIES OF SPENDING

Fixed costs Rent, utilities, debt, etc.	50–60% of take-home pay
Investments Pension, ISA	10%
Savings goals Vacations, gifts, house down payment, cash for unexpected expenses	5–10%
Guilt-free spending money Dining out, drinking, movies, clothes, shoes	20–35%

will be allocated—which means it gets thoughtlessly spent and I sob uncontrollably.

But there's a better way! It involves actually using the guidelines you established in your Conscious Spending Plan. If you did things right in Chapter 4, you already know how much money you want to contribute to your fixed costs, investments, savings, and spending money. So, if you made £100, and your plan resembled the example above, you'd put £60 toward your fixed costs, £10 into your investment account, £10 into savings, and then you'd spend the remaining £20 on whatever you felt like. Pretty cool, right? Well, it gets even better, because once everything is automated, that money will be shunted from your current account right into the appropriate accounts without you even thinking about it.

To see how it works, let's use Michelle as an example:

Michelle gets paid once a month. Her employer deducts 5 percent of her pay automatically and puts it in her pension. The rest of Michelle's paycheck goes to her checking account by direct deposit.

About a day later, her Automatic Money Flow begins transferring money out of her checking account. Her personal retirement account will pull 5 percent of her salary for itself. (That combines with the company pension contribution to complete the 10 percent of take-home pay for investing.) Her savings account will pull 5 percent, automatically breaking that money into chunks: 1 percent for a wedding sub-account and 4 percent to a house down-payment sub-account. (That takes care of her monthly savings goals.)

Her system also automatically pays her fixed costs. She's set it up so that most of her subscriptions and bills are paid by her credit card. Some of her bills can't be put on credit cards—for example, utilities and loans—so they're automatically paid out of her checking account. Finally, she's automatically e-mailed a copy of her credit card bill for a five-minute review. After she's reviewed it, the bill is also paid from her checking account.

The money that remains in her account is used for spending money.

> **IT'S WELL WORTH TAKING AN HOUR TO GET ALL YOUR ACCOUNT NUMBERS IN ONE PLACE.**

To make sure she doesn't overspend, she's focused on two big wins: eating out and spending money on clothes. She sets alerts in her online budgeting account if she goes over her spending goals, and she keeps a reserve of $500 in her checking account just in case. (The couple of times she went over her spending, she paid herself back using her "unexpected expenses" money from her savings account.) To track spending more easily, she uses her credit card as much as possible to pay for all of her fun stuff. If she uses cash for cabs or coffee, she keeps the receipts and tries to enter them into Mint as often as possible.

In the middle of the month, Michelle's calendar reminds her to check her Mint account to make sure she's within her limits for her spending money. If she's doing fine, she gets on with her life. If she's over her limit, she decides what she needs to cut back on to stay on track for the month. Luckily, she has fifteen days to get it right, and by politely passing on an invitation to dine out she gets back on track.

I work freelance and it is often difficult to plan for the future, but I set up a savings goal and now I have a cushion for the tough times. I have two jobs; one I love and one I hate. The one I love pays for the things I love, and the one I hate pays for the things I hate paying for, like bills. This means I can easily balance how I save for the future by doing extra hours when I need to, without sacrificing doing things that I love.

—**DOMINIC KELLY, 30**

By the end of the month, she's spent less than two hours monitoring her finances, yet she's invested 10 percent, saved 5 percent (in sub-buckets for her wedding and down payment), paid all of her bills on time, paid off her credit card in full, and spent exactly what she wanted to spend. She had to say "no" only once, and it was no big deal. In fact, none of it was.

Create Your Automatic Money Flow

Now that you see how it works, it's time to implement your Automatic Money Flow. You'll start by linking all your accounts together. Then, you'll set up automatic transfers to happen on various days. Below, I'll assume that you're paid once per month, but I'll also cover slight tweaks to implement if you're paid biweekly or if you're a freelancer who's paid irregularly.

To get set up, you'll need a complete list of all your accounts, their URLs, and the login/passwords. Make a chart that looks something like this.

Account	URL	Login	Password
current account			
savings account			
credit card(s)			
company pension			
personal pension or ISA			
any regular bills*			

*e.g., rent, student loans, car payments, utilities, LOVEFiLM, etc.

Alternatively, remember that on page 88 I mentioned that I use a PBwiki account to store all of this information. It's well worth taking an hour to get all these handy account numbers in one place so you never have to do this again.

Also, before you start linking your online accounts, you may need to work with your employer to get your paycheck going to the proper places. If you don't already have it, talk to your HR rep and set up a direct deposit into your current account. (For most of you lucky Brits, this is already standard.) In addition, you need to get everything squared away with your pension contribution. Ideally you already set up your pension way back in Chapter 3, but if not, DO IT NOW! Even if you already have a pension going, you may have to adjust the amount you contribute every month based on your shiny new Conscious Spending Plan.

SETTING UP EASY PAYMENTS

If you've got online accounts, you can easily set up payments between them. Otherwise, get your bank to set up regular standing orders from your current account.

This is how your easy payments system should work:

- If you're paying into a company pension scheme or a stakeholder plan that's been set up by your employer, money will automatically come out of your wages. If you've taken out your own personal or stakeholder pension, you should set up standing order payments so money comes out of your current account every month.

- Set up a regular transfer between your current account and your savings account.

- Set up a regular payment or standing order to your stocks and shares ISA

- Pay your bills by direct debit or standing order. You can pay by credit card (which may help you keep your accounts active), but direct debit or standing order give you more protection. If you want to stop a regular payment you're making with your credit card, you have to cancel it with the company you're paying (you can't ask the card provider to stop it for you).

- Some bills can't be paid by credit card (even if you wanted to). Pay these by standing order or direct debit from your current account.

- Set it up so that all your credit card accounts are paid from your current account. (This is something you need to do from your bank's website.)

Finally, there are payments that simply can't be automatically drawn from your current account. For example, if you're renting from a little old lady, she may not have a sophisticated financial infrastructure including a website where you can enter your current account information and automatically transfer money each month. Sigh. Get it together, Mildred. Anyway, you can still set up your account to transfer money into hers; you only need to get hold of her bank details including her account number and sort code. If she prefers payment by cheque, you'll have no option but to write one out and put it in the post. At the very least, you should set up alerts on your budgeting software so you don't forget to do it.

WHERE THE MONEY FLOWS

This account ...	... Should fund this account
Paycheck	■ Company pension, GPP or Stakeholder through employer ■ Current account (bank transfer)
Current account	■ Personal pension ■ Savings account and/or ISA (which is sub-divided into savings goals) ■ Credit card ■ Fixed costs that don't allow credit card payment (like rent) ■ Occasional spending cash
Credit card	■ Purchases costing £100–£30,000 ■ Guilt-free spending

SET UP YOUR REGULAR PAYMENTS

Now that all your accounts are linked, it's time to go back into your accounts and automate all transfers and payments. This is really simple: It is just a matter of working with each individual account's website to make sure your payment or transfer is set up for the amount you want (or if it's a direct debit, the amount the company is requesting) and on the date you want.

If you're paying your bills by direct debit or standing order, you can choose the date the money leaves your account. This is key, but people often overlook it. If you set your direct debits or standing orders at weird times, it will inevitably necessitate more work. If you get paid on the 1st of the month, you want to avoid having to deal with lots of different payments on different dates.

(continued on page 136)

ADVICE
FROM THE
BLOGOSPHERE

SET IT AND FORGET IT

Automate Your Finances to Focus on Long-Term Goals

by Gina Trapani of Lifehacker.com

Tech-savvy folks who want to get more done in less time don't want to fuss with tedious money tasks like writing checks and transferring funds, so financial automation is very popular among the Lifehacker readership. Personally, I'm right there: "Set it and forget it" is my guiding personal finance system principle. Well, not exactly "forget it," but I set up my accounts to run themselves to the extent they can, and check in on things monthly to make sure all the gears are turning as I intended.

I'm a busy person who doesn't want to think about money matters any more than I need to, so I rely heavily on automated transfers, deposits, and e-mail notifications to keep my dollars and cents where they need to be. Most good banks these days offer electronic bill pay, direct deposit, recurring savings account transfers, and some even offer e-mail notifications if an account balance goes above or below a certain threshold. I use all these tools. My income goes in, bill payments go out, and my credit card gets paid in full with minimal intervention. If my credit card debt in a given month goes above a certain threshold—like $3,000—I get an e-mail letting me know so I can make sure I've got that cash ready in my checking account. For week-to-week money tasks, this all works like a charm.

TOOLS OF THE TRADE. For a longer, bird's-eye view of my finances, I use a desktop copy of Quicken to suck in all my account transactions and make me pretty charts. Using Quicken, I check in on my net worth over time and see if there are any expenses that I can cut down. This kind of overview work is where I spend the most time—deciding on my savings goals, tracking them, seeing where I was at the same time last year, plotting where I want to be at the same time next year. Being a personal productivity obsessive, I'm big on having goals and using checkpoints along the way to get there. I use Google Calendar to set twelve savings goals throughout the year, with an e-mail reminder for each one. At the end of each month

I get an e-mail from my calendar saying something like, "It's October! Should be $X in the nest egg account by now!" That really keeps me on track when life has swept me away and I'm thinking about other things.

As a freelancer, things get tricky around tax time—and tax time happens four times a year for self-employed folks. I use automated monthly transfers into an income tax holding account so I can pay my quarterly estimated taxes without feeling like I just lost my shirt. (That's not a good feeling, ever—so do whatever you have to do to avoid it. In fact, keeping an attitude of confidence and prosperity is one of the best financial moves you can make, regardless of what your account balance is.) I use a simple spreadsheet to track deductions, and a big manila envelope to keep original receipts—one envelope per year.

STRATEGIES FOR DEBT. *Some of the best debt reduction strategies we've gotten from Lifehacker readers involve tricking yourself into putting money aside, and making it hard to spend. Many endorse the old-fashioned way: Cut up the credit cards, and pay down the ones with the highest interest rates most aggressively. Another strategy to avoid impulse buying is filling up online shopping carts or wishlists and then making yourself wait a week or two before you pull the trigger and hit the "Check out" button. I use this method a lot: Usually, impulse buys make much less sense when you've had some time to think about it.*

In the end, managing your finances well is a lot like developing a strong personal productivity system: You keep track of everything without making it your full-time job; you set goals; you break them down into small bite-size tasks; you save yourself time by automating manual work; and you spend your time and brainpower focusing on the big picture. That's what I try to do with my time and *money.*

Being a personal productivity obsessive, I'm big on having goals and using checkpoints along the way to get there. I use Google Calendar to set twelve savings goals throughout the year, with an e-mail reminder for each one.

Gina Trapani is the founding editor of Lifehacker.com, a daily weblog on software and personal productivity.

(continued from page 133)

The easiest way to avoid this is to get all your bills on the same schedule. To accomplish this, gather all your bills together, call the companies, and ask them to switch your billing dates. Most of these will take five minutes each to do. There may be a couple of months of odd billing as your accounts adjust, but it will smooth itself out after that. If you're paid on the 1st of the month, I suggest switching all your bills to arrive on or around that time, too. Call and say this: "Hi, I'm currently being billed on the 17th of each month, and I'd like to change that to the 1st of the month. Do I need to do anything besides ask right here on the phone?" Of course, depending on your situation, you can request any billing date that will be easy for you.

GET ALL YOUR BILLS ON THE SAME SCHEDULE BY CALLING THE COMPANIES AND ASKING TO SWITCH YOUR BILLING DATES.

Now that you've got everything coming at the beginning of the month, it's time to actually go in and set up your transfers. Here's how to arrange your Automatic Money Flow, assuming you get paid on the 1st of the month.

1st of the month: Your pension contributions are automatically deducted from your paycheck, if you're paying into an occupational pension scheme a group personal pension or a stakeholder organised by your employer. If you're paying into a pension plan that you've arranged yourself (either a personal or stakeholder plan), money should be taken from your current account as soon after your paycheck reaches your account as possible. Remember, you're treating your current account like your e-mail inbox— first, everything goes there, then it's filtered away to the appropriate place. Note: The first time you set this up, leave a buffer amount of money—I recommend £500—in your current account just in case a transfer doesn't go right. And don't worry: If something *does* go wrong, use the negotiation tips on page 24 to get any overdraft fees waived.

5th of the month: Set up your regular payment to your savings account. Log in to your savings account and set up an automatic transfer from your current account to your savings account on the 5th of every month. Waiting until the 5th of the month gives you some leeway. If, for some reason, your paycheck doesn't show up on the 1st of the month, you'll have four days to correct things or cancel that month's automatic transfer.

Don't just set up the transfer. Remember to set the amount, too. Use the percentage of your monthly income that you established for savings in your Conscious Spending Plan (typically 5 to 10 percent). But if you can't afford that much right now, don't worry—just set up an automatic transfer for £5 to prove to yourself that it works. The amount is important: £5 won't be missed, but once you see how it's all working together, it's much easier to add to that amount.

5th of the month: Regular payment to your personal pension or stocks and shares ISA. To set this up, log in to your bank's website and create a regular payment from your current account to your pension or ISA. Refer to your Conscious Spending Plan to calculate the amount of the transfer. It should be approximately 10 percent of your take-home pay, minus the amount you send to your company pension.

WHEN THE MONEY FLOWS

On this date ...	... these actions happen
1st of the month	■ Part of your salary goes into your company pension ■ The rest of your salary is transferred into your current account
5th of the month	■ Automatic transfer from current to savings account ■ Automatic transfer from current account to personal pension or ISA
7th of the month	■ Automatic payment of bills from current account via direct debit or standing order ■ Automatic transfer from current account to pay off credit card bill

7th of the month: Auto-pay for any monthly bills you have. Log in to any regular payments you have, like cable, utilities, car payments, or student loans, and set up automatic payments to occur on the 7th of each month. You can pay your bills by direct debit, standing order (if it's for a fixed amount) or by credit card. If you pay by credit card remember that you can't cancel your payments through the credit card company, only the company that's supplying the services. If you're in dispute with them, there could be problems. Track your spending on sites like www.kublax.com or by using Personal Accountz software.

7th of the month: Automatic transfer to pay off your credit card. Log in to your credit card account and instruct it to draw money from your current account and pay the credit card bill on the 7th of every month—in full. (Because your bill arrived on the 1st of the month, you'll never incur late fees using this system.) If you have credit card debt and you can't

> ## GET YOUR CREDIT CARD TO EMAIL YOU A MONTHLY LINK TO YOUR BILL, SO YOU CAN REVIEW IT BEFORE THE MONEY IS AUTOMATICALLY TRANSFERRED OUT OF YOUR CURRENT ACCOUNT.

pay the bill in full, don't worry. You can still set up an automatic payment; just make it for the monthly minimum or any other amount of your choice. (See page 39 to learn why this is a very good idea.)

If you're using an online credit card provider, you'll receive emails letting you know when our statement is ready, so you can review it before the money is automatically transferred out of your current account. This is helpful in case your bill unexpectedly exceeds the amount available in your current account—that way you can adjust the amount you pay that month.

TWEAKING THE SYSTEM

That's the basic Automatic Money Flow schedule, but you may not be paid on a straight once-a-month schedule. That's not a problem. You can just adjust the above system to match your payment schedule.

If you're paid twice a month: I suggest replicating the above system on the 1st and the 15th—with half the money each time. This is easy enough, but the one thing to watch with this is paying your bills. If the second payment (on the 15th) will miss the due dates for any of your bills, be sure that you set it so that those bills are paid in full during the payment on the 1st. Another way to work your system is to do half the payments with one paycheck (retirement, fixed costs) and half the

Review Your Credit Card Bill

I pay with my credit card as much as possible because it lets me automatically download my transactions and categorize my spending. Plus, I get travel points and extra consumer protection, like a free additional warranty for any electronic device (for more on this, see page 31).

Once a week, I take five minutes and review all the charges on my card, and once a month I get an e-mail to review my entire bill. If I take no action, my credit card reaches into my checking account and pays the full amount automatically. No late fees, no worries. If I do see an error, I just call my credit card company anytime twenty-four hours a day and get it fixed.

Let's talk about those weekly reviews for a second. I do like to keep an eye on my credit card charges whenever there's a human involved, so I keep my receipts whenever I go to restaurants, and store them in a folder on my desk.

Every Sunday night, I open the folder and spend about five minutes comparing my receipts with what my credit card's website says. I just do a "ctrl-f" for the amount (for example, $43.35) and confirm that it's correct. If I wrote down $43.35 as the full amount, but instead saw that the restaurant had charged me $50, someone's trying to make a quick buck off me. And in that case, you need to ask yourself one question:

WWAID?

(What would an Indian do?)

Answer: A quick call to my credit card company will resolve this.

The most important thing is keeping your receipt folder *on your desk.* If you have to get up to get it—even a few steps away—that's a huge barrier to getting this done consistently.

payments with the second paycheck (savings, guilt-free spending), but that can get clunky.

If you have irregular income: Irregular incomes, like those of freelancers, are difficult to plan for. Some months you might earn close to nothing, others you're flush with cash. This situation calls for some changes to

Living for Today, Too

Q: *When do I get to spend my money?*

A: Okay. You've got your automatic infrastructure set up. Each month, you've got money flowing automatically to your investing accounts and savings accounts. You've even cut your spending by focusing on a couple of big wins. So when do you get to spend all this money?

What a great question. The only people who've ever asked me this are actually concerned about saving *too much*.

The answer is simple: Once you've gotten your money under control and you're hitting your targets, you absolutely should spend your leftover money. Look to your savings goals. If you don't have something in there for "vacation" or "new snowboard," maybe you should. Otherwise, what is all this money for?

Money exists for a reason—to let you do what you want to do. Yes, it's true, every pound you spend now would be worth more later. But living only for tomorrow is no way to live. Consider one investment that most people overlook: *yourself*. Think about traveling—how much will that be worth to you later? Or attend that conference that will expose you to the top people in your field. My friend Paul has a specific "networking budget" that he uses to travel to meet interesting people each year. If you invest in yourself, the potential return is limitless.

If you're meeting your goals, another route you could take is to start saving less and increase the amount you allocate to your guilt-free spending money.

One final thing: I hope this doesn't sound too cheesy, but one of the best returns I've ever gotten has been with philanthropy. Whether it's your time or your money, I can't emphasize enough how important it is to give back, be it to your own community or to the global community. Volunteer your time at a local school or youth organization, or donate painlessly by searching the web with www.everyclick.com. Charities get a donation every time you search. For more on giving back, see page 215.

Saving too much is a good problem to have. Fortunately, there are great solutions, too.

AUTOMATING YOUR MONEY: HOW IT WORKS

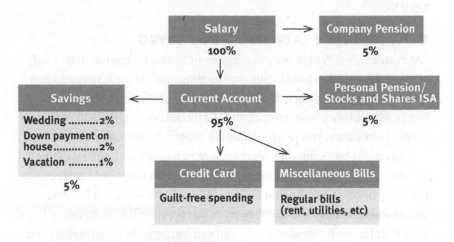

Note: For simplicity, this diagram does not include taxes.

your spending and savings. First—and this is different from the Conscious Spending Plan—you'll need to figure out how much you need to survive on each month. This is the bare minimum: rent, utilities, food, loan payments— just the basics. Those are your bare-bones monthly necessities.

Now, back to the Conscious Spending Plan. Add a savings goal of three months of bare-bones income before you do any investing. For example, if you need at least £1,500/month to live on, you'll need to have £4,500 in a savings buffer, which you can use to smooth out months where you don't generate much income. The buffer should exist as a sub-account in your savings account. To fund it, use money from two places: First, forget about investing while you're setting up the buffer, and instead take any money you would have invested and send it to your savings account. Second, in good months, any extra money you make should go into your buffer savings.

Once you've saved up three months of money as a cushion, congratulations! Now go back to a normal Conscious Spending Plan where you send money to investing accounts. Because you're self-employed, you probably don't have access to a traditional company pension, but you should look into a stakeholder or personal pension, which are great alternatives. Just keep in mind that it's probably wise to sock away a little more into your savings account in good months to make up for the less profitable ones.

I also recommend Money Made Clear's budgeting calculator: http://www.moneymadeclear.fsa.gov.uk/tools.aspx?Tool=budget_

calculator. If your income fluctuates wildly, just adjust the figures as you need to.

YOUR MONEY IS NOW AUTOMATIC

Congratulations! Your money management is now on autopilot. Not only are your bills paid automatically and on time, but you're actually saving and investing money each month. The beauty of this system is that it works without your involvement and it's flexible enough to add or remove accounts any time. You're accumulating money *by default*.

You might be wondering what's going to happen with the investment money. Right now, it's growing each month as you contribute to your company or personal pension (and possibly ISA as well), but it's just sitting there. You need to put it to work by investing it in something. In the next chapter, we'll talk about how you can become your own investment expert and how to go about getting the best return on your investment money.

ACTION STEPS

WEEK FIVE

1 List all your accounts in one place (one hour). As you start linking accounts to one another, you'll need to log in to all of them. Make your life easier by getting all the login information in one place. You'll be tweaking your accounts over the next few months, so save all the login information somewhere that you can access from home and work.

2 Link your accounts together (three to five days). To set up your Automatic Money Flow, the first step is linking accounts together. The links are free and electronic, but allow three to five days for the accounts to verify the links.

3 Set up your Automatic Money Flow (five hours). Once your accounts are linked together, set up the core of your Automatic Money Flow: automatic payments. Your system will automatically send money to your investing accounts, your savings account, and your fixed costs, and leave you money for guilt-free spending. Remember, you'll want to reset your billing cycles so you can create a well-timed Automatic Money Flow.

CHAPTER 6

THE MYTH OF FINANCIAL EXPERTISE

*Why professional wine tasters and stock pickers
are clueless—and how you can beat them*

I f I invited you to a blind taste test of a $12 wine versus a $1,200 wine, could you tell the difference? I bet you $20 you couldn't.

In 2001, Frederic Brochet, a researcher at the University of Bordeaux, ran a study that sent shock waves through the wine industry. Determined to understand how wine drinkers decided which wines they liked, he invited fifty-seven recognized experts to evaluate two wines: one red, one white.

After tasting the two wines, the experts described the red wine as *intense, deep,* and *spicy*—words commonly used to describe red wines. The white was described in equally standard terms: *lively, fresh,* and *floral.* But what none of these experts picked up on was that the two wines were *exactly the same wine.* Even more damning, the wines were actually *both* white wine—the "red wine" had been colored with food coloring.

Think about that for a second. Fifty-seven wine experts couldn't even tell they were drinking two identical wines.

There's something we need to talk about when it comes to experts.

Americans love experts. We feel comforted when we see a tall, uniformed pilot behind the controls of a plane. We trust our doctors to prescribe the right medications, we're confident that our lawyers will steer us right through legal tangles, and we devour the words of the talking heads in the media. We're taught that experts deserve to be compensated for their training and experience. After all, we wouldn't hire someone off the street to build a house or remove our wisdom teeth, would we?

> ## ALL OUR LIVES, WE'VE BEEN TAUGHT TO DEFER TO EXPERTS... BUT ULTIMATELY, EXPERTISE IS ABOUT RESULTS.

All our lives, we've been taught to defer to experts: teachers, doctors, and investment "professionals." But ultimately, expertise is about results. You can have the fanciest degrees from the fanciest schools, but if you can't perform what you were hired to do, your expertise is meaningless. In our culture of worshipping experts, what have the results been? When it comes to finances in America, they're pretty dismal. We've earned failing grades in financial literacy—in 2008, high school seniors correctly answered a gloomy 48 percent of questions on the Jumpstart Coalition's national financial literacy survey, while college seniors answered only 65 percent right. We think "investing" is about guessing the next best stock. Instead of enriching ourselves by saving and investing, most American and UK households are in debt. And the wizards of Wall Street can't even manage their own companies' risk. Something's not right here: Our financial experts are failing us.

When it comes to investing, it's easy to get overwhelmed by all the options: small-, mid-, and large-cap stocks; REITS; bonds; growth, value, or balanced funds—not to mention factoring in expense ratios, interest rates, allocation goals, and diversification. That's why so many people say, "Can't I just hire someone to do this for me?" This is a maddening question because, in fact, financial experts—in particular, fund managers and anyone who attempts to predict the market—are often no better than amateurs. They're often *worse*. The vast majority of twentysomethings can earn more than the so-called "experts" by investing on their own. No financial adviser. No fund manager. Just automatic investments in low-cost funds (which I'll get to in the next chapter). So, for the average investor, the value of financial expertise is a myth. There are several reasons for this that I'll detail below, but I urge you to think about how you treat the experts in your life. Do they deserve to be put on a pedestal? Do they deserve tens of thousands of your pounds in fees? If so, what kind of performance do you demand of them?

In truth, being rich is within *your* control, not some expert's. How rich you are depends on the amount you're able to save and on your investment plan. But acknowledging this fact takes guts, because it means admitting that there's no one else to blame if you're not rich—no advisers, no complicated investment strategy, no "market conditions." But it also means that you control exactly what happens to you and your money over the long term.

You know what the most fun part of this book is for me? No, it's not the personal-finance groupies that I constantly wish I had. It's the disbelieving e-mails I'm going to get after people read this chapter. Whenever I point out how people waste their money by investing in expensive actively managed funds or by relying on a financial adviser who generates below-market returns, I get e-mails that say, "You're full of it." Or they say, "There's no way that's true—just look at my investment returns," not really understanding how much they've made after factoring in taxes and fees. But surely they *must* be making great returns because they wouldn't continue investing if they weren't making lots of money . . . right?

In this chapter, I'm going to show you how you can actually outperform the financial pundits by sidestepping their "expertise" (and fees) and taking the simplest approach to investing. It's not easy to learn that reliance on so-called "experts" is largely ineffective, but stick with me. I've got the data to back it up, and I'll show you a simple way to invest on your own.

Experts Can't Guess Where the Market Is Going

Before we move on to discuss how you can beat the experts, let's look a little more deeply into how they operate and why their advice so often misses the mark.

The most visible financial "experts" are the financial pundits and portfolio managers (the people who choose the specific stocks in mutual funds). They love to regale us with their predictions about where the market is going: Up! Down! They go on and on about how interest rates and oil production and a butterfly flapping its wings in China will affect the stock market. This forecasting is called timing the market. But the truth is they simply cannot predict how high, how low, or even which direction the market will go. I get e-mails from people wondering what I think about oil, currency markets, or Google every single day. Who knows about those things? I certainly don't, especially in the short term. Unfortunately, the fact is that nobody can predict where the market is going. Still, the talking heads on TV make grandiose predictions every day, and whether they're right or wrong, they're never held accountable for them.

The media feeds off every little market fluctuation. On one day, the pundits are spreading gloom and doom about a multi-hundred-point loss in the market. Then, three days later, the front page is filled with images of hope and unicorns as the market climbs 500 points. It's riveting to watch, but step back and ask yourself, "Am I learning anything from this? Or am I just being overwhelmed by information about the market going up one day and down another?" More information is not always good, especially when it's not actionable and causes you to make errors in your investing. The key takeaway here is to ignore any predictions that pundits make. They simply do not know what will happen in the future.

Even though you'd think they'd know better, fund managers also fall prey to financial hype. You can see this in the trading patterns of funds themselves: Some actively managed funds "turn over" stocks frequently, meaning they buy and sell funds a lot (incurring trading fees and, if held outside a tax-advantaged account, taxes for you). The managers chase the latest hot stock, confident of their abilities to spot something that millions of others have not. What's more, they also demand extraordinary compensation. Get this: In 2006, the average Goldman Sachs employee made $622,000. That's not a typo—it's the *average amount* Goldman employees made with salary and bonuses. Despite this astronomical compensation, fund managers from all companies still fail to beat the market *75 percent of the time*.

"But Ramit," you might say, "my fund is different. The manager returned 80 percent over the last two years!" That's great, but just because someone beat the market for a year or two doesn't mean they'll beat the market the next year. Think back to the year 2000. If you had

More Examples of How "Experts" Can't Time the Market

Pundits and television shows know exactly how to get our attention: with flashy graphics, loud talking heads, and bold predictions about the market that may or may not (in fact, probably not) come true. These may be entertaining, but let's look at some actual data.

Fidelity International carried out some research between June 1994 and June 2009 and found that the annual return of the FTSE All Share index was 6.13 percent. They noted something amazing: During that fifteen-year period, if you missed the best twenty days of investing (the days where the stock market gained the most points), your return would have dropped from 6.13 percent to 5.31 – a loss of 0.82 percent. And if you missed the best *forty* days you would have made an annual loss of 5.05 percent or a loss of 54 percent over the whole period. Unfortunately, we can't know the best investing days ahead of time. The only long-term solution is to invest regularly, putting as much money as possible into low-cost, diversified funds, even in an economic downturn.

USELESS NEWSLETTERS. A 1996 study by John Graham and Campbell Harvey investigated more than two hundred market-timing newsletters. The results were, shall we say, unimpressive. "We find that the newsletters fail to offer advice consistent with market timing," the authors deadpanned as only academics can. Hilariously, by the end of the 12.5-year period they studied, 94.5 percent of the newsletters had gone out of business. Not only did these market-timing newsletters fail to accurately predict what would happen, but they couldn't even keep their own doors open. Get a life, market timers.

I'll end with a couple of more recent examples. In December 2007, *Fortune* published an article called "The Best Stocks for 2008," which contained a special entry: Merrill Lynch. "Smart investors should buy this stock before everyone else comes to their senses," they advised. They obviously weren't counting on it being sold in a fire sale a few months later. And in April 2008, *BusinessWeek* advised us, "Don't be leery of Lehman." I'm not sure about you guys, but I'm leery of worthless risky advice couched in cute alliteration. I think I'll ignore you from now on, pundits.

looked at the fifty best-returning funds then, exactly zero would have been on the same list in 1998 or 1999. And if I asked you to name the best stocks of the past ten years, you might select Apple—but would you have guessed Oshkosh Truck? What about Gilead Sciences? Holly Corp?

DESPITE THEIR ASTRONOMICAL COMPENSATION, FUND MANAGERS FAIL TO BEAT THE MARKET 75 PERCENT OF THE TIME.

The problem is that nobody can consistently guess which funds or stocks will outperform, or even match, the market over time. Anyone who claims they can is lying.

So ignore the pundits' predictions. Ignore the last year or two of a fund's performance. A fund manager may be able to perform very well over the short term. But over the long term he will almost never beat the market—because of expenses, fees, and the growing mathematical difficulty of picking outperforming stocks (more on that later in this chapter). When you're evaluating a fund, the only way to really gauge it is by looking at its track record for the last ten years or more.

How Financial Experts Hide Poor Performance

As I've shown, the "experts" are often wrong and fail to beat the market, but even more irritatingly, they know how to cover their tracks so we don't catch on to their failures. In fact, the financial industry—including both companies that administer actively managed funds and so-called experts—are sneakier than you'd imagine.

One of the biggest tricks they use is to never admit they were wrong. Daniel Solin, author of *The Smartest Investment Book You'll Ever Read*, describes a study that illustrates how financial-ratings companies like Morningstar, which provides stock ratings that investors can use to get a quick take on many stocks' performance, continue to give thumbs-up ratings even as the companies they purport to be evaluating crater and lose billions of dollars of shareholder value. (Aside from their stock

Three Legendary Investors Who Prove Me Wrong—Sort of

Now, there are indeed investors who have beaten the market consistently for years. Warren Buffett, for example, has produced a 22 percent annualized return over forty years. Peter Lynch of Fidelity returned 29 percent over thirteen years. And Yale's David Swensen has returned more than 16 percent over twenty-three years. They have phenomenal investing skills and have earned their titles as some of the best investors in the world. But just because these guys can consistently beat the market doesn't mean you or I can.

Yes, theoretically, it is possible to consistently beat the market (which typically returns around 8 percent after you account for inflation) in the same way it is *possible* for me to become a heavyweight boxing champion. With millions of people around the globe trying to beat the market, statistically there are bound to be a few extreme outliers. Who knows whether their success is due to statistics or skill? But even the experts themselves agree that individual investors shouldn't expect to equal their returns. Swensen, for example, has explained that he achieves outsize returns because of top-notch professional resources, but more important, access to investments that you and I will never have, such as the very best venture capital and hedge funds, which he can use to bolster his asset allocation. Swensen recently told the *Financial Post* about his resources versus the average investor's: "I've got 20 professionals here in New Haven devoting their careers to identifying high-quality active management opportunities," he said. "An individual who devotes a couple of hours a week in the evening, at most, trying to compete with institutions that have armies of people out there? It just doesn't make sense."

ratings, they do have an excellent website with tools that I use all the time. So it's not like they're all bad.) The study found the following:

> *Forty-seven of the fifty [advisory] firms continued to advise investors to buy or hold shares in the companies up to the date the companies filed for bankruptcy.*

Twelve of the nineteen companies continued to receive "buy" or "hold" ratings on the actual date they filed for bankruptcy.

Companies like Moody's and Morningstar offer ratings of stocks and funds that are supposedly simple reflections of their value, but the idea of Morningstar's five-star ratings is actually complete nonsense. Why? For two reasons:

First, receiving five golden stars doesn't actually predict success. A 1999 study by researchers Christopher Blake and Matthew Morey showed that although the low-star ratings were on target in predicting poor-performing stocks, the high-star ratings were not accurate. They wrote: "[F]or the most part, there is little statistical evidence that Morningstar's highest-rated funds outperform the next-to-highest and median-rated fund." Just because a company assigns five shiny stars to a fund does not mean it will perform well.

A number of mutual-fund management complexes employ the practice of starting "incubator" funds. A complex may start ten small new equity funds with different in-house managers and wait to see which ones are successful. Suppose after a few years only three funds produce total returns better than the broad-market averages. The complex begins to market those successful funds aggressively, dropping the other seven and burying their records.

—**BURTON G. MALKIEL,** *A RANDOM WALK DOWN WALL STREET*

Second, when it comes to fund ratings, companies rely on something called *survivorship bias* to obscure the picture of how well a company is doing. Survivorship bias exists because funds that fail are not included in any future studies of fund performance for the simple reason that they don't exist anymore. For example, a company may start a hundred funds, but have only fifty left a couple of years later. The company can trumpet how effective their fifty funds are, but ignore the fifty funds that failed and have been erased from history. In other words, when you see "Best 10 Funds!" pages on actively managed-fund websites and in magazines, it's just as important to think about what you *aren't* seeing as what you are: The funds on that page are the ones that didn't close down. Out of that pool of already successful funds, *of course* there will be some five-star funds.

Financial companies know very well about survivorship bias, but they care more about having a page full of funds with great performance numbers than revealing the whole truth. As a result, they've consciously created several ways to test funds quickly and market only the best-performing ones, thus ensuring their reputation as the brand with the "best" funds.

How to Engineer a Perfect Stock-Picking Record

Since we know it's almost impossible to beat the market over the long term, let's turn to probability and luck to explain why some funds seem irresistibly compelling. Although a fund manager might be lucky for one, two, or even three years, it's mathematically unlikely he'll continue beating the market. To examine probability theory, let's take a simple example of an unscrupulous scammer who wants to sell his financial services to some naive investors.

He e-mails 10,000 people, half of whom are told that Stock A will go up, the other half Stock B. "This is just a freebie e-mail to demonstrate my insider knowledge," he might say. After a couple of weeks, he notices that Stock A has indeed gone up by chance. He eliminates the Stock B group and focuses on the Stock A group, e-mailing them an "I told you so" e-mail. This time, he splits the mailing in half again. Twenty-five hundred people are told about Stock C and 2,500 are told about Stock D. If either C or D goes up, on the next cycle, at least 1,250 people will have seen him pick two stocks successfully. And each cycle will make the recipients increasingly awed by his "ability."

Because we like to create order where there is none, we will ascribe magical stock-picking abilities to the scammer—even though it was literally by chance—and buy whatever "investment success kit" he's selling. The same is true of the pages of "five-star funds" you see. Moral of the story: Don't trust purported financial expertise just because of a few impressive stats.

Pundits Worth Reading

Q: *What are your favorite personal-finance blogs?*

A: Despite all my criticism of pathetic pundits who don't know what they're talking about, there are still people who provide a fresh perspective on money issues. Here are three of my favorite bloggers.

Get Rich Slowly (www.getrichslowly.org/blog), by J. D. Roth, is a great blog covering the basics of personal finance. With a name like that, you can imagine that J. D. believes in long-term growth. He writes about managing money, investing, and even starting a side job.

The Simple Dollar (www.thesimpledollar.com) is written by Trent Hamm. He covers the saving, investing, and debt sides of personal finance. He's got great book reviews and posts about regular financial situations that people like you and I find ourselves in all the time. Plus, he posts a lot.

JLP at AllFinancialMatters (http://allfinancialmatters. com) does an excellent job of using charts and data to show how low-cost investing beats brokers. JLP is usually pretty laid back, but occasionally he loses it and can't resist calling out financial companies that take advantage of regular people (those are my favorite posts).

I also keep a public list of *all* my personal-finance bookmarks at http://delicious.com/ramitsethi/finance.

These tricks are especially insidious because you'd never know to look out for them. When you see a page full of funds with 15 percent returns, you naturally assume they'll keep giving you 15 percent returns in the future. And it's even better if they have five-star ratings from a trusted company like Morningstar. But now that we know about survivorship bias and the fact that most ratings are meaningless, it's easy to see that financial "experts" and companies are just looking to fatten their wallets, not ensure that you get the best return for your money.

I Bet You Don't Need a Financial Adviser

You've heard my rants against the media hype surrounding investment and the poor performance of most professional investors. Now there's one more category of financial professionals that I want to warn you about: financial advisers.

Some of you might say, "But Ramit, I don't have time to invest! Can't I just use a financial adviser?" Ah, yes, the old outsourcing argument. We outsource our car cleaning, laundry, and housekeeping. So why not the management of our money?

Most young people don't need a financial adviser. We have such simple needs that with a little bit of time (a few hours a week over the course of, say, six weeks) we can get an automatic personal-finance infrastructure working for us.

Plus, financial advisers don't always look out for your interests. They're supposed to help you make the right decisions about your money, but keep in mind that unless they're independent, they don't have to do what's best for you. Some of them will give you very good advice, but many of them are pretty useless. If they're paid on commission, they will usually direct you to expensive, bloated funds to earn their commissions. By contrast, fee-based financial advisers simply charge a flat fee and are much more reputable. (Neither is necessarily better at providing good investment returns, or your top line; they simply charge differently, affecting your bottom line.)

SOME FINANCIAL ADVISERS WILL GIVE YOU GOOD ADVICE, BUT MANY ARE PRETTY USELESS.

The key takeaway is that most people don't actually need a financial adviser—you can do it all on your own and come out ahead. But if your choice is between hiring a financial adviser or not investing at all, then sure, you should hire one. People with really complex financial situations, those who have inherited significant amounts of money, and those who truly are too busy to learn about investing for themselves also should consider seeking an adviser's help. It's better to pay a little and get

So You Really Think You Need a Financial Adviser?

If you really want to look into hiring a financial adviser, here's an introductory e-mail you can adapt and send:

Hi, Mike,

I'm looking for a fee-based financial planner, and I found you on www.financialplanning.org.uk. A little bit about me: I'm 29 and have about £15,000 in total assets. At the moment my money is split between a stocks and shares ISA and a stakeholder pension, although I also have some cash. I don't need the money any time soon, so I'm looking for investments that will maximize long-term returns while minimizing costs.

If you think you can help me, I'd like to meet for half an hour and ask you some specific questions. I'd also like to hear details on other situations in which you've worked with similar people with similar goals. Would next Friday, 2/6, at 2 P.M., work at your office? Alternatively, Monday, 2/9, is wide open for me.

Thanks, Ramit

For your thirty-minute meeting—which shouldn't cost you anything—you'll want to come prepared with questions. There are hundreds of sample questions available online (search for "financial adviser questions"), but at the very least, ask these three:

- How do you make your money? Is it through commission or strictly fee based? Are there any other fees? *(You want a fee-based adviser with no hidden fees.)*

- Have you worked with other people like me in similar situations? What general solutions did you recommend? *(Get references and call them.)*

- What's your working style? Do we talk regularly or do I work with an assistant? *(You want to know what to expect in the first thirty days, sixty days, and ninety days.)*

started investing than to not start at all. If you're determined to get professional help, begin your search at the Institute of Financial Planning (www.financialplanning.org.uk). These planners are fee based (either a flat fee or an hourly rate) and are licensed. They want to help you, not profit off their recommendations.

But remember, many people use financial advisers as a crutch and end up paying tens of thousands of pounds over their lifetime simply because they didn't spend a few hours learning about investing. If you don't learn to manage your money in your twenties, you'll cost yourself a ton one way or another—whether you do nothing, or pay someone exorbitant fees to "manage" your money.

After seeing for four years that my financial planner wasn't providing any special return on my investment, but costing me 1.5 percent in fees each year, I made the decision to open an online brokerage account and take charge of my money.

—SARAH PURA, 24

Active vs. Passive Management

Please know that even with all of this doom and gloom about professional investor performance, I'm not in any way saying that investing is a waste of money. You just have to know where to invest.

Actively managed funds—which are simply collections of stocks (and sometimes bonds, but usually just stocks)—are often considered the simplest and best way for most people to invest. But, as we've seen, fund managers fail to beat the market 75 percent of the time, and it can be hard to tell which funds will actually perform well over the long term. And no matter how good an actively managed fund is, the returns are hampered by the large fees they charge. (Sure, there are some low-cost actively managed funds, but because of the way they compensate their own portfolio managers and other employees, it's virtually impossible for them to compete with the low costs of passively managed tracker funds, which I'll talk more about in a minute.)

When it comes to investing, fees are a huge drag on your returns. This is a little counterintuitive since we're used to paying for service, like our gym membership or admission to Disneyland. If we're getting something out of it, we should pay a fair price, right? The key is *fair*, and many of the financial "experts" we turn to for guidance make an effort to squeeze every last cent out of us.

You see, actively managed funds employ a fund manager (or sometimes a whole team to actively try and pick the best stocks and give you the best return. Sounds good, right? But even with all the fancy analysts and technology they employ, portfolio managers still make fundamentally human mistakes like selling too quickly, trading too much, and making rash guesses. These fund managers trade frequently so they can show short-term results to their shareholders and prove they're doing something—anything!—to earn your money. Not only do they usually fail to beat the market, but they charge a fee to do this. Actively managed funds typically charge 1.5 to 2 percent of assets managed each year. (This percentage is known as the annual management charge.) In other words, with a 2 percent expense ratio and a £10,000 portfolio, you'd pay £200 per year in fees. Some funds even tack on additional sales charges, or "loads," to the purchase price (called an initial charge) or sales price (back-end load) of the fund. These are just some of the tricky ways actively managed fund managers make money whether they perform or not.

> **NOT ONLY DO MOST FUND MANAGERS FAIL TO BEAT THE MARKET, THEY CHARGE A FEE TO DO THIS.**

Two percent doesn't sound like much until you compare it with the alternative: "passive management." This is how tracker funds (a cousin of actively managed funds) are run. These funds work by replacing portfolio managers with computers. The computers don't attempt to find the hottest stock. They simply and methodically pick the same stocks that an index holds—for example, the 350 stocks in the FTSE 350 index—in an attempt to match the market. (An index is a way to measure part of the stock market. For example, the FTSE 100 represents the UK's 100 largest publicly-owned companies; other UK indexes track technology companies or smaller businesses. There are international indexes and even retail indexes.)

Most tracker funds stay close to the market (or to the segment of the market they represent). Just as the stock market may fall 10 percent one year and gain 18 percent the next year, tracker funds will rise and fall with the indexes they track. The big difference is in fees: Tracker funds are not as cheap in the UK as they are in the US, but that is beginning to change and you can get trackers that charge less than 0.25 percent.

Remember, there are all kinds of tracker funds. International tracker funds are relatively volatile since they follow indexes that were just recently established. General U.S.-based tracker funds, on the other hand, are more reliable. Since they match the U.S. stock market, if the market goes down, tracker funds will also go down. During the financial crisis, many tracker funds plummeted as they matched the market, which underwent a global drop. But over the long term, the overall stock market has consistently returned about 8 percent.

Let's look at the performance from two sides: the downside (fees) and the upside (returns). First, let's compare the fees for a passively managed fund with those for an actively managed fund.

WHAT'S A BETTER DEAL?

Assuming 7% return on £100 a month	Passively managed tracker fund (0.25% annual management charge)	Actively managed fund (1.5% annual management charge)	Investors pay this much more in fees with an actively managed fund
After 5 years, you'd have ...	£7,112.03	£6,878.92	£233.11
After 10 years, you'd have ...	£16,963.10	£15,829.40	£1,133.70
After 25 years, you'd have ...	£75,687.05	£62,344.65	£13,342.40

source: thismoney.co.uk. NB figures don't take account of initial charges.

If your decision was determined by fees alone, tracker funds would be the clear choice. But let's also consider another important factor: returns.

Despite my hammering home the fact that actively managed funds fail to beat the market 75 percent of the time, I will say that they do occasionally provide great returns. In some years, some actively managed funds do extraordinarily well and far outperform tracker funds. In a good year, for example, a fund focused on Russian stocks might return 70 percent—but one or two years of great performance only gets you so far. What you really want is solid, long-term returns. So, if you're thinking about using a broker or actively managed fund, call them and ask them a simple, point-blank question: "What were your after-tax, after-fee returns for the last ten, fifteen, and twenty years?" Yes, their response must include all fees and taxes. Yes, the return must be at least ten years, because the last five years of any time period are too volatile to matter. And yes, I promise they won't give you a straight answer, because that would be admitting that they didn't beat the market consistently. It's *that* hard to do.

So, the safe assumption is that actively managed funds will too often fail to beat or match the market. In other words, if the market returns 8 percent, actively managed funds won't return at least 8 percent more than three-fourths of the time. In addition, when combined with their high expense ratios, actively managed funds have to outperform cheaper, passively managed funds by at least 2 or 3 percent just to break even with them—and that simply doesn't happen.

In his book *The Smartest Investment Book You'll Ever Read,* Daniel Solin cites a study conducted by Professor Edward S. O'Neal from the Babcock Graduate School of Management. O'Neal tracked funds whose sole purpose was to beat the market. What he discovered was that from 1993 through 1998, less than half of these actively managed funds beat the market. And from 1998 through 2003, only 8 percent beat the market. But there's more. When he looked at the number of funds that beat the market in *both* time periods, the results were "sad indeed. The number of funds that beat the market in both periods was a whopping ten—or only 2 percent of all large-cap funds . . . Investors, both individual and institutional, and particularly pension plans, would be far better served by investing in passive or passively managed funds than in trying to pick more expensive active managers who purport to be able to beat the markets."

Bottom line: There's no reason to pay exorbitant fees for active management when you could do better, for cheaper, on your own.

Now that you've read about the myth of expertise, it's time to see exactly how you can invest your own money to get better returns for lower cost. In the next chapter, I'll teach you everything you need to know about investing, and we'll cover all the technical aspects of selecting and automating your investments. Let's do this.

P.S.—If you're looking for Action Steps, keep reading. This chapter is informational but in the next section you'll make some major decisons.

CHAPTER 7

INVESTING ISN'T ONLY FOR RICH PEOPLE

Spend the afternoon picking a simple portfolio that will make you rich

Ⅰ n the previous chapter, you read about how useless investing "experts" are—and how we can do better on our own. Now we've arrived at the Promised Land, the chapter where you'll learn how to choose your own investments, pay less in fees, and get superior performance. You're going to determine your investing style by asking yourself some key questions: Do you need your money next year or can you let it grow for a while? Are you saving up for a house? Can you withstand big day-to-day changes in the stock market, or do they make you queasy? Then you're going to research funds and pick exactly the right investments to meet your goals. This includes all your investment accounts, like your defined contribution and stakeholder pensions. (When someone boasts, "I have £50,000 in

(continued on page 162)

What's Your Investor Profile?

Do you sweat like Joe Calzaghe when you look at your investment returns? Do you have a robotic, emotionless demeanor when surveying gains or losses? Take this quiz to determine your investment personality:

1. YOU TURN ON YOUR COMPUTER AND LEARN THAT THE MARKET HAS LOST 350 POINTS. YOU:

   a. Laugh at the fools who track day-to-day changes and go watch *Have I Got News For You.*

   b. Get a little nervous, log in to your investment account to check out your portfolio, and decide to sit tight and ride it out.

   c. Feel your heart start to race, bite off your fingernails, log in to your account, and scream, "Sell, sell, sell!" while clicking furiously.

2. IF SOMEONE ASKED YOU WHEN YOU'D NEED THE MONEY YOU'RE INVESTING, YOU'D SAY . . .

   a. "Maybe when I have wrinkles all over, a gleaming white yacht, and a twenty-five-year-old girlfriend who feeds me peeled grapes."

   b. "Probably some time in the next five to fifteen years."

   c. "I want it there whenever I need it, like within the next three to five years."

3. HOW DO YOU WANT TO HANDLE YOUR INVESTMENTS?

   a. You want to optimize every asset of your investments and tweak your asset allocation to exactly what you want.

   b. You know you should do something with your money but aren't sure yet exactly what.

   c. Can't someone please handle this for me?

IF YOU CHOSE MOSTLY (A), you're a type-A power investor who's focused on the long term. You're willing to give up convenience in exchange for control over every aspect of your portfolio. I recommend you pick your own asset allocation through tracker funds. See how on page 188.

IF YOU CHOSE MOSTLY (B)S, you're like most people reading this book: You don't need your money for the next few years, but after that, it's hard to tell what you'll need. You know you should do *something* to invest but it's not clear what—and you don't want to spend your life managing your money. This is actually a great position to be in because, while most people will give in to inertia and do nothing, you can take action. You're a perfect candidate for the 85 Percent Solution: You just want to invest and let your money grow without having to think about or monitor it all the time. I recommend a lifecycle fund for your pension (or a multi-asset fund as an alternative to a tracker if it's an ISA).

IF YOU CHOSE MOSTLY (C)S, you need to get your head on straight. It's one thing to be conservative—if you're afraid of losing money, you can pick investments that limit your exposure (such as a lifecycle fund that's geared towards cautious investors, or a heavier emphasis on more stable, large-cap funds in your portfolio). But the more common problem is that you haven't given investing much thought at all! You want to invest and get your money out in three to five years? What the hell is wrong with you? Nobody can consistently make money in the short term.

More typically, people who answered (c) haven't invested at all. Confusion and fear of losing money gets in the way. Let's be clear: If you're not investing, in the long term you're losing money every day. It actually costs you money to park your money in a savings account as inflation eats into your earnings. Look at the chart on page 5 to see why investing makes such a difference—especially when you start early. If you're truly risk-averse, you can always balance your portfolio with more conservative investments. But don't succumb to irrational fear and not invest at all. Ironically, the people who do that are the ones who end up without enough money in the end. Check out the chart on page 75 and see why it pays to start investing today.

(continued from page 159)

my portfolio," which they would say only if they were a jackass, they're probably referring to money in their pension funds, and perhaps even other investment accounts.) By the end of this chapter, you'll know exactly what to invest in—and why. And you'll do it with minimal human involvement, incurring minimal expense.

My goal for this chapter is to help you pick the simplest investment to get started—and to make your portfolio easy to maintain. By doing just those two things, you'll be on the way to getting rich. Another benefit is that you will, quite simply, become a cooler person than all of your friends. Hey, I can't deny it. You'll realize that your friend who makes £50,000 a year has no savings or investments. You'll start noticing the excuses people make to justify not investing, including "I don't have time" and "Stocks can go down, and I don't want to lose my money." Most people don't know the first thing about how to pick investments— but now you will! Ah, the Promised Land is sweet.

A Better Way to Invest: Automatic Investing

Let's be honest. Nobody really loves managing their money. I'd rather be *using* my money, like eating at Taco Bell or flying to New York to hang out with friends. Basically, I'm always on the lookout for ways to spend less time and get better results. When I was in high school and applying to colleges, for example, I created a system to write three scholarship applications per day and ended up winning more than $200,000 in six months to pay for school. These days, I manage more than seven hundred e-mails per day about PBwiki, my blog, and this book. This isn't to brag about how busy I am, but to show that when it comes to money, I'm very, very interested in paying less attention while getting better returns. I've taken pains to research investments that don't take lots of time to maintain and also pay off. That's why I urge you to combine a classic low-cost investing strategy with automation.

Automatic Investing is not some revolutionary technique that I just invented. It's a simple way of investing in low-cost funds that is recommended by Nobel laureates, billionaire investors such as Warren

Buffett, and most academics. It involves spending most of your time choosing how your money will be distributed in your portfolio, picking the investments (this actually takes the least amount of time), and then automating your regular investments so you can sit and watch TV while growing your money. Hey, we're lazy. We might as well embrace it and use it to our advantage.

Automatic Investing works for two reasons:

LOWER EXPENSES. As I discussed in Chapter 6, nothing kills your investment performance more than expensive funds that invisibly drain your returns. Investing in them is especially ridiculous when you can earn better returns with lower fees. Why would you pay for the privilege of losing your money? With Automatic Investing, you invest in low-cost funds—which replace worthless, expensive portfolio managers—and you save tens of thousands of pounds in trading fees, taxes, and overall investment expenses, outperforming most investors.

IT'S AUTOMATIC. Automatic Investing frees you from having to pay attention to the latest "hot stock" or micro-change in the market. You pick a simple investment plan that doesn't involve any sexy stocks or guessing whether the market is going up or down, and then set up automatic contributions to your investment accounts. In this way, you effectively trick yourself into investing because it requires no work from you. This means you can focus on living your life—doing your job well, spending time with friends, traveling to different countries, eating at great restaurants—instead of worrying about your money. I might well call this Zen Investing for People Who Have Real Lives. (And that is why I'll never be a naming consultant.)

TOO GOOD TO BE TRUE? The way I described Automatic Investing was basically the same as saying, "Puppies are cute." Nobody would ever disagree with it. Automatic Investing sounds perfect, but what happens when the market goes down? It's not as easy to go along for the ride then. For example, I know several people who had automatic investment plans and when the stock market incurred huge losses in late 2008, they immediately canceled their investments and took their money out of the market. Big mistake. The test of a real Automatic Investor is not when things are going up, but when they are going down. It takes strength to know that you're basically getting shares on sale—and, if you're investing for the long term, the best time to make money is when everyone else is getting out of the market.

Do You Believe Everything Your Friends Tell You?

Q: *My friends tell me that investing is too risky and that I could lose all my money. Is that true?*

A: That's an instinctive, emotional reaction, not a well-reasoned, logical response. But you have to admit: It does make sense to be scared of investing right now, especially if you don't understand how it works. With headlines screaming about sharp drops, it's easy to practice the "DNA" style of investing—the Do Nothing Approach. It's very unfortunate that the very same people who are afraid of investing in the market right now are usually the same people who buy when prices are soaring. As Warren Buffett has said, investors should "be fearful when others are greedy and greedy when others are fearful."

For you, it's different. You understand how investing works, so you can put a long-term perspective into practice. Yes, in theory it's possible for you to lose all your money, but if you've bought different investments to create a balanced (or "diversified") portfolio, you won't.

You'll notice that your friends are concerned with the downside: "You could lose everything! How will you have time to learn to invest? There are so many sharks out there to take your money."

What about the downside of the money they're losing every day by not investing?

Ask your friends what the average return of the S&P 500 has been for the past seventy years. How much money would they have if they invested $10,000 today and didn't touch it for ten years—or fifty years? They won't know because they don't even know the basic return rate to assume (try 8 percent). When people say investing is too risky, it's because they don't know what they don't know.

BOTTOM LINE: Automatic Investing may not seem as sexy as trading in hedge funds and biotech stocks, but it works a lot better. Again, would you rather be sexy or rich?

More Convenience or More Control: You Choose

I want investing to be as painless as possible for you, so here's what I'm going to do: I'll give you an easy version and a more advanced version. If you're the kind of person who wants your money to grow with the least possible effort on your part and you don't care about all the theory, turn to page 180. There you'll find a step-by-step guide for picking a single investment—a lifecycle fund—and you'll get started investing in just a few hours.

But if you're a Type A nerd like me who wants to learn how it works— and maybe even customize your own portfolio for more control—read on. I'll walk you through the building blocks of a portfolio, and I'll help you construct a portfolio that's both aggressive and balanced.

Investing Is Not About Picking Stocks

Really, it's not. Ask your friends what they think investing means and I bet they'll say, "Picking stocks." Guys, you cannot reliably pick stocks that will outperform the market over the long term. It's way too easy to make mistakes such as being overconfident about choices or panicking when your investments drop even a little. As we saw in Chapter 6, even experts can't guess what will happen to the stock market. Because they've heard it repeatedly from the many investment magazines and TV shows, people think that investing is about picking winning stocks and that anyone can be successful. They can't. I hate to say it, but not everyone is a winner. In fact, most of these so-called financial "experts" are failures.

Actually, I don't hate saying that. I'll say that to their faces again and again. Yeah, I'm a frail Indian man throwing verbal punches here on page 165 of a personal-finance book. This is how battles should be fought.

Anyway, the little-known but true fact is that the major predictor of your portfolio's volatility is not due, as most people think, to the individual stocks you pick, but instead your *mix* of stocks and bonds. In 1986, researchers Gary Brinson, Randolph Hood, and Gilbert Beebower published a study in the *Financial Analysts Journal* that rocked the financial world. They demonstrated that more than 90 percent of your portfolio's volatility is a result of your asset allocation. I know *asset allocation* sounds like a B.S. phrase—like *mission statement* and *strategic alliance*. But it's not. Asset allocation is your plan for investing, the way you organize the investments in your portfolio between stocks, bonds, and cash. In other words, by diversifying your investments across different asset classes (like stocks and bonds, or, better yet, stock funds and bond funds), you could control the risk in your portfolio—and therefore control how much money, on average, you'd lose due to volatility. It turns out that the amounts you buy—whether it's 100 percent stocks or 90 percent stocks and 10 percent bonds—make a profound difference on your returns. Later, other researchers tried to measure how closely *volatility* and *returns* were correlated, but the answer ends up being pretty complicated. Suffice it to say that asset allocation is the most significant part of your portfolio that you can control.

Think about that remarkable fact: *Your investment plan is more important than your actual investments.*

Take, for example, this book. If we apply the same principle here, it means that the way I organized this book is more important than any given word in it. That makes sense, right? Well, the same is true of investing. If you allocate your money properly—for example, not all in one stock, but spread out across different kinds of funds—you won't have to worry about a single stock possibly cutting your portfolio's value in half. Indeed, by diversifying your investments, you'll make more money as an individual investor. To know how to allocate your assets, you have to know the basic options you have for investing, which is where we're headed next.

"Since you cannot successfully time the market or select individual stocks, asset allocation should be the major focus of your investment strategy, because it is the only factor affecting your investment risk and return that you can control."

—WILLIAM BERNSTEIN, *THE FOUR PILLARS OF INVESTING: LESSONS FOR BUILDING A WINNING PORTFOLIO*

The Building Blocks of Investing

Again, if you're not interested in the mechanics of investing and want to skip ahead to see what the simplest investment choice is, turn to page 180. But if you want to know more about what's going on under the hood, stay with me.

THE PYRAMID OF INVESTING OPTIONS

LIFESTYLE FUNDS
More convenience
Less control
More predictable returns over the long term

MULTI-ASSET FUNDS
(for ISAs)
Broad mix of investments
Investments may not change with your age
Should reduce risk

TRACKER FUNDS / ACTIVELY MANAGED FUNDS
Somewhat convenient
Can be low fees (tracker funds) or high fees (many actively managed funds)
More control than lifestyle funds, less control than stocks/bonds
Returns are fairly predictable over the long term

SHARES / BONDS / CASH
Individual stocks and bonds are very inconvenient to choose and maintain
High control
Shares offer extremely unpredictable returns that typically fail to beat the market
Bonds offer extremely predictable returns, but on average return less than shares

This Pyramid of Investing Options represents your choices for different investments. At the bottom is the most basic level, where you can invest in stocks or bonds or just hold your money in cash. I'm oversimplifying because there are tons of different kinds of stocks and bonds, but you get the idea. Above them are tracker and actively managed funds. And finally, at the top of the pyramid, are lifestyle funds. Let's look at each category (also known as *asset class*) to see what lies beneath.

STOCKS

When you buy stock, you buy shares of a company. If the company does well, you expect your stock in it to do well. When people talk about "the market," they're talking about a collection of thirty large-cap stocks—the Dow Jones Industrial Average Index. The S&P 500 is another index of 500 stocks that I'll frequently refer to.

Overall, stocks as an entire category provide excellent returns. As we know, on average the stock market returns about 8 percent per year. In fact, you can do significantly better than the market if you pick a winning stock—or significantly worse if you pick a loser. Although stocks as a whole provide generally excellent returns, individual stocks are less clear. If you invest all your money in one stock, for example, you *might* make a huge return, but it's also possible the company could tank and you could lose it all.

Stocks have been a good way to earn significant returns over the long term, but I discourage you from picking individual stocks, because it's extremely difficult to choose winning ones on your own. The tricky thing about stocks is you never know what will happen. For example, in 2005 eBay announced that it missed Wall Street's earning expectations by *a penny* per share. The stock immediately plunged 20 percent. Was it 20 percent less useful the next day? Of course not.

In Chapter 6, I demonstrated that even professionals whose livelihoods depend on it can't predict stock returns. And remember, these are highly trained analysts who can read stock prospectuses like I can read an Indian restaurant menu—flawlessly. If these experts—who devour annual reports and understand complicated balance sheets—can't beat the market, what chance do you have of picking stocks that will go up?

You have very little chance. That's why individual investors like you and me should not invest in individual stocks. Instead, we'll choose funds, which are collections of stocks (and sometimes, for diversification, bonds). They let you reduce your risk and create a well-balanced portfolio that will let you sleep at night . . . but more on that later.

BONDS

Bonds are essentially IOUs from companies or the government. (Technically, bonds are longer-term investments of ten-plus years, whereas fixed-rate bonds involve lending money to a bank. Because they're very similar, let's just call them both *bonds* to simplify things.) If you buy a one-year bond, it's the same as if the bank says, "Hey, if you lend us £100, we'll give you £103 back a year from now."

The advantages of bonds are that you can choose the term, or length of time, you want the loan to last (two years, five years, ten years, and so on), and you know exactly how much you'll get when they "mature" or pay out. Also, bonds, especially government bonds, are generally stable and let you decrease the risk in your portfolio (UK government bonds, which are seen as very safe, are called gilts). See, the only way you'd lose money on a government bond is if the government defaulted on its loans—and it doesn't do that. If it runs low on money, it just prints more of it. Now *that's* gangsta.

IN GENERAL, RICH PEOPLE AND OLD PEOPLE LIKE BONDS.

But because bonds are such a safe, low-risk investment, the return—even on a highly rated bond—is much lower than it would be on an excellent stock. Investing in bonds also renders your money illiquid, meaning it's locked away and inaccessible for a set period of time. Technically, you can withdraw early, but you'll face severe penalties, so it's a bad idea.

With these qualities, what kind of person would invest in bonds? Let's see: extremely stable, essentially guaranteed rate of return, but relatively small returns . . . Who would it be?

In general, rich people and old people like bonds. Old people like them because they like to know exactly how much money they're getting next month for their medication or whatever it is they need. Also, some of these grannies and grampies can't withstand the volatility of the stock market because they don't have much other income to support themselves and/or they have very little time left on this earth to recover from any downturn.

Rich people, on the other hand, tend to become more conservative because they have so much money. Put it this way: When you have £10,000, you want to invest aggressively to grow it because you want to make more money. But when you have £10 million, your goals switch from aggressive growth to preservation of capital. You'll accept lower investment returns in exchange for security and safety. So a guaranteed bond at 3 percent or 4 percent is attractive to a wealthy person—after all, 3 percent of £10 million is still a lot.

CASH

In investing terms, cash is money that's sitting on the sidelines, uninvested and earning only a little money in interest from money-market accounts. Be aware that some 'cash-based' funds have invested in some complex and risky financial instruments, and have been riskier than investors realised. Traditionally, cash has been the third part of a portfolio beyond stocks and bonds. You want to have totally liquid cash on hand for emergencies, and as a hedge if the market tanks. Cash is the safest part of your portfolio, but it offers the lowest reward. If you factor in inflation, you actually *lose* money by holding cash in most accounts.

That's why I say it's *traditionally* been part of a portfolio. As long as you're contributing toward your savings goals as I described in Chapter 5, you're fine. Don't worry about having a separate cash account as part of your investments. Let's keep this simple.

Asset Allocation: The Critical Factor That Most Investors Miss

If you bought all different kinds of stocks or stock funds, you'd be diversified—but still only within stocks. That's like being the hottest person in Friendship, Wisconsin—better than not being hot, but not going to get you cast in *Hollyoaks*. (Friendship is actually a real place. My friend grew up there, and he told me what he and his buddies used to use as a gang sign: two hands clasping in friendship. I mocked him endlessly for that.)

It is important to diversify within stocks, but it's even more important to allocate *across* the different asset classes—like stocks and bonds. Investing in only one category is dangerous over the long term. This is where the all-important concept of asset allocation comes into play. Remember it like this: Diversification is *D* for going *deep* into a category (for example, buying different types of stocks: large-cap, small-cap, international, and so on), and asset allocation

80 YEARS OF AVERAGE ANNUAL RETURNS FOR STOCKS AND BONDS

The group at Vanguard Investment Counseling & Research in America recently analyzed eighty years of investment returns to help individual investors understand how to allocate their money. These numbers, which don't include inflation, give us a hint on how to maximize our investment returns.

Stocks	Bonds	Cash
Higher risk	Lower risk	Ultra-low risk. Stored in an interest-generating money-market account, not under your mattress.
10.5%	5.2%	3.8%

is *A* for going *across* all categories (for example, stocks *and* bonds).

In determining where to allocate your assets, one of the most important considerations is the returns each category offers. Of course, based on the different types of investments you make, you can expect different returns. Higher risk generally equals higher potential for reward. Take a look at the chart above.

At first glance, it seems clear that stocks return the most. So let's all invest there!!

Not so fast. Remember, higher rewards entail higher risk, so if you're loaded up on stocks and your portfolio dips 25 percent next year, all of a sudden you're financially immobile, eating only Pot Noodle, waiting to see whether your money climbs back up or you die first. Hey, it had to be said.

But seriously, many of the fifty- and sixty-year-olds who have seen catastrophic drops in their portfolios should never have invested in all equities. Timing matters. If you're twenty-five years old and have dozens of years to grow your money, a portfolio made up of stock-based funds probably makes sense. But if you're older retirement is coming up within a few decades and you'll want to tamp down your risk. I heard from tons of people in their forties, fifties, and sixties who were rocked by the stock market's decline in 2008. I can't help but feel sorry for them, but you should learn from their mistakes. Even if the market tanks, you have control over your asset allocation. If you're older—especially if you're in your sixties, for god's sake—a sizeable portion of your portfolio should be in stable bonds.

Bonds act as a counterweight to stocks, rising when stocks fall and reducing the overall risk of your portfolio. By investing part of your money in bonds, you reduce some of your overall risk. Sure, if that biotech stock went up 200 percent, you'd wish your bond money was all in the stock—but if the stock went down, you'd be glad your bonds were there as a buffer against losing everything. Although it may seem counterintuitive, your portfolio will actually have better overall performance if you add bonds to the mix. Because bonds will generally perform better when stocks fall, bonds lower your risk a lot while limiting your returns only a little.

"But Ramit," you might say, "I'm young and I want to invest aggressively. I don't need bonds." I agree. Bonds aren't really for young people in their twenties. If you're in your twenties or early thirties, and you don't necessarily need to reduce your risk, you can simply invest in share-only funds and let time mitigate any risk. But in your thirties and older, you'll want to begin balancing your portfolio with bonds to reduce risk. And what if stocks as a whole don't perform well for a long time? That's when you need to own other asset classes—to offset the bad times.

The Importance of Being Diversified

Now that we know the basics of the asset classes (stocks, bonds, and cash) at the bottom of the pyramid, let's explore the different choices within each asset class. Basically, there are many types of stocks, and we need to own a little of all of them. Same with bonds. This is called diversifying, and it essentially means digging in to each asset class—stocks and bonds—and investing in all their subcategories.

As the table on the next page shows, the broad category of "stocks" actually includes many different kinds of stock, including large-company stocks ("large-cap"), mid-cap stocks, small-cap stocks, and international stocks. To add yet another wrinkle, none of them performs consistently. In the same year, small-cap stocks might gain huge percentages, but international stocks might tank—and this performance can vary from year to year. For example, William Bernstein notes, in 1998 U.S. large-cap stocks gained 28.6 percent, international stocks gained 20 percent, and REITs

STOCKS AND BONDS HAVE MANY FLAVORS

Stocks	Bonds
LARGE-CAP Big companies with a market capitalization ("market cap," which is defined as outstanding shares times the stock price) over £3 billion or members of FTSE 100 index	**GILTS** An ultra-safe investment that's backed by the government. In exchange for their low risk, government bonds tend to return less than stocks as a general rule of thumb.
MID-CAP Midsized companies that fall within the FTSE 250 (the next largest companies after the FTSE 100)	**CORPORATE** A bond issued by a company. These tend to be riskier than government bonds, but safer than stocks.
SMALL-CAP Smaller companies with a market cap less than £100 million	**SHORT-TERM** Bonds with terms of usually less than three years
INTERNATIONAL INVESTMENTS Stocks from companies in other countries, including emerging markets (like China, India, and Mexico) and developed markets (like the United States, Germany, and France). You can buy these directly, or may have to buy them through funds.	**LONG-TERM** These bonds tend to mature in twenty or more years and, accordingly, offer higher yields than shorter-term bonds.
GROWTH Stocks whose value may grow higher than other stocks, or even the market as a whole	**LOCAL AUTHORITY** These are bonds issued by local governments.
VALUE Stocks that seem bargain priced (i.e., cheaper than they should be)	**INDEX-LINKED** Index-linked gilts are ultra-safe investments that protect against inflation.

Note that REITs, "real-estate investment trusts"—which are types of investments that let you invest in real estate through a fund that's quoted on the stock market, just like a stock—don't neatly fall into any of these categories because of their complicated structure.

WHAT A GRANNY NEEDS:
TYPICAL ASSET ALLOCATIONS BY AGE

Here's what typical investors' asset allocations—remember, that's the mix of different investments—might look like as they get older. These figures are taken from Vanguard's lifecycle funds.

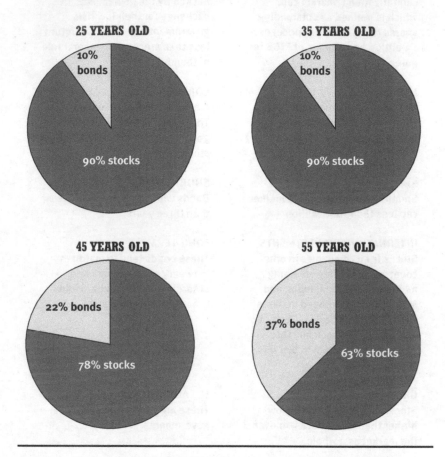

25 YEARS OLD
10% bonds
90% stocks

35 YEARS OLD
10% bonds
90% stocks

45 YEARS OLD
22% bonds
78% stocks

55 YEARS OLD
37% bonds
63% stocks

(collections of real estate stocks) lost 17 percent. But in 2000, just two years later, U.S. large-cap stocks *lost* 9.10 percent, foreign stocks *lost* 14.17 percent, and REITS *gained* 31.04 percent. Similarly, different types of bonds offer different benefits, including rates of return and tax advantages.

The fact that performance varies so much in each asset class means two things: First, if you're trying to make quick money off investing, you'll usually lose money because you have no idea what will happen in the near future. Anyone who tells you they do is a fool or a commission-based salesman. Second, you should own different categories of stocks (and maybe bonds) to balance out your portfolio. You don't want to own only U.S. small-cap stocks, for example, or funds that own only small-cap stocks. If they didn't perform well for ten years, that would really suck. If, however, you own small-cap stocks, plus large-cap stocks, plus international stocks, and more, you're effectively insured against any one area dragging you down. So, if you were to invest in stocks, you'd want to *diversify,* buying all different types of stocks or stock funds to have a balanced portfolio.

These allocations are just general rules of thumb. Some people prefer to have 100 percent in stocks until they're in their thirties or forties. Others are more conservative and want some money in bonds. But the big takeaway here is that, if we're in our twenties and thirties, we can afford to be aggressive about investing in stocks and stock funds—even if they drop temporarily—because time is on our side.

And honestly, if you're twenty-five and just starting out, your biggest danger isn't having a portfolio that's too risky. It's being lazy and overwhelmed and not doing any investing at all. That's why it's important to understand the basics but not get too wrapped up in all the variables and choices.

Over time, you can manage your asset allocation to reduce risk and get a fairly predictable return on investments. Thirty years from now, you're going to need to invest very differently from how you do today. That's just natural: You invest much more aggressively in your twenties than in your fifties, as you get older and tell long-winded stories about yourself. So although it seems sexy to pull out a pipe and phone in your favorite stock choices to your broker, the real work in investing comes with creating an investment plan that's appropriate for your age and comfort level with risk.

All of this sounds completely reasonable: "I invest more aggressively when I'm younger, and as I get older, I get more and more conservative."

There's just one problem.

How the hell are you actually supposed to do it? What specific investments should you choose? Should you invest in individual stocks? (No.) Most people stop here, superficially thinking that investing is only about stocks, leading to frustration. Not surprisingly, when they try to think more deeply about this, they get confused and shut down, killing any impetus to invest, becoming destitute and wandering around a tumbleweed-laden desert in their twilight years. Well, almost all of that.

Don't let this happen to you! Let's go further up the Pyramid of Investing Options to cover another key to investing: funds.

Actively Managed Funds: Not Bad, Pretty Convenient, but Often Expensive and Unreliable

The financial industry isn't stupid. Those people are ingenious at creating products to meet investor needs (or what the industry *wants* people to need). The first investment fund was launched in 1931. It was just a basket of around two dozen stocks. Instead of requiring investors to perform the Herculean task of picking individual stocks themselves, actively managed funds allowed average investors to simply choose types of funds that would suit them. For example, there are large-cap, mid-cap, and small-cap actively managed funds, but also actively managed funds that focus on biotechnology, communication, and even Europe or Asia. Actively managed funds are extremely popular because they allow you to pick one fund, which contains different stocks, and not worry about putting too many eggs in one basket (as you likely would if you bought individual stocks), monitoring prospectuses, or keeping up with industry news. The funds provide instant diversification because they hold many different stocks. Most people's first encounter with actively managed funds is through their pension, where they choose from a bewildering array of options. You buy shares of the fund and the fund's manager picks the stocks he thinks will yield the best return.

Actively managed funds are incredibly useful financial tools—over the past eighty-five years, they have proven to be very popular and extremely profitable. Compared with other investments, they've been a cash cow for Wall Street. That's because in exchange for "active management" (having an expert choose a fund's stocks), the financial companies charge big fat fees (also known as annual management charges). These fees eat a hole in your returns and make me want to poke a steel-tipped ice-lolly stick into my eye. Sure, there are some low-fee funds out there, but most actively managed funds have high expense ratios.

You can avoid the charges associated with actively managed funds by putting money into an investment trust, rather than a unit trust or OEIC. Investment trusts are sold as shares (rather than 'units') and they have lower annual management charges and no initial charge; although you do pay stamp duty when you buy. The downside is they can be riskier because managers are allowed to borrow against their value (called 'gearing') and the shares can trade at a discount or premium to the value of the trust.

Advantages of a managed fund: Hands-off approach means an expert money manager makes investment decisions for you. Managed funds hold many varied stocks, so if one company tanks, your fund doesn't go down with it.

Disadvantages: Annual fees can equal tens of thousands of pounds or more over the lifetime of an investment using expense ratios, front-end loads (worthless sales charges that add nothing to your returns)—all tricky ways to make managed funds more money. Also, if you invest in two managed funds, they may overlap in investments, meaning you may not really be diversified. Worst of all, you're paying an "expert" to manage your money, and 75 percent of them do not beat the market.

In short, actively managed funds are prevalent because of their convenience, but because actively managed funds are, by definition, expensive, they're not the best investment any more. Active management can't compete with passive management, which takes us to tracker funds, the more attractive cousin of managed funds.

Tracker Funds:
The Attractive Cousin in an
Otherwise Unattractive Family

I n 1975, John Bogle, the founder of Vanguard, introduced the world's first tracker fund. These simple funds use computers to buy stocks and match the market (such as the S&P 500 or NASDAQ). Instead of having an actively managed fund's expensive staff of "experts" who try to beat the market, tracker funds set a lower bar: A computer matches the indexes by automatically matching the makeup of the market. For example, if a stock represents 2 percent of the S&P 500, it will represent 2 percent of the tracker fund. Tracker funds are the financial equivalent of "If you can't beat 'em, join 'em." And they do so while also being low cost and tax efficient, and requiring hardly any maintenance at all. In other words, tracker funds are simply collections of stocks that computers manage in an effort to match the market. There are tracker funds for the S&P 500, for Asia-Pacific funds, for real-estate funds, and for anything else you can imagine.

In a radical move he originally crafted in his senior thesis at Princeton, Bogle argued that tracker funds would offer better performance to individual investors. Actively managed fund managers could not typically beat the market, yet they charged investors maintenance fees and incurred tremendous amounts of taxes on their frequent trading.

Just as we each think we're above average when it comes to being attractive, every actively managed fund manager believes *he* can beat the market. To accomplish this, managers use fancy analysis and data, and trade frequently. Ironically, this results in lots of taxes and trading fees, which, when combined with the expense ratio, makes it virtually impossible for the average fund investor to beat—or even match—the market over time. Bogle opted to discard the old model of actively managed funds and introduce tracker funds.

Today, tracker funds are an easy, efficient way to make a significant amount of money. Note, however, that tracker funds simply match the market. If you own all equities in your twenties (like me) and the stock market drops (like it has), your investments will drop (like mine, and

HIGH EXPENSE RATIOS COST MORE THAN YOU THINK

Amount in your portfolio	Annual expenses of a low-cost tracker fund (.25%)	Annual expenses of an actively managed fund (2%)
£5,000	£12.50	£100
£25,000	£62.50	£500
£100,000	£250	£2,000
£500,000	£1,250	£10,000
£1,000,000	£2,500	£20,000

Professionals Agree—
Tracker Funds Are
Great Investments

You don't have to take my word for it. Here, a few experts on the benefits of tracker funds:

"I believe that 98 or 99 percent—maybe more than 99 percent—of people who invest should extensively diversify and not trade. That leads them to [a tracker] fund with very low costs."

—WARREN BUFFETT,
ONE OF AMERICA'S GREATEST INVESTORS

"When you realize how few advisers have beaten the market over the last several decades, you may acquire the discipline to do something even better: become a long-term [tracker] fund investor."

—MARK HULBERT,
EDITOR OF HULBERT FINANCIAL DIGEST

"The media focuses on the temporarily winning active funds that score the more spectacular bull's eyes, not [tracker] funds that score every year and accumulate less flashy, but ultimately winning, scores."

—W. SCOTT SIMON, *AUTHOR OF* INDEX MUTUAL FUNDS:
PROFITING FROM AN INVESTMENT REVOLUTION

everyone else's, did). Tracker funds reflect the market, which is going through tough times but, as history has shown, will climb back up. As a bonus for using tracker funds, you'll anger your friends in finance because you'll be throwing up your middle finger to their entire industry—and you'll keep their fees for yourself. Wall Street is terrified of tracker funds and tries to keep them under wraps with increased marketing of actively managed funds and nonsense like "5-Star Funds" and TV shows that highlight action, not results.

Advantages of the tracker Fund: Extremely low cost, easy to maintain, and tax efficient.

Disadvantages: When you're investing in tracker funds, you typically have to invest in multiple funds to create a comprehensive asset allocation (although owning just one is better than doing nothing). If you do purchase multiple tracker funds, you'll have to rebalance (or adjust your investments to maintain your target asset allocation) regularly, usually every twelve to eighteen months. Each fund typically requires a minimum investment, which is reduced to between £20 and £50 with automatic monthly investments.

Okay, so tracker funds are clearly far superior to buying either individual stocks and bonds or actively managed funds. With their low fees, they are a great choice if you want to create and control the exact makeup of your portfolio.

But what if you're one of those people who knows you'll just never get around to doing the necessary research to figure out an appropriate asset allocation and which tracker funds to buy? Let's be honest: Most people don't want to construct a diversified portfolio, and they certainly don't want to rebalance and monitor their funds, even if it's just once a year.

If you fall into this group, there is an option—for pension funds—at the very top of the investment pyramid. It's an investment option that's drop-dead easy: lifestyle funds.

Lifestyle Funds: Pension Investing the Easy Way

Whether you're just arriving here direct from page 165, or you've read through the basics of investing and decided you want to take the easy way after all, no problem—the lifestyle option may be the easiest investment choice you'll ever need to make.

In America, we have something similar called lifecycle funds and they are my favorite investment of all because they embody the 85% solution: not exactly perfect, but easy enough for anyone to get started—and they work just fine.

Lifecycle funds are simple funds that automatically diversify your investments for you based on age. Instead of having to rebalance stocks and bonds, lifecycle funds do it for you. If more Americans owned lifecycle funds, for example, far fewer retirees would have seen precipitous drops in their retirement accounts, because the lifecycle funds would have automatically changed to a more conservative asset allocation as they approached their golden years. Lifecycle funds are actually "funds-of-funds," or collections made up of other funds, which offer automatic diversification. For example, a lifecycle fund might include large-cap, mid-cap, small-cap, and international funds. (And those funds, in turn, will hold stocks from each of those areas.) In other words, your lifecycle fund will own many funds, which all own stocks and bonds. It sounds complicated, but believe it or not, this actually makes things simple for you, because you'll have to own only *one* fund, and all the rest will be taken care of for you.

Lifecycle funds are different from tracker funds, which are also low cost but require you to own multiple funds if you want a comprehensive asset allocation. Multiple funds mean you have to rebalance your funds regularly, usually every year, which is a laborious process of redistributing your money to different investments so you get back to your target asset allocation. What a pain.

> **IF MORE AMERICANS OWNED LIFECYCLE FUNDS, FOR EXAMPLE, FAR FEWER RETIREES WOULD HAVE SEEN PRECIPITOUS DROPS IN THEIR RETIREMENT ACCOUNTS.**

In the UK, there are only a handful of providers to offer lifecycle funds as a retirement option (Fidelity International is one). But many pension funds (whether it's occupational defined contribution schemes, group personal pensions or stakeholder plans that you take out yourself) have at least one lifestyle fund (sometimes called a 'lifestyle option'). These aren't as sophisticated as lifecycle funds in the States in that they usually tend to move your investments away from equities in the last five or ten years of the term of the plan. So, if you set your retirement date to age 60 and choose a lifestyle fund that is active ten years before the end of the term, your money will be moved away from shares and into less risky investments from when you reach 50.

The criticism of lifestyle funds is that they are a 'one size fits all' approach. They will move money away from shares, no matter what the stock market is doing (and if they sell shares after a major fall in share prices, you'll lose money). But they're definitely better than keeping the

What About Other Kinds of Investments?

There are many different investments besides stocks, bonds, and tracker and lifecycle funds. You can buy precious metals, real estate, or even art; just don't expect very good returns. And despite all my dire warnings, you can also buy a couple of stocks you really like.

REAL ESTATE. For most Americans, their home is their biggest "investment", and yet, as investments go, real estate is not a very good one for individual investors. Why? Because the returns are generally poor, especially when you factor in costs like maintenance and property taxes—which renters don't pay for, but homeowners do. I'll cover real estate more in Chapter 9, but in general, most people confuse their house with an investment that they buy and sell for profit. Think about it. Who sells their house for profit and keeps the money? If your parents ever sold their house, did they move into a smaller house and enjoy the rest of that money? No! They rolled it over to the down payment for their next, more expensive house.

You want to keep each part of your portfolio balanced so no one area overshadows the rest. If you're spending £2,000 per month on your mortgage and don't have enough left over to diversify into other areas, that's not a balanced portfolio. If you do buy real estate, regardless of whether it's to live in or to invest in, be sure to keep funding the rest of your investment areas—whether that's a lifestyle fund or your own portfolio of tracker funds.

ART. A 1998 study at New York University produced some surprising results about art as investment. It showed that art is reliable, profitable (fine art returned 10.4 percent), and an effective hedge against portfolio volatility. However, by choosing particular art pieces as investment, you're doing essentially the same thing as trying to predict winning stocks, and after reading Chapter 6 you know how difficult that is to do. In aggregate, art investments may be quite profitable, but the trick is choosing which individual pieces will appreciate—and as you can imagine, that isn't easy.

HIGH-RISK, HIGH-POTENTIAL-FOR-REWARD INVESTMENTS. Life isn't just about lifestyle funds and tracker funds. Lots of people understand that, logically, they should create a well-diversified portfolio of low-cost funds. But they also want to have *fun* investing. If you feel this way, sure, use a small part of your portfolio for "high risk" investing—but treat it as fun money, not as money you need. I set aside about 10 percent of my portfolio for fun money, which includes particular stocks I like, know, and use (companies like Amazon.com that focus on customer service, which I believe drives shareholder value); sector funds that let me focus on particular industries (I own a tracker fund that focuses on health care); and even angel investing, which is personal venture-capital investing for private ultra-early-stage companies. (I occasionally see these angel opportunities because I work in Silicon Valley and have friends who start companies and look for early friends-and-family money.) All these are very-high-risk investments and they're funded by just-for-fun money that I can afford to lose. Still, there is the potential for great returns. If you have the rest of your portfolio set up and still have money left over, be smart about it, but invest a little in whatever you want.

same asset allocation (the same percentages in shares, bonds, cash etc) right up until you retire.

If you don't make an active decision about where to invest your pension contributions when you're investing in your employer's defined contribution scheme, your money will end up in the default fund (and, guess what – over 90% of people who sign up to a pension scheme end up in the default fund). Default funds often have a lifestyle option, but they don't all take the same approach. Some may not start moving money until five years before retirement.

It's definitely worth finding out a little about how the lifestyle option works on the fund you're thinking of investing in and also (importantly) what it's investing your money in to start off with. Some pension providers have half a dozen or more different lifestyle fund options, based on how much of a risk-taker you are when you invest, but – depending on the type of pension scheme you're saving for your retirement with – you may not be offered such a wide choice.

To get an idea of how lifestyling and lifecycling compare, let's check out two different funds. In the table below, you can see how the allocations in both funds change based on your age.

LIFECYCLE FUNDS AUTOMATICALLY ADJUST AS YOU GET OLDER

Here's a comparison of a lifecycle fund with a lifestyle option, so you can see how they work. It's important to understand that not all lifestyle funds are the same. Some are suitable for people who have a very cautious approach to investment, others are targeted at those who are prepared to take on more risk. You should look at what the funds invest in during the early years as well as at what point they start to move your money away from shares.

Age of investor (assuming retirement age of 65)	Asset allocation: Fidelity Weathbuilder Target Date funds	Asset allocation: Legal & General UK Equity Index Lifestyle
Up to age 55	Shares: 63.91%, bonds: 6.6%, cash: 2.41%, other: 27.01% (includes commodities, property etc)	100% invested in shares tracking FTSE All-Share index
Age 55 (56 for L&G fund)	Shares: 49.67%, bonds: 0.17%, cash: 4.77%, other: 41.64%	90% UK Equity Index fund, 7.5% fixed interest fund, 2.5% cash fund
Age 60	Shares: 34.92%, bonds: 22.32%, 11.64%, 31.12%	50% UK Equity Index fund, 37.5% fixed interest fund, 12.5% cash fund
Age 65	Shares: 11.97%, bonds: 32.26%, cash: 38.6%, other: 16.7%	75% Fixed interest, 25% cash

Source: Fidelity International/Legal & General. Fixed interest refers to investments that generate a fixed rate of return and normally include bonds and cash deposits. With Legal & General's fund, money is gradually moved to less risky investments from age 55.

The major benefit of a lifecycle or lifestyle fund is that your money won't be left invested in shares right up until the last minute. In America, lifecycle funds move money into different assets throughout your life, but in the UK they tend to do so in the last 10 years before retirement.

Lifestyle funds don't generally change the asset allocation while you are in your twenties, thirties or forties, and some experts argue that you'd get a much better result if you timed the move from shares to bonds yourself. But bearing in mind how inactive most investors are, this is definitely better than doing nothing at all.

Non-retirement investments: Choosing and Buying Your Investments

Lifestyle and lifecycle funds are generally only available to you as an option if you are taking out a pension (whether it's an employer-based defined contribution scheme or a personal or stakeholder plan). That means if you want to put your money into something like a stock and shares ISA, you may not be able to use a lifecycle or lifestyle fund. Another option is to invest in multi-asset funds. These split your money between bonds, shares and cash-based investments.

The advantage of using a multi-asset fund is that you don't have to worry about having too much money in shares—the asset allocation is done for you. The disadvantage is that the way your money is split doesn't usually change according to your age. The fund manager should make changes in relation to what's happening in the economy, but it's definitely not a completely hands-off approach.

The Investment Most People Have: A Pension

As I mentioned earlier, not everyone who has a pension gets to choose where their money is invested. If your employer offers a final salary (otherwise known as a defined benefit) pension scheme, the money you pay in is just mixed together with everyone else's.

You can't insist that it's invested in a particular way. That means there's one less decision for you to make about your investments. It's down to those running the pension to make sure they get it right.

Money Purchase or 'Defined Contribution' Pensions

If your workplace offers you a defined contribution pension, you will have already opened your plan and paid money into it. At the time, you'll have had to choose a fund to put your money in (I suggested a cash-based or money market fund). Your human resources manager will tell you how you can switch your money into a different fund if the information isn't on your employer's website.

You know how I love reducing choice to get people to take action? Well, the companies that offer defined contribution pensions take this to an extreme: They offer a few investment funds for you to choose from—usually the options are called something like *aggressive fund* (which will be a fund of mostly shares), *balanced fund* (this fund will contain shares and bonds), and *cautious fund* (a more conservative mix of mostly bonds).

If you're not sure what the different choices mean, ask your HR representative for a sheet describing the differences in funds. Note: Stay away from "money market funds," which is just another way of saying your money is sitting, uninvested, in cash. You want to get your money working for you.

As a young person, I encourage you to pick the most aggressive fund they offer that you're comfortable with. As you know, the more aggressive you are when younger, the more money you'll likely have later. This is especially important for a pension, which is an ultra-long-term investment account.

Depending on what pension provider your employer uses, the charges on these funds may be a little pricey, but on balance, you're getting huge tax advantages and employer-match benefits. So, it's worth it to invest in these funds, even if they aren't perfect.

Group Personal Pensions or Employer-Based Stakeholder Schemes

If you're paying into a pension at work where you get a choice of different funds to invest your money into, you may assume it's a defined contribution pension, but it might not be. Employers can also set up personal or stakeholder pension schemes for their workers. If you don't already know what type of pension you're paying into, find out now. The information should be on the paperwork that you were given when you joined the scheme.

Group personal pensions offer a far bigger choice of funds than work-based stakeholder plans. Stakeholders typically might have up to 25 different funds for you to choose from, whereas a group personal pension (GPP) might have up to two hundred. Don't get overwhelmed by the choice that's on offer. You don't need to worry about the ones you don't put your money into; just pick funds that you're happy with

If there are no multi asset funds on offer, you can set up your own mix of

The Rule of 72

The Rule of 72 is a fast trick you can do to figure out how long it will take to double your money. Here's how it works: Divide the number 72 by the return rate you're getting, and you'll have the number of years you must invest in order to double your money. (For the math geeks among us, here's the equation: $72 \div$ return rate $=$ number of years.) For example, if you're getting a 10 percent return rate from a tracker fund, it would take you approximately seven years ($72 \div 10$) to double your money. In other words, if you invested £5,000 today, let it sit there, and earned a 10 percent return, you'd have £10,000 in about seven years. And it doubles from there, too. Of course, you could have even more by adding a small amount every month using the power of compounding.

funds that will give you the right mixture of shares, cash and bonds for your own risk profile. If you took out your pension with the help of an independent financial adviser, you should have received detailed advice about the type of investment mix that would be suitable for you, giving you the best return while not taking on more risk than you feel comfortable with.

Investing directly into a personal or stakeholder pension

In Chapter 3 I talked about how personal and stakeholder pensions were something you could buy directly from a pensions company, or pay into through your workplace. If you're self-employed or your employer doesn't make contributions to the group personal pension or stakeholder scheme they offer, you may have your own personal or stakeholder pension plan.

The brochure or website should include a few lines about what each fund does. There should also be some information about your own risk profile (whether you're a cautious, balanced or adventurous investor) and a suggestion of the funds that would suit you.

Depending on the scheme and pension provider you're with, you may have access to a range of tracker funds (including FTSE index trackers, European index trackers and trackers that invest in a mixture of companies that make up the FTSE index and those that make up overseas indexes). You should also be offered several funds with a lifestyle option. With a stakeholder pension, you can switch funds at any time without penalty. It means you don't have to worry about 'getting it wrong'.

Investing in a SIPP

If you've taken out a SIPP (a self invested personal pension), it's probably because you want to have much more control over your money. That means you're unlikely to want to pay your contributions into your SIPP every month and leave your money where it is. Potentially, you could have access to thousands of different investment options when you open one up. That's because you can put your money into shares in individual companies as well as investment funds ranging from the ordinary to very specialist (and probably quite risky).

If you go for this strategy, make sure you don't switch round your investments just for the sake of doing something. Yes, having control of your pension money can be a good thing, but you should check out the costs of switching your investments to make sure you don't end up eating away your return with the charges.

So You Want to Do It on Your Own

S o, you don't have access to a lifecycle or suitable lifestyle fund and you want to pick your own index funds to construct your own pension portfolio. That means you're going to have to accept the fact you'll have more work on your hands. If you pick your own portfolio, you can't just ignore your funds and hope they'll produce the returns you're counting on. (That's why I'm such a fan of lifecycle funds back home!).

Remember, most people who try to manage their own portfolios fail at even matching the market. They fail because they sell at the first sign of trouble, or because they buy and sell too often, thereby diminishing their returns with taxes and trading fees. (Think of all the people who sold off their shares in late 2008, not really understanding that there were bargains to be had by simply continuing their consistent investing. It was fear—not strategy.) The result is tens of thousands of pounds lost over a lifetime. Plus, if you buy individual tracker funds, you'll have to rebalance every year to make sure your asset allocation is still what you want it to be (more on this in a minute).

But if you want more control over your investments and you just *know* you're disciplined enough to withstand market dips and to take the time to rebalance your asset allocation at least once a year, then choosing your own portfolio of tracker funds is the right choice for you.

All right, let's do this. If you've read this far, I guess my warnings and harassment didn't dissuade you from building your own portfolio. If I can't scare you, I might as well help you.

As we discussed earlier, the

THE KEY TO CONSTRUCTING A PORTFOLIO IS NOT PICKING KILLER STOCKS! IT'S FIGURING OUT A BALANCED ASSET ALLOCATION THAT WILL LET YOU RIDE OUT STORMS AND SLOWLY GROW OVER TIME.

key to constructing a portfolio is not picking killer stocks! It's figuring out a balanced asset allocation that will let you ride out storms and slowly grow, over time, to gargantuan proportions. To illustrate how to allocate and diversify your portfolio, we're going to use David Swensen's recommendation as a model. Swensen is pretty much the Warren G of money management. He runs Yale's fabled endowment, and for more than twenty years he has generated an astonishing 16.3 percent annualized return, whereas most managers can't even beat 8 percent. That means he has doubled Yale's money every 4.5 years from 1985 to today. Best of all, Swensen is a genuinely good guy. He could be making hundreds of millions each year running his own fund on Wall Street, but he chooses to stay at Yale, making just over $1 million per year, because he loves academia. "When I see colleagues of mine leave universities to do essentially the same thing they were doing but to get paid more, I am disappointed because there is a sense of mission," he's said. I love this guy.

Anyway, Swensen suggests allocating your money in the following way:

THE SWENSEN MODEL OF ASSET ALLOCATION

- 15% Index-linked gilts
- 15% Government bonds
- 20% Real estate funds
- 5% Emerging-market equities
- 30% Domestic equities
- 15% Developed-world international equities

30 percent—Domestic equities: UK equity funds, including small-, mid-, and large-cap stocks

15 percent—Developed-world international equities: funds from developed foreign countries, including the United States, Germany, and France.

5 percent—Emerging-market equities: funds from developing foreign countries such as China, India, and Brazil. These are riskier than developed-world equities, so don't go off buying these to fill 95 percent of your portfolio.

20 percent—Real estate funds: also known as REITs, short for real estate investment trust. REITs are funds that invest in residential and commercial property, both in the UK and overseas.

15 percent—Government bonds: also known as gilts, these provide predictable income and balance risk in your portfolio. As an asset class, bonds generally return less than stocks.

15 percent—Index-linked gilts: these bonds protect against inflation. Eventually you'll want to own these, but they'd be the last ones I'd get after investing in all the better-returning options first.

A significant amount of math went into Swensen's allocation, but the most important takeaway is that no single choice represents an overwhelming part of the portfolio. As illustrated by the tech bubble of 2001 and the real estate crash of 2007, any sector can drop at any time. When it does, you don't want it to drag your entire portfolio down with it. As we know, lower risk generally equals lower reward. But the coolest thing about asset allocation is that you can actually reduce your risk while maintaining an equivalent return.

Swensen's theories are great, but how do we make them real and pick funds that match his suggestions? By picking a portfolio of low-cost funds, that's how.

Choosing your own tracker funds means you'll need to dig around and identify the best tracker funds for you. I always start researching at the most popular companies: Legal and General is probably one of the best known providers of tracker funds in the pensions market, but Barclays Global Investors (due to be renamed Blackrock Global Investors following a planned takeover) and HSBC are also key players. HSBC has reduced its charges on trackers and Vanguard, which is a very popular provider of tracker funds in America, has recently launched low cost trackers in the UK (although as I write this these funds are not available for investors to buy directly, but have to be purchased via a financial adviser). There are other providers of trackers, so you should be able to find something that suits you.

The first thing you want to do when picking tracker funds is to minimize fees. Look for the management fees ("expense ratios") to be low, around 0.2 percent, and you'll be fine. Really, anything lower than 0.75 percent is

Keep It Manageable

Q: *How many funds should I invest in?*

A: It's a little complicated in the UK because it will depend on whether you're offered more than one lifestyle fund as a pension option. I'd certainly advise you to go fewer, rather than more funds. But if you're picking your own tracker funds, as a general guideline, you can create a great asset allocation using anywhere from three to seven funds. Remember, the goal isn't to be exhaustive and to own every single aspect of the market. It's to create an effective asset allocation and move on with your life. And if you're looking for those funds, check page 180.

YOU CANNOT JUST PICK RANDOM FUNDS AND EXPECT TO HAVE A BALANCED ASSET ALLOCATION.

okay. Most of the tracker funds at Vanguard, Fidelity, and HSBC have relatively low costs. Remember: Expense ratios are one of the few things you can control, and higher fees cost you dearly—and they just put money in Wall Street's pocket. See the chart on page 157 for a comparison of how these fees can affect you.

Second, you want to make sure the fund fits into your asset allocation. After all, the reason you're choosing your own tracker funds is to have more control over your investments. Use David Swensen's model as a baseline and tweak as necessary if you want to exclude certain funds or prioritize which are important to you. For example, if you have limited money and you're in your twenties, you'd probably want to buy the stock funds first so you could get their compounding power, whereas you could wait until you're older and have more money to buy the bond funds to mitigate your risk. In other words, when you look for various funds, make sure you're being strategic about your domestic equities, international equities, bonds, and all the rest. You cannot just pick random funds and expect to have a balanced asset allocation. I use the Instant X-Ray tool (www.morningstar.co.uk/uk/instantxray/default.aspx?lang=en-GB), which lets me compare various funds' asset allocations to see how well they

Pound-Cost Averaging: Investing Slowly Over Time

When I want to sound smart and intimidate people, I calmly look at them, chew on a muffin for a few seconds, and then abruptly throw it against a wall and scream, "DO YOU DOLLAR-COST AVERAGE???" People are often so impressed that they slowly inch away, then turn around and whisper to people around them. I can only surmise that they are discussing how clever and knowledgeable I am.

Anyway, *dollar-cost averaging* (that's pound-cost averaging to you Brits) is a fancy phrase that refers to investing regular amounts over time, rather than investing all your money into a fund at once. This is the essence of Automatic Investing, which lets you consistently invest in a fund so you don't have to guess when the market is up or down. For example, if you have £12,000 available to invest, you could invest £1,000 per month for a year.

But if you have the cash, why would you invest at regular intervals instead of all at once? Imagine if you invest £10,000 tomorrow and the stock drops 20 percent. At £8,000, it will need to increase 25 percent (not 20 percent) to get back to £10,000. By investing over time, you hedge against any drops in the price—and if your fund does drop, you'll pick up shares at a discount price. In other words, by investing over a regular period of time, you don't try to time the market. Instead, you use time to your advantage.

This can all be automated, of course. In Chapter 5, we covered your automatic infrastructure. To set up Automatic Investing, configure your investment accounts to automatically transfer money in from your current account each month. See page 131 for details.

cover domestic investments, foreign investments, bonds, and more. It's a great tool to help drill into your asset allocation and make sure your funds are well diversified.

Third, note that you should absolutely look at how well the fund has returned over the last ten or fifteen years, but remember that, as they say, past performance is no guarantee of future results.

It's much better to look at returns over the last ten or fifteen years than it is to pick a shorter time frame. What you're aiming for is a fund that has been consistent. Remember, this isn't simple. Creating your own portfolio takes significant research.

As an example of what you might end up with, here's a sample from Legal & General's index tracking funds:

Shares ("Equities")

30 percent—L&G UK Equity Index Fund

20 percent—L&G World (Excluding UK) Equity Index Fund

20 percent—L&G Ethical Global Equity Index Fund

Fixed Interest Stocks ("Bonds")

15 percent—L&G AAA-AA-A Corporate Bond Over 15 Year Index Fund

5 percent—L&G Over 15 Year Gilts Index Fund

5 percent—L&G All Stocks Index-Linked Gilts Index Fund

5 percent—L&G Overseas Bond Index Fund

These are just a few of the literally thousands of tracker funds that exist. You can be flexible with the funds. If you want to be more or less aggressive, you can change the allocation to match your risk tolerance. For example, if you look at those funds and say, "Man, I'll never get around to owning seven funds," then be realistic with yourself. Maybe you want to buy the stock funds but just one bond fund for now. Maybe you don't need to think about index-linked gilts yet. Pick the number of funds that will let you get started, realizing that you can adjust it later on to get a balanced asset allocation.

Spend time identifying the funds that will help you build a full, balanced asset allocation over time. You don't need to get all seven funds listed above—even one is better than nothing. But you should have a list of funds that you'll eventually buy to round out your allocation.

EXCHANGE TRADED FUNDS

There is an alternative to tracker funds that you might find in your pension or ISA and that's exchange traded funds or ETFs. These have lower charges than many tracker funds and are traded throughout the day like shares. They also have the advantage of following the chosen index more closely than a number of tracker funds do.

The problem is that these funds are only available to pension investors who buy a SIPP (self invested personal pension). If you've joined your employer's defined contribution scheme or taken out a personal or stakeholder plan, you'll only be offered a limited range of funds.

FINAL CHECKS BEFORE YOU BUY A TRACKER FUND

You might think that the only difference between tracker funds is the index they mirror, but you'd be wrong. So here are a few points to think about before you make your tracker fund choice:

How closely does the fund track the chosen index? If a fund tracks the index it is aligned to closely, it's said to have a low 'tracking error'. The lower the tracking error, the easier it will be for you to follow what's happening to your investments (and therefore to your retirement fund).

Do you replicate the index or just invest in a selection of stocks that make up the index? Say you buy a tracker fund that tracks the FTSE All-Share index; if it's going to buy every stock that makes up the index, it would have to purchase shares In around 850 different companies, which is way higher than the number that most investment funds hold. So, to cut costs, some funds buy investments that are designed to reproduce the performance of the index. This means you don't get the same guarantees that the fund will mirror the particular index it's aligned to.

Note: Once you own all the funds you need, you can split the money across funds according to your asset allocation—but *don't* just split it evenly. Remember, your asset allocation determines how much money you invest in different areas. For example, if you have £250 per month and you buy seven tracker funds, the average person who knows nothing (i.e., most people) would split the money seven ways and send £35 to each. That's wrong. Depending on your asset allocation, you'd send more or less money to various funds, using this calculation: (Your monthly total amount of investing money) $\times$ (Percentage of asset allocation for a particular investment) = Amount you'll invest there. For example, if you're investing £1,000 per month and your Swensen allocation recommends 30 percent for domestic equities, you'd calculate (£1,000) $\times$ (0.3) = £300 toward your domestic-equity fund. Repeat for all other funds in your portfolio.

Finally, if you opt for investing in your own tracker funds, you'll have to rebalance about once a year, which will keep your funds in line with your target asset allocation. I'll cover that in the next chapter.

HOW TO WRESTLE WITH A BEAR—AND WIN

Why I'm Not Worried About the Economy

by J.D. Roth of www.getrichslowly.org

As I write this, the U.S. is in the midst of a financial crisis. The stock market has dropped more than 22 percent in the past two weeks. It's down 36 percent for the year. People are panicked. They're pulling money out of mutual funds at record rates—$46 billion last week alone.

I'm not one of them.

In fact, I just made the largest investment of my life, moving $46,000 in my Roth IRA [pension] from cash into a Fidelity index fund. Am I scared? You bet. $46,000 is a hell of a lot of money. But I'm taking my cues from Warren Buffett, the world's richest man, who in 2004 gave this advice: "Be fearful when others are greedy and greedy when others are fearful."

Or, to put it in more familiar terms, "Buy low, sell high."

I think the market is low right now, so I've made a lump-sum investment. But buying low can be intimidating. Suppose the markets never go back up? Nobody wants to wrestle with a bear. I'm taking a risk by attacking the beast head on.

Moves like this don't bother me as much as they might bother other people (my wife, for example) because my risk tolerance is high. I have twenty or thirty years to go before retirement. That's two or three decades to recover from any further market drops.

Risk and reward go hand in hand. The historically high returns of the stock market are impossible without risk; anyone who tells you otherwise is lying. But not everyone can stomach having all of their investments in stocks and mutual funds.

If your risk tolerance is low (if you're scared of bears), or you're approaching retirement, it's best to keep your money someplace safe, such as bond funds or high-yield savings accounts. I keep cash equal to a few months of expenses in *savings. I have a friend who is far less risk-tolerant than I am who keeps an entire year of expenses in savings. (Please, if you're going to set this much money aside, put it into a high-yield savings account or certificates of deposit!)*

Even if your risk tolerance isn't all that high, you can still invest in the stock market, even during downturns. Dollar-cost averaging is an excellent way to do this. Dollar-cost averaging simply means making regular, scheduled investments instead of buying into the stock market all at once. It's a way to mitigate risk. An indexed mutual fund decreases risk because your money is diversified across many stocks. Dollar-cost averaging decreases risk even further because your money is diversified across time.

Buying low can be intimidating. Suppose the markets never go back up?

When I was dollar-cost averaging, I set up a system through ShareBuilder (sharebuilder.com), an online brokerage that's a subsidiary of ING Direct, though there are many other ways to do it. On the first of every month, ShareBuilder pulled $250 from my credit union and used the money to buy shares of index funds inside my [personal pension]. The process was painless. I invested every month, whether the market was up or down. It let me ignore the news and enjoy life knowing my long-term plan was in motion.

Dollar-cost averaging makes investing easy: you set it and forget it.

But don't just take my word for it. Here are a handful of sites that offer tools and tricks to help you tangle with bear markets:

■ *http://tinyurl.com/dollarcostaveraging—Michael Fischer's video presentation about the virtues of dollar-cost averaging*

■ *http://tinyurl.com/fearofinvesting—Erin Burt offers five tricks to conquer your fear of investing*

■ *http://tinyurl.com/riskquiz—Rutgers University helps you assess your risk tolerance*

■ *http://tinyurl.com/stupidinvestors—Ben Stein on why "smart" investors are sometimes stupid*

■ *http://tinyurl.com/DCAbenefits—A great introduction to the benefits of dollar-cost averaging*

In Why Smart People Make Big Money Mistakes and How to Correct Them, *Gary Belsky and Thomas Gilovich point to research that shows "the pain people feel from losing $100 is much greater than the pleasure they experience from gaining the same amount." Don't let the bear scare you. You can wrestle with him and come out ahead.*

J.D. Roth writes about smart personal finance at getrichslowly.org.

1 **Figure out your investing style (30 minutes).** Decide whether you want to invest in lifecyle or lifestyle funds (if your pension plan or scheme offers them) or whether you'd prefer tracker funds. If you opt for tracker funds, you have to be prepared for the extra work.

2 **Research your investments (3 hours to 1 week).** If you've decided on a lifecycle or lifestyle fund, check out different funds that are offered by your pension scheme and choose one that matches your risk profile. If you're investing in a stakeholder or personal pension (or ISA) directly with a pensions provider, you can choose a company that offers the best range of funds. Use the Swensen model as a basic template and once you decide on asset allocation, spend some time researching the funds.

3 **Transfer money into your fund(s) (1 hour to 1 week).** Hopefully, you'll have set up your pension plans as I described in chapter 3. If you put your money into a cash-based or money market account while you tried to decide what to do with your money, you should either log onto the pension scheme's website or that of your pension provider (or phone them if you can't do it online). You should be able to transfer money into tracker, lifecycle or lifestyle funds.

Yes! You're now an investor! And not only that, but you've reached the end of the six-week program. You've optimized your credit cards and bank accounts and started investing—and, even better, you've tied your system together so it works automatically with hardly any effort on your part. There's just a little more: In the next chapter we'll focus on how to maintain your investments. Then, in the last chapter, I'll address all those random questions you have about money and life in general. But the truth is, by making it all the way through this chapter, you've already done all the hard work.

CHAPTER 8

EASY MAINTENANCE

*You've done the hard work: Here's how to maintain
(and optimize) your financial infrastructure*

You may have noticed that this chapter is one of the shortest in the book. That's because you've already put the 85 Percent Solution into place and dealt with the most important parts of your finances: your credit cards, bank accounts, spending, and investments. Most people are still struggling with paying their monthly bills. So congratulations. But—of course there's a *but*—if you're seriously nerdy and want to know more about enhancing your finances, this is the chapter for you. We'll cover a few topics that will help you optimize your investments even further. Remember, though: This is extra credit, so don't feel the need to follow the advice in this chapter unless you really want to.

Feed Your System

In the previous chapter, you chose your investments and set things up so they run automatically. The automatic system is great, but it's fueled by only one thing: the money you feed it. That means that your system is only as strong as the amount you put in it. The earlier chapters in this book were about implementing the 85 Percent Solution—getting started was the hardest and most important step. It didn't matter if you were contributing only £100 per month. But now it's about the raw volume you put into your system—more in, more out. Do you really want to wait twenty-five years to have £100,000? If not, feed your system as much money as possible now. Every pound you invest today will be worth many more tomorrow.

HOW RICH WILL I BE IN . . .

How much will your monthly investment be worth, assuming 5 percent a year (this is a conservative rate, the official rate set by the FSA is 7 percent)?

IF YOU INVEST . . .	£100/ month	£500/ month	£1,000/ month
After 5 years . . .	£6,800	£34,003	£68,006
After 10 years . . .	£15,528	£77,641	£155,282
After 25 years . . .	£59,551	£297,755	£595,510

Don't just take it from me, though. Go to www.thisismoney.co.uk and open up their investment calculator. Enter in your monthly investment contribution, assuming a 5 percent return—don't forget to factor in taxes if you're not using a pension or an ISA. You'll likely see that your current contributions will grow more slowly than you thought. But by adding a small amount per month—even £100 or £200 more—the numbers will change dramatically.

In Chapter 4, I outlined a Conscious Spending Plan that suggested general percentages of income to allocate for savings and investing. Your first goal was to aim for those percentages. Now it's time to move beyond those amounts so you can save and invest as much as possible. I can hear you screaming, "Are you kidding? I can't squeeze out another cent. I hate you, Ramit!" This is not about me wanting to deprive you. Actually, quite the opposite: Because compounding works so effectively, the more you save now, the more you'll have later (by a huge amount). You saw this in the thisismoney.co.uk calculator. Now, go in and play around with your Conscious Spending Plan to see how you can eke out a little more to put toward your investments every month. Optimizing your plan might involve doing some serious bargaining when you make major purchases like a car or house (see Chapter 9). Or you might need to cut your expenses as ruthlessly as possible. (Don't forget to check out my "Save $1000 in 30 Days Challenge" at www.iwillteachyoutoberich.com/30daychallenge.) You may even think about negotiating a higher salary or getting a higher-paying job (see page 234). No matter how you go about it, be sure that you're shoveling the maximum amount possible into your system every month. Remember, it's never easier to do this than when you're in your twenties and thirties—and the more you feed into your system now, the sooner you'll be rich.

Ignore the Noise

Now that you've mastered the basics of personal finance and set up your automated system, you're going to start noticing how badly most other people are managing their money. Here, for example, are three real recent quotes from my highly educated friends:

Q: *"I don't know what to do with my personal pension. I was advised to put it all in a cash-based fund for now since equity funds are not doing well. Is this right? How do you know when the downturn has hit bottom? Somebody said that it may take five years to get this mortgage mess turned around!"*

MY RESPONSE: The day-to-day movements of the market shouldn't concern you. If you have a long time horizon, you're automatically investing each month. When the market is going up, your system will automatically buy fewer shares. When the market is going down, it will buy more shares. Over time, you'll do far better than speculators who try to predict where the market will go.

Q: *"Forget tracker funds. I made a 67 percent return with my Russian managed fund last year, and that's after fees."*

MY RESPONSE: It doesn't matter what happened last year, it matters what happens in the next ten to twenty years. Plus, if a fund goes up, it can also go down. That's why asset allocation is more important—and less risky—than a superstar fund.

Q: *"Dude, you're wasting your money on renting in San Francisco. Why don't you buy a house?"*

MY RESPONSE: Renting is actually an excellent decision in certain markets—and real estate is generally a poor financial investment, which I cover on page 250.

Look, you've decided on Automatic Investing because it's a simple, low-cost way of investing. You've seen the research indicating that it beats traditional fund managers. And yet, every time your friends ask you one of those questions or you see a report about the "plunging" stock market, you'll be tempted to change your investing style. Buy that tech company's stock! Sell oil, it's no good! The sky is falling!!! This is especially true in tumultuous

> **UNLIKE OTHER PEOPLE, WHO WORRY ABOUT MONEY (BECAUSE THEY NEVER LEARNED HOW IT WORKS), YOU GET TO FOCUS ON THE THINGS YOU LOVE.**

times, like during the global financial crisis of 2008. One day the market dropped 700 points, the next week it soared 900 points. As a result, the pundits were out in full force, making all sorts of absurd claims. The volatility spooked people, and ordinary Americans started withdrawing from the market. For most people, fear guides their investment decisions.

Ignore it all. As I discussed in Chapter 6, the benefit of Automatic Investing is that you don't have to focus on these heart-pounding stock reports from pundits and magazines every day! Unlike other people, who will clasp their hands and worry about money (because they never took a couple of hours to learn how it works), you get to focus on the things you love: hanging out with friends, visiting your family, traveling, or whatever you want to do. Ignore the noise. Force yourself to resist logging in to your investment account more than once a month—that's it. If you've set up your asset allocation and are consistently funding it, stick to your guns. You're investing for the long term, and when you look back, day-to-day changes (even the cataclysmic plunges of 2008) will seem like minor blips—which they are.

Rebalancing Your Investments

I f you have a diversified portfolio, some of your investments, such as international stocks, may outperform others. To keep your asset allocation on track, you'll want to rebalance once a year so your international stocks don't become a larger part of your portfolio than you intended. Think of your investment portfolio like your backyard: If you want your zucchini to be only 15 percent of your backyard, and they grow like crazy and end up taking over 30 percent, you'll want to rebalance by either cutting the zucchini back, or by getting a bigger yard so that the zucchini is back to covering only 15 percent. I know, I know—I should become an organic gardener. Ladies, it's hard to deny that I am a Renaissance man.

Most funds can't be left alone for too long, so you'll need to rebalance every 12 to 18 months. But if you've chosen to manage your own asset allocation, you'll need to rebalance every twelve to eighteen months. Otherwise, within a couple of years, your allocation will be completely skewed. For example, let's say you create an asset allocation based on the Swensen model:

TARGET ASSET ALLOCATION

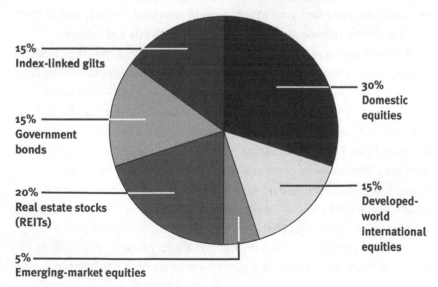

15%
Index-linked gilts

15%
Government
bonds

20%
Real estate stocks
(REITs)

5%
Emerging-market equities

30%
Domestic
equities

15%
Developed-
world
international
equities

Now let's assume that domestic equities gain 50 percent one year. (For easy calculations, let's hold all other investments constant.) All of a sudden, domestic equities represent a larger part of your portfolio, and all the other numbers are out of whack.

ALLOCATION AFTER DOMESTIC EQUITIES JUMP 50%

- 12% Index-linked gilts
- 12% Government bonds
- 16% Real estate stocks (REITs)
- 4% Emerging-market equities
- 12% Developed-world international equities
- 45% Domestic equities

Although it's great that one of your investment areas is performing well, you want to keep your allocation in check so one sector isn't disproportionately larger or smaller than the others. Rebalancing your portfolio will make sure your assets remain allocated properly and protect you from being vulnerable to one specific sector's ups and downs.

The best way to rebalance is to plow more money into the other areas until your asset allocation is back on track. How? Assuming your domestic equities now represent 45 percent of your asset allocation—but should actually be only 30 percent— stop sending money there temporarily and redistribute that 30 percent of your investment contribution evenly over the rest of your investment categories. You can do this by "pausing" your automatic investment to particular funds from within your investment account. Log onto your account or ring your pensions provider. Find out what's happened to your asset allocation. If there's one fund that's pushed your asset allocation out of balance, find out—from your pension provider or your pension scheme—what the options are for pausing contributions to particular funds so you can bring your investments back into balance.

Check out the chart on the next page to see how it works. As you can see, in this case, after eight months you're back on target, more or less, and can go back to your original allocations.

Note: There's another way to rebalance, but I don't like doing it. You can rebalance by selling the outperforming equities and plowing the money into other areas to bring the allocation back under control. I hate selling because it involves trading fees, paperwork, and "thinking," so I don't recommend this.

Don't forget to set a calendar reminder to resume your automatic payments. With two minutes of math, which you may consider torture (unless you're Asian), you can know exactly when to resume your payments.

If, on the other hand, one of your funds has *lost* money, that will also knock your asset allocation out of whack. In this case, you can pause the other funds and add money to the loser until it returns to where it should be in your portfolio. To keep the math simple, I recommend the Portfolio Allocator at www.morningstar.co.uk to help guide your rebalancing.

Stop Worrying About Taxes (and the 85 Percent Solution for Handling Them)

People worry about taxes too much, and they make all kinds of bad decisions to avoid them. Listen to me: You pay taxes only if you make money. If you're paying 30 percent in taxes on something, it means you made 70 percent elsewhere, so do not freak out about taxes. Plus, it's your damned civic duty. Want to complain about taxes? Go take a ride on a road anywhere in Africa or Southeast Asia. After two hours of bouncing in the back of a rickshaw, the top of your skull will be permanently dented and you'll look like a coal worker from the *Titanic*. So give me a break, pay your taxes, do your civic duty.

Okay, that was a weird tangent. I hate to say this, but aside from the very basics of saving on taxes (like taking advantage of tax-deferred

(continued on page 210)

Rebalancing Your Portfolio

£10,000 PORTFOLIO AFTER GAIN OF 50% IN DOMESTIC EQUITIES

Value	£12,727	← New portfolio value

	Allocation	Value	
Domestic	45%	£5,727	←
International	12%	£1,500	←
Emerging Markets	4%	£500	←
REITs	16%	£2,000	←
Bonds	12%	£1,500	←
TIPS	12%	£1,500	←

	Month 2		Month 3		Month 4	
Value	£13,727		£14,727		£15,727	
	Allocation	Value	Allocation	Value	Allocation	Value
Domestic	42%	£5,727	39%	£5,727	36%	£5,727
International	12%	£1,710	13%	£1,920	14%	£2,130
Emerging Markets	4%	£610	5%	£720	5%	£830
REITs	16%	£2,260	17%	£2,520	18%	£2,780
Bonds	12%	£1,710	13%	£1,920	14%	£2,130
TIPS	12%	£1,710	13%	£1,920	14%	£2,130

Note: In some cases, the numbers in the above columns don't add up to 100%

Because your domestic equities now represent 45 percent of your portfolio, rather than the targeted 30 percent, you have to take action. Pause your automatic contribution to domestic equities and reallocate that 30 percent by distributing it evenly to the other five asset classes (e.g., each would get an additional 6 percent). £1,000 monthly contributions will now be allocated as follows:

—— 0%: Put this investment on pause and evenly distribute the 30% across the other asset classes (i.e., 6% for each).

—— 21%: The target is 15%, so add 6% and you'll get 21%.
Monthly contribution: £210

—— 11%: The target here is 5%, so you again add 6%. Monthly contribution: £110

—— 26%: Target is 20%. Monthly contribution: £260

—— 21%: Target is 15%. Monthly contribution: £210

—— 21%: Target is 15%. Monthly contribution: £210

Month 5		Month 6		Month 7		Month 8	
£6,727		£17,727		£18,727		£19,727	
ocation	Value	Allocation	Value	Allocation	Value	Allocation	Value
%	£5,727	32%	£5,727	31%	£5,727	29%	£5,727
%	£2,340	14%	£2,550	15%	£2,760	15%	£2,970
	£940	6%	£1,050	6%	£1,160	6%	£1,270
%	£3,040	19%	£3,300	19%	£3,560	19%	£3,820
%	£2,340	14%	£2,550	15%	£2,760	15%	£2,970
%	£2,340	14%	£2,550	15%	£2,760	15%	£2,970

because of the variables of rounding.

ADVICE FROM THE BLOGOSPHERE

MANAGING ASSET ALLOCATION WITH MULTIPLE ACCOUNTS AND MINIMAL EFFORT

by nickel of www.fivecentnickel.com

*I*nvestment experts have argued for years that asset allocation is one of the most important factors in determining your success as an investor. In other words, picking the proper mix of investment types in the proper proportions is the key to maximizing your returns while minimizing your risk. While entire books have been written about how to determine a proper allocation, much less attention has been paid to the ins and outs of maintaining this balance, especially when you (and perhaps a spouse) are managing multiple investment accounts.

Consider the case of a married couple with a taxable investment account, two Roth IRAs, and two 401(k) accounts. Even with a relatively simple allocation of X percent in domestic stocks, Y percent in international stocks, and Z percent in bonds, maintaining the proper allocation can get complicated. If you've chosen a lifecycle fund, none of this is really relevant, since you can just choose the same fund in all of your accounts. But if you're handling your own asset allocation, how do you keep managing multiple investments simple?

THE ONE POT SOLUTION. *The solution is simple: Treat all of your accounts as one big pot of money. Instead of trying to hit the proper X/Y/Z allocation in each account, shoot for maintaining that allocation overall. In order to make this work with the least effort possible, keep one account as your "variable" account and make the others static. The variable account will contain a mix of different funds, which you can rebalance based on your target asset allocation. The static accounts will each contain a single type of investment, whether it's domestic equities, international equities, or bonds. For example, your Roth IRA could contain a few different funds (and would be the variable account), while your wife's 401(k)* could be a static account, which you'd only use to buy domestic equities.*

* Roth IRA and 401(k) are different types of pensions in the US

If you need to rebalance your overall portfolio, log in to your variable account and make changes. For example, if your international equities have grown faster than your other investments, and are now disproportionately higher than you want, log into your variable account and exchange some of your international holdings into domestic stocks and/or bonds. Alternatively, you can change your ongoing contributions to put the international funds on "pause" until things even out.

So how should you decide which assets go where? I have several guiding principles: First and foremost, tax-inefficient (i.e., income-generating) assets such as bonds should go into a tax-advantaged account like an IRA or 401(k). Conversely, taxable accounts should only hold tax-efficient investments like equity index funds, and you should try to make these accounts static to minimize the tax consequences associated with selling your investments when rebalancing. Finally, since withdrawals from Roth accounts such as a Roth IRA or Roth 401(k) will be completely tax free, you should seek to maximize growth in those accounts by picking aggressive investments.

> **Keeping one asset type per account eliminates the need to rebalance within each individual account.**

The real benefit here is that keeping one asset type per account eliminates the need to rebalance within each individual account. Instead, rebalancing becomes a matter of tweaking the holdings within your variable account to bring your overall allocation back into line.

You'll handle ongoing contributions in much the same way. All contributions made into a static account go directly into its chosen asset class. For instance, all contributions into a 100 percent bond account would go to purchase bonds—and so on. You can then balance out your contributions across your variable account(s) so that your total contributions are in proportion with the desired X/Y/Z mix.

THE DOWNSIDE. *The only real drawback to this strategy is that, in an extremely turbulent market, your allocation might get so far out of line that you can't correct it by rebalancing your overall holdings across accounts. For example, in the latter half of 2008, stocks dropped dramatically. So if you wanted to rebalance by selling bonds and buying more stocks, you might not have had enough bonds available to exchange into stocks in your variable account(s). In such cases, you'd have to "unlock" one of your static accounts and use that to help rebalance your portfolio. For the most part, however, you won't have to do this, and this strategy will save you a ton of headaches.*

nickel writes about personal finance at http://www.fivecentnickel.com.

(continued from page 205)

accounts and not selling investments before holding them for a year), chances are you don't make enough to worry about them. You certainly don't need to make investment decisions—like buying tax-efficient investment bonds—to save on taxes. People in their twenties who do this have usually read something in some magazine and then they start scheming ways to avoid the tax man. Let's be honest. Once you've paid the maximum into tax-efficient ISAs and pensions, you'll need more help in this department. But for now, follow that old adage: "Don't let the tax tail wag the investment dog."

THE ONE THING YOU NEED TO KNOW ABOUT TAXES AND INVESTMENTS

Invest as much as possible into tax-deferred accounts like your pension and ISA. Because retirement accounts are tax advantaged, you'll enjoy significant rewards. Your pension money won't be taxed until you withdraw it many years down the line, and your ISA earnings won't be taxed at all. More important, you won't have to worry about the minutiae, including picking tax-efficient funds or knowing when to sell to beat end-of-year distributions. By taking this one step of investing in tax-advantaged accounts, you'll sidestep the vast majority of tax concerns.

Investing in tax-advantaged accounts is the 85 Percent Solution for taxes. Sure, you could create complicated tax structures, start putting money away in off-shore accounts, and use the annual gift allowance to give thousands away to others in gifts—but who the hell needs to do that right now? Investing as much as possible in tax-deferred accounts is the answer to 85 percent of your tax questions.

WHY YOU SHOULD THINK TWICE ABOUT SELLING

If you have money invested in a pension, you don't have to pay capital gains tax if you sell some of your investments (such as a fund or individual company shares, if you have put money into a self-invested personal pension, for example). And you don't pay capital gains or income tax on profits from money that's invested in an ISA. But even if you have money in taxable accounts, you won't necessarily have to pay tax if you plan carefully.

Every year you get a capital gains tax allowance—a level of profit that you're allowed to generate on your investments before you pay tax. As I write this it's worth £10,100 (in the tax year that runs from April 6th 2009 to April 5th 2010). That means you're allowed to make £10,100 profit before you pay a penny in tax. But any profit you make above that is taxed.

You're also allowed to offset profits you make against losses for capital gains tax purposes. It means that with a bit of careful organisation, you can plan how you withdraw money or sell investments so you don't get stung with an unexpected tax bill. The trick is to make sure you don't leave it until the last minute (i.e. a few days before the tax year ends), to think about what you want to do.

Since you presumably made a good investment, why not hold it for the long term? In Chapter 6, we covered how people can't time the market. In Chapter 3, I showed you how buy-and-hold investing produces dramatically higher returns than frequent trading. And once you've factored in taxes, the odds are stacked against you if you sell. This is yet another argument for not buying individual stocks, and instead using lifestyle, lifecycle or tracker funds to create a tax-efficient, simple portfolio. Remember, all of this assumes that you made a *good investment*.

Bottom line: Invest in retirement accounts and hold your investments for the long term. Until your portfolio swells to roughly $100,000, that's about all you need to know.

Knowing When to Sell Your Investments

In your twenties and thirties, there are only three reasons to sell your investments: You need the money for an emergency, you made a terrible investment and it's consistently underperforming the market, or you've achieved your specific goal for investing.

YOU NEED THE MONEY FOR AN EMERGENCY

If you suddenly need money for an emergency, here's your hierarchy of where to get it.

1. Use your savings account. You should have built up a large enough cushion of money to be able to use some of it if you really need it.

Hopefully, that money will be in an account that you can access within a few days, but even if it isn't (if it's in a notice account, for example), you'll only sacrifice the interest you would have earned in that period.

2. Sell any valuables that aren't critical to you. Seriously—use eBay. I'll be honest: You probably won't get a lot of money from selling valuables (people have a tendency to overvalue their own property compared with what others will pay for it). But selling some of your own goods is an important psychological step—it will let you prove how serious you are both to yourself and to your family (which will help if you're asking them for help).

3. Ask your family if you can borrow the money from them. *Note:* This doesn't work if your family is crazy.

4. Use your credit card or a loan if you have no other option. I said earlier in the book that I wasn't a fan of going for 0 percent deals on credit cards, but if you're really desperate it might be worth trying to see if you can get your money interest-free. Only do this once—don't think this is a habit you can repeat or you could damage your credit score.

YOU MADE A TERRIBLE INVESTMENT THAT'S CONSISTENTLY UNDERPERFORMING

This point is largely moot if you invested in a tracker fund or series of tracker funds, because they reflect the entire market's performance. If it's going down, that means the entire market is down. If you believe the market will recover, that means investments are on sale for cheaper prices than before, meaning not only should you *not* sell, but you should keep investing and pick up shares at a cheaper price.

But let's talk about this conceptually to understand when to sell an investment for poor performance. If you pulled up a list of your investments and saw the chart at the top of the next page, what would you do?

"Ramit," you might say frantically. "This stock sucks! I need to sell it before I lose all my money!"

Not so fast. You have to look at the context before you decide what to do. For instance, knowing that the example is a consumer-goods stock, how is the rest of the consumer-goods industry doing? (*Note:* You can research industries by going to DigitalLook (www.digitallook.com) and clicking on "investing" then "UK Shares," and finally "sectors and

CONSUMER-GOODS STOCK

Date	Price	Date	Price
3/6/2002	33.43	3/1/2006	23.78
2/1/2003	31.53	1/6/2006	23.90
2/6/2003	31.01	3/1/2007	26.29
2/1/2004	35.55	1/6/2007	27.68
1/6/2004	35.45	2/1/2008	22.91
3/1/2005	26.45	2/5/2008	20.61
1/6/2005	28.17		

indices." You'll have to register for sector research, but it's free to do.)

By looking at the stock *and* the surrounding industry (see chart below), you see that the entire industry Is In decline. It's not your particular investment. They're *all* doing poorly. Now, this raises questions about the industry, but it also gives you a context to explain your stock's plunging returns. And just because they're plunging, by the way, doesn't mean that you should sell immediately. All Industries experience declines at one time or another. In fact, looking at the chart below, I'd dig in more to see what was happening with the industry. Is it still viable? Are there competitors replacing it? (For example, If you own shares in a company

CONSUMER-GOODS INDUSTRY TRACKER

Date	Price	Date	Price
3/6/2002	50	3/1/2006	38
2/1/2003	49	1/6/2006	36
2/6/2003	45	3/1/2007	32
2/1/2004	42	1/6/2007	30
1/6/2004	44	2/1/2008	31
3/1/2005	40	2/5/2008	29
1/6/2005	38		

that's producing cassette-playing Walkmans, chances are that business is not coming back.) From looking at the above chart, it appears that the stock is performing in line with the rest of the industry. If you think the industry or investment is simply going through a cyclical downturn, then hang on to the investment and continue regular purchases of shares. If, however, you think the industry won't recover, you may want to sell the investment.

Now if your stock looked like *this,* I might consider selling:

STOCK FROM INDUSTRY A

Date	Price	Date	Price
3/6/2002	43	3/1/2006	23.78
2/1/2003	31.53	1/6/2006	23.9
2/6/2003	31.01	3/1/2007	26.29
2/1/2004	35.55	1/6/2007	27.68
1/6/2004	35.45	2/1/2008	22.91
3/1/2005	26.45	2/5/2008	20.61
1/6/2005	28.17		

INDUSTRY A TRACKER

Date	Price	Date	Price
17/6/2002	335.97	3/1/2006	372.26
2/1/2003	317.39	1/6/2006	355.64
2/6/2003	324.38	3/1/2007	388.98
2/1/2004	351.22	1/6/2007	425.47
1/6/2004	358.26	2/1/2008	406.19
3/1/2005	346.81	2/5/2008	372.74
1/6/2005	363.26		

As you can see, this stock really had been underperforming against its industry tracker.

If you were to decide to sell your investment, the process is easy, but varies slightly depending on whether you have a self-select ISA (which lets you invest in single-company shares) or a SIPP. If you're selling outside of a tax-efficient account (such as an ISA or a pension), there are tax implications. Go back to page 210 if you need to refresh your memory. I want to emphasize that I almost never have to sell investments because I rarely make specific stock investments. If you pick a lifecycle or lifestyle fund or build a portfolio of tracker funds instead, you rarely have to think about selling. My advice: Save your sanity and focus on more important things.

YOU ACHIEVED YOUR SPECIFIC GOAL

Buy and hold is a great strategy for ultra-long-term investments, but lots of people invest in the medium to short term to make money for specific goals. For example, "I'm going to invest for a dream vacation to Thailand. . . . I don't need to take the trip any time soon, so I'll just put $100/month into my investing account." Remember, if your goal is less than five years away, you should set up a savings goal in your savings account. But if you've invested money for a longer-term goal and you've achieved it, sell and don't think twice. That's a great investing success, and you should use the money for whatever your original goal was.

Giving Back: Elevating Your Goals Beyond the Day-to-Day

Most people spend their entire lives handling the day-to-day issues of money and never get ahead. How am I going to pay off that loan? Oh man, why did I buy that £300 jacket? Damn, I thought I canceled that subscription.

If you've followed the steps in this book, you've moved past these basic questions. Your accounts work together automatically. You know how much you can afford to spend going out and how much you want to save each month. If something goes wrong, your system lets you easily see if you need to cut costs, make more money, or adjust your lifestyle. It's all there.

Financial Options for Super-Achievers: Make the Ten-Year Plan That Few Others Do

I'm always surprised by the e-mails I get from people who have optimized every part of their investing strategy and are nonetheless *still* looking for more ways they can optimize their finances. It's easy: Just ask people five to ten years older than you what they *wish* they had started earlier, then do that. You'll get three answers right off the bat:

1. CREATE AN EMERGENCY FUND. An emergency fund is simply another savings goal that is a way to protect against job loss, disability, or simple bad luck. Most people in their twenties don't need emergency funds because we can just borrow money from our other savings goals or, worst case, go home to Mom and Dad. But if you have a mortgage or you need to provide for your family, an emergency fund is a critical piece of being financially secure. To create one, just set up an extra savings goal and then funnel money to it in the same way you would your other goals. Eventually, your emergency fund should contain six months of spending money (which includes *everything:* your mortgage, other loans, food, transportation, taxes, gifts, and anything else you would conceivably spend on).

2. INSURANCE. As you get older and more crotchety, you'll want more and more types of insurance to protect yourself from loss. This includes home-owner insurance (fire, flood, and earthquake) and life insurance. If you own a home, you need insurance, but young, single people don't need life insurance. First of all, statistically, we hardly ever die, and the insurance payout is useful only for people who depend on your livelihood, like your spouse and kids. Beyond that, insurance is really out of the scope of this book, but if you're truly interested, I encourage you talk to your parents and their friends, and search for "life insurance" online to research the various options. You probably don't need to buy a bunch of insurance options right now, but you can certainly set up a savings goal so when you *do* need them, you'll have money to use. One last thing: Insurance is almost never a good investment, despite what financial salespeople (or clueless parents) will tell you. So use it as protection from downside risk— like for fires or accidental death when you have a family—but don't think of it as a growth investment.

3. CHILDREN'S EDUCATION. Whether or not you have children yet, your first goal should be to excel financially for yourself. I always get confused when I see people on TV who are in debt yet want to save for their children's education. What the hell? Listen up, Momma: First, get out of debt and save for your own retirement. *Then* you can worry about your kids. That said, just as pensions are a great way of saving for retirement accounts, stocks and shares ISAs and child trust funds have tax advantages that make them great for saving for children's education. If you've got kids (or know that one day you will) and some spare cash, pour it into an ISA.

These are just a few of the things you'll be forced to think about in the next ten years. The best way to prepare yourself is to talk to successful people who are somewhat older than you and have their act together. Their advice can be invaluable—and can give you an edge on planning for the next decade.

That means it's time to think about elevating your goals beyond the day-to-day. Whereas most people might be so consumed with the minutiae of money that they've never thought about getting rich ("I just want to pay off this debt."), you can set larger goals of doing the things you love using money to support you.

I'm afraid this will sound sanctimonious to some of you, but I really don't mean it to be. I believe that part of getting rich is giving back to the community that helped you flourish. There are lots of traditional ways to do this, like volunteering at a soup kitchen or becoming a child mentor. I wanted to try to contribute on a bigger scale (plus I find that my jokes are not so welcome at soup kitchens). So, in 2006, I created The Sethi Scholarship (scholarships.ramitsethi.com), which awards money and mentoring to one entrepreneurial young person per year. (Fun fact: The first year I launched it, not one person applied.) When I told friends I had launched a scholarship, they looked at me in disbelief. "That's ridiculous," they said. "I could never have enough money to launch a scholarship." They said this while wearing $150 jeans and eating a $40 dinner. How easy would it be for them to set a savings goal and sock away money to give to others? Look, my scholarship is for $1,000. You don't need to be rich to give back. Even £100 helps. And it doesn't have to be a scholarship, either. Sites like Kiva.org let you give directly to poor third-world communities. Or you can donate to your high school, local library, environmental action groups, the Red Cross—whatever means the most to you. And if you're short on cash, donate your time, which is often more valuable than money.

If you think about it, philanthropy mirrors the very same *I Will Teach You to Be Rich* principles you read in this book: The simplest step can get you started. But, as with managing their money, people over-complicate things and create artificial barriers to prevent themselves from giving back. You don't have to be rich to be a philanthropist, just as you don't have to be rich to invest. The point is that now you've got a personal-finance system that few others have. This allows you to elevate your goals beyond making it through the daily grind. When you think back to last year, what was the one big thing you accomplished for others? What will it be this year?

If I could hope for one thing from this book, it would be that you become a master of conscious spending—and then apply those skills to help those around you. Maybe it will be by establishing a scholarship, or mentoring a needy kid, or even just helping your friends manage their money for free. Whatever it is, you're now in the very top tier of investing knowledge. You've moved beyond managing your money for short-term goals and you're thinking strategically about your money and how it can help you to be rich—and how to share that with others.

If this were a movie, it would be raining, violin music would be swelling in the background, and a young soldier would slowly raise his hand to salute an elderly general. With all this talk about giving back, it would be very emotional, and a single tear would be rolling down someone's cheek.

But we've got one last chapter to read. From the thousands of e-mails and blog comments I've received over the years, I know there are a few common issues that come up regularly. Apparently, life isn't all about dissecting the nuts and bolts of asset allocation and creating compound-growth charts. Who knew? In the next chapter, I'll cover the specifics of money and relationships, buying a car and your first house, and managing the daily questions that come up in your financial life. Last chapter! Let's do it.

CHAPTER 9

A RICH LIFE

*The finances of relationships,
weddings, buying a car, and your first house*

What does *rich* mean to you? I brought this up in the introduction, but throughout this book we've spent a lot of time talking about *money*. As I've said before, that's great, but I believe being rich is about much more than that. For me, it's about freedom—it's about not having to think about money all the time and being able to travel and work on the things that interest me. It's about being able to use money to do whatever I want—and not having to worry about my budget, asset allocation, or how I'll ever be able to afford a house.

But that's just me. Being rich probably means something different to you. In this chapter, I'm going to address some of the most common questions I've received about life and money. I hope my answers will help you live a richer life.

Student Loans— Pay Them Down or Invest?

Student loans are a big kick in the face that the real world has arrived. CNN reports that the average college graduate has around $20,000 of student loans—plus, as the U.S. Public Interest Research Group recently indicated, more than $2,500 of credit card debt. It can seem hard to get ahead when you have the baggage of student loans weighing you down. The good news is that student loans were probably an excellent financial decision (unless you ended up being an artist or actor . . . In those cases, get a real job). University graduates far outearn those with only GCSEs or A levels. Still, if you have $20,000 of debt hanging over your shoulders, you're going to want to know how to handle it. Although we already talked about getting out of student debt in Chapter 1, there's one additional question I constantly get asked: "Should I invest or pay off my student loans?"

INVESTING VS. PAYING OFF STUDENT LOANS

It can be difficult to hear the drumbeat of "invest early!" when you're scrambling to pay £100 or £200 in student debts each month. But when it comes to putting money toward investing or your student loans, you really have three choices:

- *Pay the minimum monthly payment on your student loans and invest the rest.*

- *Pay as much as possible toward your student loans and then, once they are paid off, start investing.*

- *Do a hybrid 50/50 approach, where you pay half toward your student loans (always paying at least the minimum) and send the other half into your investment accounts.*

Technically, your decision comes down to interest rates. If we're talking about your loan with the Student Loan Company (rather than a bank overdraft), you'd want to pursue option one: Pay your student loans off as slowly as possible because you can make an average of 8 percent by investing in low-cost funds. However, notice I said *technically*. That's because money management isn't always rational. Some people aren't comfortable having any debt at all and want to get rid of it as quickly as possible. If having debt keeps you awake at night, follow option two and pay it off as soon as possible—but understand that you could be losing lots of growth potential just so you can be more comfortable.

I recommend you take a close look at option three, and here's why: The interest rate on your graduate loans from a bank (once you've gone past the interest-free period) will be higher than what you'd earn from the stock market, but your Student Loans Company loan is likely to be lower, so frankly your decision will be a toss-up. All things being equal, the money you would stand to make by investing would be about the same amount that you'll pay out in interest on your student loan, so basically it's a wash. It won't really matter whether you pay off your student loans or invest, because you'll get roughly the same return. *Except for two things:* compound interest and tax-advantaged retirement accounts. When you invest in your twenties and early thirties, you get huge benefits from compound interest. If you wait until you're older to invest, you'll never be able to catch up on those earnings. Plus, if you're investing in tax-advantaged accounts like pensions and ISAs (see Chapter 3), you're getting gains from tax benefits. That's why I would consider a hybrid split, paying off your debt with part of your money and investing with the rest. The exact split depends on your risk tolerance. Most people will simply choose a 50/50 split to keep things simple, but if you're more aggressive, you'll probably want to invest more.

LOVE AND MONEY

MONEY HAS A HUGE EFFECT ON RELATIONSHIPS. JUST TAKE A LOOK AT your day-to-day life: I bet you have a friend who never leaves enough of a tip at restaurants or never pays you back when you lend him money. Nothing is more annoying than someone who mistreats you with money—and those are just your *friends*! Imagine when you have a husband or wife, and you have to share bank accounts and responsibilities for rent and car payments and everything else. You better believe money will be an issue.

That's why I want to spend some time talking about how to handle money in your different relationships—your relationship with your parents, your boyfriend or girlfriend, your future spouse. I thought about dealing with money and your children, too, but considering I am planning to buy my kids paper towels instead of shoes, I may not be the best person to talk about that.

Letting Your Parents Manage Your Money Is Dumb

You wouldn't believe how many questions I get from smart, educated people who think it's fine to let their parents manage their money. When you think about it, it is not that surprising. Parents who offer to let their kids send cash to the family money manager have probably coddled their kids for their entire lives. Do you want to let your folks feed you with a bottle and change your diaper, too? Don't be one of these jackasses.

It's time to grow up. Even though parents have good intentions, offering to handle money management is one of the worst things they can do for their kids. At our age, we should be learning how to manage our money ourselves. No financial advisers, no B.S. And if we make mistakes, that's okay—maybe we lose £100 or even £1,000 now and again, but we learn from those mistakes. By doing this we get confident enough to be increasingly aggressive with our investments. Plus, chances are good that after reading this book you know more than your parents do about managing money anyway.

> **IT'S TIME TO GROW UP. AT OUR AGE, WE SHOULD BE LEARNING HOW TO MANAGE OUR MONEY OURSELVES. NO FINANCIAL ADVISERS, NO B.S.**

If you take the lazy route and send your money to your parents, a few things happen. First, you develop a hands-off mentality: "Well, I don't have to worry about it." GOD, IF I HEAR THIS ONE MORE TIME, I AM GOING TO JUMP UP AND BEAT SOMEONE WITH AN ONION. (That way it's unclear why they're crying.) But as I've said over and over, investing is largely hands off once you do the initial research. Buy and hold means buy something and . . . hold it! Not too hard once you've done your homework. Plus, if it's your own money and you made the investment yourself, you'll actually *want* to track its progress. Trust me, it's kind of fun.

Second, if your parents invest your money, you don't get the kind of transparent information you would if it were your own investment. Sure, you could probably get your parents' password and log in every once in a while and check . . . but would you? Also, if their entire portfolio went up 30 percent, what does that mean for your money (which was probably invested at a different time than their money)? How much did you actually make? I hate math, so I would avoid having to calculate this at all costs.

Third, you want to give yourself bottom-line accountability for any gains or losses. No blaming your parents, their financial adviser (who is paying *his* bills using the fees he charges you), or your parents' fancy full-service account for charging you fees. Your investments should be yours, and so should the wins or losses. It's fine to rely on your parents for advice, and your friends and the Internet are always there to help with evaluating investments, too. But in the end, the decisions should be yours.

Finally, now that you've read this book, you can probably beat your parents' return. (Go to Chapter 6 and revisit the myth of financial expertise to see why.) So please, if your parents suggest you just invest with them, tell them why you'd rather do it on your own.

How to Help Parents Who Are in Severe Debt

As you could probably tell from my rant on parents and money, I'm a big fan of being self-sufficient with your money—whether or not your parents offer to help you out.

But sometimes your parents are in financial trouble of their own. If your parents are in a lot of debt, it can be very tough on your relationship with them—especially if they reach out to you and ask for help. In this case, your biggest challenge is not going to be coming up with a technical personal-finance solution for their problem. Instead, it's going to be persuading them to change decades of bad money-management habits. Work through this delicately but firmly. They'll probably be coping with the crushing guilt of having to rely on their son or daughter to help them with their finances, but don't let them get caught up in feeling bad. Instead, identify where their money is going, set up a plan using the hierarchy of investing (see page 76), and then help your parents make the tough decisions that will be necessary. My readers have used what I've taught them to persuade their parents to do anything from finally setting up a retirement account (when they were in their fifties) to selling their house and downsizing their entire lives.

Every situation is different, but here are some questions you can ask. (Remember: Tread gently. Nobody likes talking about money—especially if it means having to admit to their kids that they need help.)

- *How do they feel about their money? Why?*

- *How much do they make per month? How much do they spend?*

- *What percentage of their income are they saving?*

- *Do they pay fees for their bank accounts and credit cards?*

- *What's their average monthly credit card balance? Why isn't it zero? How could they get it there?*

- *Do they have any investments? If so, how did they choose them?*

- *Do they own actively managed fund(s)? How much are they paying in fees?*

- *Are they maximizing their company pension, at least as much as their company matches?*

- *What about other investment vehicles like a stakeholder or personal pension or stocks and shares ISAs? Do they have one?*

- *Do they read www.iwillteachyoutoberich.com? NO? WHY NOT, POPS?!?! (Note: I highly recommend that you scream this really loudly at them.)*

Your parents might not have answers to all these questions, but listen closely to what they *do* tell you. I'd encourage you to take the 85 Percent Solution approach and figure out one or two major actions they could take to improve their financial situation. Maybe it means setting up an automatic savings account, or focusing on paying off one credit card so they can feel a small sense of accomplishment. Think back to when you didn't know anything about money and it was incredibly overwhelming. Now you can use what you've learned to help your parents make small changes that will have big results.

The Dreaded "DTR" Conversation with Your Boyfriend or Girlfriend—About Money

Remember how painful those "Define the Relationship" conversations were back in college? Now imagine you have to sit down and talk about money while wishing you could use the sweat from your forehead to drown yourself. Sure, you and your boyfriend or girlfriend might have had an occasional chat about money. But when you're getting serious—whether you're recently engaged or moving in together or just at a point where your decisions start to really affect each other—it's important to spend some time talking about your money and your financial goals. Talking about money with your partner might sound painful, but I promise you it doesn't have to be awkward. As corny as it sounds, it can actually bring you closer together—*if* you know what to ask and stay calm. And if your girlfriend/boyfriend isn't a nut job with £300,000 in credit card debt.

THE KEY IS TO START BY ASKING THEIR ADVICE. YES, EVEN IF YOU DON'T NEED IT!

The specific tactics aren't as important as your attitude going in. The key is to start by *asking their advice*. Yes, even if you don't need it! Bring the topic up lightly. "Hey, I've been trying to learn about money lately . . . What do you think about investing versus saving?" If you don't get an answer, try this: "Okay, hey, I have another question . . . What do you think about my spending? Is there anything you think I should change?" I guarantee you they'll have an opinion on *that*—and although you're sacrificing yourself, at least it'll get the conversation started.

After a few days, ask for their financial advice again: "What do you think—should I pay off my credit card or my student debt?" (Of course, you already know the answer from page 220.) Then, a few days later, tell them you've been doing some more research. "I picked up a book on personal finance and it had some really interesting stuff in it," you can say. "What do you think about talking about our money together?"

(It is optional to add something like, "The book is by an amazing, weird, gracious author named Ramit Sethi, and I visit his website every day.")

When you sit down to talk, once again start by asking your partner's opinions: "I know you use cash to pay for everything, but this guy says we should use credit cards to build our credit and track spending. What do you think?" The goal of this meeting should be to agree that money is important to both of you, and that you want to work together to help each other with finances. That's it!

If things go well during your first conversation, ask if your boyfriend or girlfriend would be willing to sit down again to go over both of your finances together. Remember, it's not about criticizing or noting things that are being done wrong—it's about figuring out ways to help each other so you can grow together. Some phrases you can use:

- *"You're really good at [X] and I want you to help me with my finances."*
- *"We're going to join our lives together, and I want money to be a part of that."*
- *"One plus one equals three,"* which explains why you two can combine money smarts to create synergies. *Note:* Only MBAs or consultants can use this line with a straight face.

THE BIG MEETING

This is the big day when you both lay bare all your finances and work through them together. But remember, it's not really such a dramatic step, since you've been slowly working toward this for weeks.

It should take about four or five hours to prepare for this meeting. You'll each want to bring the following:

- *A list of your accounts and the amount in each*
- *A list of debts and what the interest rates are*
- *Monthly expenses (see page 104 for details)*
- *Your total income*
- *Any money that is owed to you*
- *A list of short-term and long-term financial goals*

When you sit down, put the paper aside and start by talking about goals. From a financial perspective, what do you want? What kind of lifestyle do you expect? What about vacations in the next year? Does either of you need to support your parents?

Then look at your monthly spending. This will be a sensitive conversation because nobody wants to be judged. But remember, keep an open mind. Show yours first. Ask, "What do you think I could be doing better?" And then it's your partner's turn.

Spend some time talking about your attitudes toward money. How do you treat money? Do you spend more than you make? Why? How did your parents talk about money? (One of my friends has horrible money-management skills, which is confusing because she's so disciplined and smart. After years of knowing her, one day she told me that her dad had declared bankruptcy *twice*, which helped me understand the irrational way she approached money.)

> **SPEND SOME TIME TALKING ABOUT YOUR ATTITUDES TOWARD MONEY. HOW DO YOU TREAT MONEY? DO YOU SPEND MORE THAN YOU MAKE? WHY?**

The most important goal of this conversation is to set up a plan to manage your money, including your credit cards, bank accounts, budget, and investment accounts. Essentially, you want to work through this book with your partner.

Your immediate goal should be to set up a few short- and long-term savings goals, such as a year-end trip and/or something a little more major like buying a car or putting a down payment on a house. At this point, it's probably better not to run through all the numbers for a really large purchase because it can get overwhelming. Just set up a savings goal or two and set up an automatic monthly transfer for each of you. Longer term, you and your girlfriend/boyfriend should work together to get on the same page with your money attitudes. When you set a goal together ("We're going to save enough to put a £30,000 down payment on a house"), you'll both be able to commit to working toward it.

LIVING TOGETHER: WHAT TO DO IF ONE OF YOU MAKES MORE MONEY THAN THE OTHER

The first question to ask is "Do you realize you're living in sin?" Just kidding, I don't give a damn.

Once you and your girlfriend or boyfriend start sharing expenses, questions will invariably come up about how to handle money on a daily basis—especially if one of you has a higher income than the other. When it comes to splitting bills, there are a couple of options.

The first, and most intuitive, choice is to split all the bills 50/50. But that doesn't work for everyone.

As an alternative, how about this fresh idea from Suze Orman? She encourages dividing expenses based proportionately on income. For example, if your monthly rent is £1,000, here's how you might split it up:

DIVIDING EXPENSES BASED ON INCOME

	You	Your partner
Monthly income	£3,000	£2,000
Rental payment	£600 (3,000 / 5,000 = 60%)	£400 (2,000/5,000 = 40%)

WHAT TO DO IF YOUR PARTNER SPENDS MONEY IRRESPONSIBLY

This is the most common complaint I hear from newlywed readers. "Ramit," they write, "my husband spends way too much money on video games. How are we supposed to save money? When I tell him this, he tunes me out and the next day, he's buying something else."

The solution to this is to *elevate the conversation beyond you and your partner.* If you keep trying to tell your partner not to spend money on something, he or she will resent it and ignore you. More than anything, people hate to be judged for their spending, so if you continue making it personal ("You can't spend that much on shoes each month!"), you'll get nowhere.

Instead, keep it simple. Turn to page 106 in Chapter 4 and look at how much it costs to save for common purchases like vacations, Christmas gifts, or a new car. Then have a conversation about what your savings goals are and how much you need to save to reach them—and come to a savings plan that you both agree on.

If you do this, the next time you have an argument about spending, you can steer it away from you and your partner and instead make it about *the plan*. Nobody can get defensive when you're pointing to a piece of paper (rather than pointing at the other person). Say, "Hey, cool iPhone. Are we still on track to hit our savings goal?" This is hard to argue with if you say it in an innocent voice. In fact, they definitely can't get defensive, because they agreed to the plan! By focusing on the plan, not the person, you sidestep the perception of being judgmental and work on bringing spending in line with your goals. This is the way handling money is supposed to work.

The £20,000 Question: Why We're All Hypocrites About Our Wedding (and How to Save for Yours)

A while back, I was out with some friends, including one who was planning her wedding. Because both my sisters had recently gotten married, I suggested she check out a nearby stationery store for her invitations. "It's really expensive, like fourteen dollars per invitation," I told her. "But at least you can get some ideas for design." She looked at me and without a hint of arrogance said, "Oh, I'll check it out. I actually talked to my family and we have an unlimited budget for the wedding."

That one sentence rendered me speechless. She wasn't bragging. She was just saying it matter-of-factly: Her wedding could cost *anything* and that was totally fine. She comes from a very wealthy family, so this isn't so unusual. What *is* unusual, however, is that so many people will scoff at the above story—and then proceed to spend ungodly amounts on their own wedding while steadfastly insisting how absurd "most" people are. I want to help plan for these large life events. But be prepared—you're going to have to confront the hypocrisy that we all have when it comes to these purchases.

OF COURSE *YOUR* WEDDING WILL BE SIMPLE

When my sister called me to tell me that she'd gotten engaged, I was out with my friends. I ordered champagne for everyone. When my other sister told me she was getting married a few months later, I told all my friends again. Then I found out they were each having both an East Coast wedding and a West Coast wedding—for a total of four Indian weddings in a few months! I ordered a round of cyanide and made mine a double.

That's what got me started thinking about weddings. The average UK wedding costs almost £20,000, which is not much less than the average annual salary of £24,000. Hold on: Just wait a second before you start rolling your eyes. It's easy to say, "These people should just realize that a wedding is about having a special day, not about putting yourself in crippling debt."

But guess what? When it's your wedding, you're going to want everything to be perfect. Yes, you. So will I. It'll be your special day, so why *not* spend the money to get the extra-long-stemmed roses or the filet mignon? My point isn't to judge people for having expensive weddings. Quite the opposite: The very same people who spend £20,000 on their weddings are the ones who, a few years earlier, said the same thing you're saying right now: "I just want a simple wedding. It's ridiculous to go into debt for just one day." And yet, little by little, they spend more than they planned—more than they can afford—on their special day. Look, there's nothing wrong with wanting your day to be perfect. Let's just acknowledge it and figure out how to achieve our goals.

SO WHAT SHOULD YOU DO?

Knowing the astonishingly high costs of weddings, what can you do? I see three choices:

Cut costs and have a simpler wedding. Great idea, but frankly, most people are not disciplined enough to do this. I don't say this pejoratively, but statistically: Most people will have a wedding that costs tens of thousands of pounds.

Do nothing and figure it out later. This is the most common tactic. I spoke to a recently married person who spent the previous eight months planning her wedding, which ended up becoming a very expensive day. Now, months later, she and her husband don't know how to deal with the resulting debt. If you do this, you are a moron. But you are in good company, because almost everybody else does it, too.

Budget and plan for the wedding. Ask ten people which of these choices they'll make, and every single one of them will pick this one. Then ask them how much money they're saving every month for their wedding (whether they're engaged or not). I guarantee the sputtering and silence will be worth it. This is a great idea in theory but is almost never followed in practice.

If you think about it, we actually have all the information we need. The average age at marriage is about thirty-two for men and thirty for women. We know that the average amount of a wedding is about £20,000. So, if you really are committed to not going into debt for your wedding, here's the astonishing amount you should be saving (whether you're engaged or not):

SCARY FIGURES

Your Age	Months until wedding	Monthly amount needed to save
25	84	£238
26	72	£278
27	60	£333
28	48	£417
29	36	£556
30	24	£833
31	12	£1,667
32	1	£20,000

Most of us haven't even conceived of saving this amount for our weddings. Instead, we say things like

- *"Wow, that's a lot. There's no way I can save that. Maybe my parents will help. . . ."*
- *"My wedding won't be like that. It'll be simple and elegant."*

- *"I'll think about it when I get engaged."*
- *"Luckily, I won't have to pay for it."* (Who will? Is your future spouse also thinking like this?)
- *"I have to marry someone rich."* (I've heard people say this, and they were only half joking.)

More commonly, though, we don't think about this at all: one of the most major expenditures of our lifetimes, which will almost certainly arrive in the next few years, and we don't even sit down for ten minutes to think about it. Something's broken here.

SURPRISING WEDDING MATH

This is pretty cool in a sickening, gut-wrenching kind of way. I set up a simulation to see which levers were the most powerful in reducing wedding costs. To be honest, I thought reducing the number of guests would produce the biggest result.

I was wrong.

Interestingly, changing the number of guests doesn't change the cost as much as you'd imagine. In the example on the next page, reducing the headcount by 50 percent reduces the cost only 25 percent.

Beyond the obvious—negotiating for better prices on the venue and food—the best suggestion I've heard about cutting wedding costs is to tackle the *fixed* costs. One of my friends, for example, actually flew in a photographer from the Philippines for his wedding. It sounds extravagant, but even with the flight, he saved $4,000. In another example, my sister had her invitations designed and printed in India for a fraction of what it would have cost in the United States.

In Chapter 4, I encouraged you to pick the one or two biggest problem areas in your spending and address them. Your wedding is no different: You want to look at the biggest expenses with a fine-toothed comb. Pick the biggest two or three expenditures and relentlessly cut their costs. Your honeymoon is going to cost £5,000? See if you can get someone to give you frequent flier miles as a wedding gift, check for travel deals online, enlist your second cousin who's a travel agent, or see if your credit card offers any perks you can use. Bridesmaids' dresses cost £400? Cut it in half by going with a local dress store. Chances are, it's better to optimize the three biggest cost areas by 30 percent than to get a 10 percent reduction in everything (and it'll keep you sane).

SAMPLE WEDDING COSTS

The table below shows the average fixed costs for a wedding of 80 guests. Obviously the cost of your wedding is going to change if you want to invite everyone you've ever met, including all your Facebook and Twitter friends.

FIXED COSTS	
Rings	£630
Wedding Dress	£1,590
Hair & Beauty	£170
Bridal Bouquet	£100
Groom's Outfit	£200
Attendants' Outfits	£600
Flowers	£685
Invitations and Stationary	£465
Transportation	£480
Civil/Church Fees	£520
Photography	£905
Videography	£905
Wedding Cake	£370
Reception Decorations	£460
Wedding Reception (inc. venue, food, & drinks)	£4,000
Evening Reception (inc. venue, food, & drinks)	£1,700
Entertainment	£850
Wedding night hotel	£200
Honeymoon	£2,000
Wedding Insurance	£110
Misc.	£1,000
TOTAL	£17,940

You can run the simulation yourself to check out how your own planning stacks up. Visit the live wedding-cost spreadsheet at www.iwillteachyoutoberich.com/wedding.

WORK AND MONEY

I'VE SAID IT BEFORE AND I'LL SAY IT AGAIN: FUNDAMENTALLY, THERE ARE two ways to get more money. You can earn more or you can spend less. Cutting costs is great, but I personally find increasing earnings to be a lot more fun. Because most of our income comes from work, it's an excellent place to optimize and earn more. In fact, negotiating your salary at a new job is the fastest legal way to make money. Your starting salary is even more important than you think because it sets the bar for future raises and, in all likelihood, your starting salary at future jobs. A £1,000 or £2,000 salary increase, in other words, can equal many times that over your career. Now let me show you how to get thousands by negotiating for a better salary.

Negotiating Your Salary, I Will Teach You to Be Rich Style

In Chapter 4, I wrote about asking for a raise at your current job. But the single best time to negotiate salary is when you're starting a *new* job. You have the most leverage then and—with some basic preparation—you can earn £3,000 or £6,000 in a simple ten-minute conversation, then retire to a nearby café for a light lunch. Delightful.

When I coach people on negotiation, I pretend to be the hiring manager and ask the toughest questions they might get. My friends don't like this, possibly because I also repeatedly crack jokes about taking the "role play" further than I should, but I force them to do it and they later thank me. When we're finished—four to five hours later—they're exhausted and cranky. But the people I've coached end up negotiating, on average, $6,000 more in salary.

Negotiating is 90 percent about mind-set and 10 percent about tactics. Most people don't believe they should negotiate. They're afraid of being "rude" or of having the employer rescind their offer. That almost never happens,

HIGHLIGHT THE WAYS YOU'LL HELP YOUR COMPANY HIT ITS GOALS.

especially because the company may have already spent up to £5,000 recruiting you. If you negotiate, you explicitly communicate that you value yourself more highly than the average employee. Are you average? If not, why would you settle for an average salary?

The basics of negotiating are very simple:

1. Remember that nobody cares about you.

Most new employees come to the table talking about how much *they* want to make. To be totally honest, as a hiring manager, I don't really care what you want to make. I would like to sit in the back of a Bentley with two hot twins and be fed a Taco Bell Grill Stuft Burrito with extra jalapeños. So when you're negotiating, remember this: When it comes to you, your manager cares about two things—how you're going to make him look better, and how you're going to help the company do well.

NEGOTIATING TACTIC: Always frame your negotiation requests in a way that shows how the *company* will benefit. Don't focus on the amount you'll cost the company. Instead, illustrate how much *value* you can provide to the company. If your work will help them drive an initiative that will make £1 million for the company, point that out. Tie your work to the company's strategic goals—and show the boss how you'll make him look good. Highlight how you'll make your boss's life easier by being the go-to person he can hand anything to. And remember that your company will make much more off your work than they pay you, so highlight the ways you'll help your company hit its goals. Your key phrase here is "Let's find a way to arrive at a fair number that works for both of us."

2. Have another job offer—and use it.

This is the single most effective thing you can do to increase your salary. When you have another job offer, your potential employers will have a newfound respect for your skills. It's like seeing the hot girl in the bar who's surrounded by guys. You want her more because everyone else does, too.

(continued on page 238)

CASE STUDY

How My Friend Got a 28 Percent Raise by Doing Her Homework

I recently helped my friend Rachel, twenty-five, negotiate a job offer, and at my request, she wrote up the process:

First the big picture: I got a 28 percent raise in base salary, which comes out to more than $1,000/hour based on how much time I spent getting the job. Plus stock options, which at least allow me the luxury of dreaming about being a gazillionaire.

I've applied to, and been ignored for, many, many job openings— more than I care to share. Despite this, I decided to jump back into the job market a few months ago after doing marketing for a large hotel in San Francisco. I found a marketing manager position on a site called VentureLoop (Craigslist for startups) and through it I sent in a resume, which snagged a phone interview, which was followed by an in-person interview, which was followed by an offer letter.

Sounds like a cakewalk, right? Actually, the VP of Marketing told me that I had the least experience of anyone she was interviewing— then she hired me anyway. I can't pinpoint exactly why I was successful in getting this job in contrast to all of my past attempts, but I can think of a few things that probably made the difference. My strategies weren't rocket science but they involved time and effort, two things that definitely make a difference separating you from the pack.

1. I BROKE DOWN THEIR JOB POSTING line by line and wrote down my skills and projects I'd worked on that directly related to their description.

2. I RESEARCHED THEIR WEBSITE EXTENSIVELY, read articles about the company, and looked up the management teams' backgrounds so that I could speak knowledgeably about the company and why I was a good fit.

3. I PREPARED A SPIEL ABOUT MY SOMEWHAT ECLECTIC RESUME, which can look unfocused if not set in the proper context.

4. I CALLED AN EXPERT ON START-UPS, finance, bargaining, and a half dozen other things to get some outside counsel. Ramit gave me some key advice, including, "Tell them you want to get your hands dirty," and "Suggest three things you would do to improve/enhance their marketing efforts." Yes, he does talk just like he writes on his blog.

5. I ACTUALLY TOOK RAMIT'S ADVICE, which is where a lot of my work came in. I dreamed up three proposals for generating greater interest at trade shows, better responses to direct marketing efforts, and increased name recognition in the general population.

Wow! So the interview must have gone really well, right? Not quite ... and Rachel's description of what she did is a classic case of turning a missed opportunity into a chance to win.

I never actually found a good opportunity to mention my ideas (this despite a four-hour interview). I e-mailed the proposals to my potential boss instead. I then individually e-mailed every person I spoke to that day to thank them for their time. Might have been overkill, but then again, my e-mail flurry may have been the tipping point for my hiring.

My references later told me that the VP had been impressed with my energy and intelligence, and had decided she would rather train someone with potential than hire a more experienced, and perhaps less flexible, individual. Three weeks of research and planning paid off with an entirely new career— a pretty stellar return on the investment of my time.

Just notice how this is the exact embodiment of everything this book stands for. Rachel carefully researched her options, took action, reached out to more experienced people for advice, and came in with a presentation that was better than everyone else's (so much so that she actually didn't have to negotiate much). And when she didn't get a chance to show off all of her presentation, she sent it by e-mail—even though some people would think that was "weird."

Getting rich isn't about one silver bullet or secret strategy. It happens through regular, boring, disciplined action. Most people see only the results of all this action—a winnable moment or an article in the press. But it's the behind-the-scenes work that really makes you rich.

(continued from page 235)

NEGOTIATING TACTIC: Interview with multiple companies at once. Be sure to let each company know when you get another job offer, but *don't* reveal the amount of the exact offer—you're under no obligation to. In the best case, the companies will get into a bidding war and you'll profit while watching two multinational firms rumble over you. I can think of no better way to spend a casual weekday.

3. Come prepared (99 percent of people don't).

Don't just pick a salary out of thin air. First, visit www.mysalary.co.uk and www.payscale.com to get a median amount for the position. Then, if you can, talk to people currently at the company (if you know someone who has recently left, even better—they'll be more willing to give you the real information) and ask what the salary range really is for the job. Finally—

> **BRING A STRATEGIC PLAN OF WHAT YOU WANT TO DO IN THE POSITION AND HAND IT TO YOUR HIRING MANAGER.**

and this is important—bring a plan of how you'll hit your goals to the negotiating session.

NEGOTIATING TACTIC: Most of the negotiation happens outside the room. Call your contacts. Figure out the salary amount you'd love, what you can realistically get, and what you'll settle for. And don't just ask for money. Literally bring a strategic plan of what you want to do in the position and hand it to your hiring manager. Do you realize how few people come to a negotiation with a plan for their role? This alone could win you $2,000 to $5,000. And, of course, it allows you to negotiate on the value you're going to bring to the company, not just the amount they'll pay you.

4. Have a toolbox of negotiating tricks up your sleeve.

Just as in a job interview, you'll want to have a list of things in your head that you can use to strengthen your negotiation. Think about your strong points and figure out ways you might be able to bring them to the hiring manager's attention. For example, I often ask, "What qualities make someone do an extraordinary job in this position?" If they say, "The

(continued on page 242)

Five Things You Should Never Do in a Negotiation

1. DON'T TELL THEM YOUR CURRENT SALARY. Why do they need to know? I'll tell you: So they can offer you just a little bit more than what you're currently making. If you're asked, say, "I'm sure we can find a number that's fair for both of us." If they press you, push back: "I'm not comfortable revealing my salary, so let's move on. What else can I answer for you?" (*Note:* Typically first-line recruiters will ask for these. If they won't budge, ask to speak to the hiring manager. No recruiter wants to be responsible for losing a great candidate, so this will usually get you through the gatekeeper. Also, some government jobs require you to reveal your salary. But if a place insists that you reveal your prior salary, it's a pretty good sign that it's not a great job.)

2. DON'T MAKE THE FIRST OFFER. That's their job. If they ask you to suggest a number, smile and say, "Now come on, that's your job. What's a fair number that we can both work from?"

3. IF YOU'VE GOT ANOTHER OFFER FROM A COMPANY THAT'S GENERALLY REGARDED TO BE MEDIOCRE, DON'T REVEAL THE COMPANY'S NAME. When asked for the name, just say something general but true, like, "It's another tech company that focuses on online consumer applications." If you say the name of the mediocre company, the negotiator is going to know that he's got you. He'll tear down the other company (which I would do, too), and it will all be true. He won't focus on negotiating, he'll just tell you how much better it will be at his company. So withhold this information.

4. DON'T ASK "YES" OR "NO" QUESTIONS. Instead of "You offered me fifty thousand pounds. Can you do fifty-five thousand?" say, "Fifty thousand pounds is a great number to work from. We're in the same ballpark, but how can we get to fifty-five thousand?"

5. NEVER LIE. Don't say you have another offer when you don't. Don't inflate your current salary. Don't promise things you can't deliver. You should always be truthful in negotiations.

ADVICE FROM THE BLOGOSPHERE

MAKE SURE A RAISE GOES TO YOUR BOTTOM LINE, NOT TO YOUR HEAD

How to Turn Small Raises into Long-Term Financial Success

by Trent Hamm of www.thesimpledollar.com

*E*very year, many Americans receive a welcome addition to their paycheck: a cost-of-living raise. This raise is a small percentage (between 3 and 4 percent) of salary that is added to keep pace with the increase in inflation. Some of us get even luckier, and receive a performance-based raise or a promotion.

I know the joys of receiving a raise—and I also know how tempting it can be to spend the extra money. When I received my first significant raise as a working adult, which amounted to roughly a 10 percent increase in my salary, I celebrated. I bought an iPod and a pile of video games, and then later I "invested" the rest of that raise in some vintage baseball cards.

To a small degree, that kind of behavior is fine. It's great to celebrate our successes in life—when our hard work pays off, it's natural and healthy to do something fun to mark that occasion, whether it's to buy something new or to go out on the town.

CELEBRATE A LITTLE—AND THEN GET SMART. *As with many things in life, however, true success is achieved by finding a healthy balance. So when you receive a raise, don't feel bad about celebrating—but do it modestly. Go out for a dinner date with your partner, or buy a DVD you've been thinking about picking up. And that's where the celebration should stop. A mere increase in your income is not a call to change your standard of living.*

Instead, use your raise to put yourself in a better financial position. Start by calculating how much your take-home pay will increase each month after your raise and then plan on setting aside most of that extra money. The next step is to automatically transfer that amount from your checking account to your savings account each time you're paid, so that you're never tempted to check your account balance and spend more than you should.

What do you do with that saved amount? You have a lot of options. If you're still carrying student loans or credit card debt, you can use it to accelerate your repayment plan, which will allow you to systematically eliminate your personal debt more quickly. Another smart move is to simply let it build up in your savings account as an emergency fund. This cash will come in handy if you need a major car repair or if you lose your job, for example. Another tactic is to invest it toward a long-term goal, like a home for yourself and your (potential) family or for retirement.

BE LIKE WARREN BUFFETT. Storing away your extra income also has a second benefit: it keeps you from growing your standard of living in step with the growth in your paycheck. While it can be very tempting to do this, I encourage you to look at the story of Warren Buffett. His abilities as a businessman and investor have made him the richest man in America, yet he still lives in the same modest house in Omaha, Nebraska, that he's lived in for much of his adult life. Buffett realized long ago that having money doesn't require you to spend it and that the money you don't spend can be invested, growing from a small amount today into a large amount tomorrow. His $50 billion net worth certainly attests to it.

Trent Hamm, author of *365 Ways to Live Cheap,* blogs about applying frugal living tactics to everyday life at www.thesimpledollar.com

> When you receive a raise, don't feel bad about celebrating— but do it modestly. ...A mere increase in your income is *not* a call to change your standard of living.

(continued from page 238)

person should be very focused on metrics," I say, "That's great that you said that—we're really on the same page. In fact, when I was at my last company, I launched a product that used an analytical package to . . ."

NEGOTIATING TACTIC: Have a repertoire of your accomplishments and aptitudes at your fingertips that you can include in your responses to commonly asked questions. These should include the following:

- Stories about successes you've had at previous jobs that illustrate your key strengths

- Questions to ask the negotiator if the conversation gets off track ("What do you like most about this job?" "Oh, really? That's interesting, because when I was at my last job, I found . . .")

5. Negotiate for more than money.

Don't forget to discuss whether or not the company offers a bonus, stock options, flexible commuting, or further education. You can also negotiate vacation and even job title. *Note:* Startups don't look very fondly on people negotiating vacations, because it sets a bad tone. But they *love* negotiating stock options, because top performers always want more, as it aligns them with the company's goals.

NEGOTIATING TACTIC: Your line is "Let's talk about total comp," which refers to your total compensation—not just salary, but everything. Treat them each as levers: If you pull one up, you can afford to let another fall. Use the levers strategically—for example, by conceding something you don't really care about—so you can both come to a happy agreement.

6. Be cooperative, not adversarial.

If you've gotten to the point of negotiating a salary, the company wants you and you want them. Now you just need to figure out how to make it work. It's not about you demanding more or them screwing you for less. Negotiation is about finding a cooperative solution to creating a fair package that will work for both of you. So check your attitude: You should be confident, not cocky, and eager to find a deal that benefits you both.

NEGOTIATING TACTIC: The phrase to use here is "We're pretty close . . . Now let's see how we can make this work."

7. Smile.

I'm not joking. This is one of the most effective techniques in negotiation. It's a disarming technique to break up the tension and demonstrates that you're a real person. When I was interviewing for college scholarships, I kept getting passed over until I started smiling—and then I started winning a bunch of them.

NEGOTIATING TACTIC: Smile. Really, do it.

8. Practice negotiating with multiple friends.

This sounds hokey, but it works better than you can imagine. If you practice *out loud,* you'll be amazed at how fast you improve. Yet nobody ever does it because it feels "weird." I guess it also feels "weird" to have an extra $10,000 in your pocket, jackass. For example, one of my friends thought it was too strange to practice negotiating, so when he faced a professional hiring manager, he didn't have a prayer. Later, he came to me like a clinically depressed Eeyore, whining about how he didn't negotiate. What could I say? This lack of practice can cost, on average, $5,000 to $10,000.

CHECK YOUR ATTITUDE: YOU SHOULD BE CONFIDENT, NOT COCKY, AND EAGER TO FIND A DEAL THAT BENEFITS YOU BOTH.

NEGOTIATING TACTIC: Call over your toughest, most grizzled friend and have him grill you. Don't laugh during the role play—treat it like it's a real negotiation. Better yet, videotape it—you'll be surprised how much you learn from this. If it sounds ridiculous, think about the benefits of not only the additional money, but the respect you'll get from your boss for a polished, professional negotiation.

9. If it doesn't work, save face.

Sometimes, the hiring manager simply won't budge. In that case, you need to be prepared to either walk away or take the job with a salary that's lower than you wanted. If you do take the job, always give yourself an option to renegotiate down the line—and get it in writing.

NEGOTIATING TACTIC: Your line here is "I understand you can't offer me what I'm looking for right now. But let's assume I do an excellent job over the next six months. Assuming my performance is just extraordinary, I'd like to talk about renegotiating then. I think that's fair, right?" (Get him to agree.) "Great. Let's put that in writing and we'll be good to go."

If you want to learn more about negotiation, I've put together a package of in-depth negotiation videos and tips. Check out www.iwillteachyoutobe rich.com/negotiate-like-an-Indian for details.

HOW TO SAVE THOUSANDS ON BIG-TICKET ITEMS

WHEN IT COMES TO SAVING MONEY, BIG PURCHASES ARE YOUR CHANCE to shine—and to dominate your clueless friends who are so proud of not ordering Cokes when they eat out, yet waste thousands when they buy large items like furniture, a car, or a house. When you buy something major, you can save massive amounts of money—£2,000 on a car or £200,000 on a house—that will make your other attempts to save money pale in comparison. Big-ticket items like these, however, are where people most commonly make mistakes. They don't comparison shop, they overpay because a salesperson cons them into spending too much, and worst of all they then think they got a good deal. Don't be one of these people!

A Fresh Look at Buying a Car

It's strange how many people make an effort to save on things like clothes and eating out, but when it comes to large purchases like cars, make poor decisions and erase any savings they've accumulated along the way.

Let me first tell you that the single most important decision associated with buying a car is not the brand or the mileage or the rims (please jump off a bridge if you buy specialty rims). Surprisingly, from a financial perspective, the most important factor is *how long you keep the car before selling it*. You could get the best deal in the world, but if you sell the car after four years, you've lost money. Instead, understand how much you can afford, pick a reliable car, maintain it well, and drive it for as long as humanly possible. Yes, that means you need to drive it for more than ten years, because it's only once you finish the payments that the real savings start. And by taking good care of your car, you can save even more enormous piles of money over the long term—and you'll have a great car.

There are four steps to buying a car: Budgeting, Picking a Car, Negotiating Like an Indian, and Maintaining Your Car.

First, ask yourself how buying a car fits into your spending and saving priorities (see Chapter 4). If you're satisfied with a used Toyota Corolla and would rather put your extra money toward investing for growth, great. On the other hand, if you really love BMWs and can afford to buy one, then you should do it. This is conscious spending, applied.

Once you've thought about where your car fits into your priorities, you need to look at your Conscious Spending Plan and decide what you're willing to allocate toward your car each month. This is the number you keep in your back pocket as the number you can afford *to spend up to*. Ideally you'll spend less. (*Note:* Ignore the advertisements for "$199/month." Those are scammy introductory rates that are simply not real.)

So, knowing that there will be other expenses involved in the total expense of having a car, you want to decide how much you want to spend on the car itself. For example, if you can afford a total monthly payment of $500 toward your car, you can probably afford a car that costs $200 to $250 per month. (For example, my monthly car payment of $350.75 actually adds up to around $1,000 when I factor in insurance, gas, maintenance, and $200/month San Francisco parking.) With a budget of around $200 per month for your car itself, that means you can afford a car that costs around $12,000 over five years. Pretty sobering compared with what most people think they can afford, right? This shows you how easy it is to overspend on a car.

IF YOU PICK A CRAPPY CAR, YOU ARE A MORON

Please, pick a good car. There are some cars that are just objectively bad decisions that nobody should ever buy. For example, has anyone with an IQ over 42 ever consciously chosen to buy a Chevy Lumina? Sadly, many

Dos and Don'ts for Your First Car

Do

■ **DO YOUR RESEARCH** by looking at car brokers, internet companies and car supermarkets. Check out online sites of car magazines like *What Car* to get information about the car you're thinking of buying.

■ **CALCULATE TOTAL COST OF OWNERSHIP** (TCO). This means you figure out how much you'll be spending over the life of the car—these expenses can have a big effect on your finances. Besides the cost of the car and the interest on your loan, the TCO should include maintenance, gas, insurance, and resale value. By understanding even a rough ballpark of how much these "invisible" costs will run you, you'll be able to save more accurately—and avoid surprises when you get a $600 car-repair fee.

■ **BUY A CAR THAT WILL LAST YOU AT LEAST TEN YEARS,** not one that looks cool. Looks fade and you're still going to be stuck with the payments. Optimize for the long term.

Don't

■ **PERSONAL CONTRACT PURCHASE OR LEASE.** These deals nearly always benefits the dealer, not you. They appeal to people who want the newest car and are willing to pay exorbitant amounts and get nothing to show for it—so, wealthy people who want new cars every two years, and in some cases, businesses for tax reasons. Not you! Buy a car and hold it for the long term. *Consumer Reports* research recently "determined that buying a car—in this case, the best-selling 2008 Honda Accord EX, at $24,495—would cost $4,597 less over five years than closed-end leasing for exactly the same model." If that doesn't persuade you not to lease, I don't know what will.

> ■ **SELL YOUR CAR IN FEWER THAN SEVEN YEARS.** The real savings come once you've paid off your car loan and driven it for as long as possible. Most people sell their cars far too early. It's much cheaper to maintain your car well and drive it into the ground.
>
> ■ **ASSUME YOU HAVE TO BUY A USED CAR.** Run the numbers. Over the long term, a new car may end up saving you money, if you pick the right new car, pay the right price, and drive it for a long time. See below for my story on buying a new car.
>
> ■ **STRETCH YOUR BUDGET FOR A CAR.** Set a realistic budget for your car and don't go over it. Be honest with yourself. Other expenses will come up—maybe car related, maybe not—and you don't want to end up struggling because you can't afford your monthly car payment.

people I know are seduced by the shiny new cars at the dealership. But it's important to remember that you're not just buying the car for today—you're buying it for the next ten-plus years. Buying a flashy car can be like dating a hot yet vapid girl: The hotness will wear off after a little while, and all you'll be left with is the unsatisfying person beneath. That is why when I'm checking girls out, I always exclaim loudly to my friend, "HEY, MAN, REMEMBER, WE HAVE TO OPTIMIZE FOR THE LONG TERM." Trust me, when girls overhear that, they can't resist me.

First, any car you evaluate must fit within your budget. This will eliminate most cars automatically. Do not even look at cars you can't afford.

Second, the car must be a *good car*. "But Ramit," you might say, "who can say what a good car is? One man's trash is another man's treasure." Listen, there is one person who will say what a good car is: me. Here's what makes a good car:

■ **RELIABILITY.** When I bought my car, above all, I wanted one that would not break down. I have enough stuff going on in my life, and I want to avoid car-repair issues that cost time and money as much as possible. Because this was a high priority, I was willing to pay slightly more for it.

- **A CAR YOU LOVE.** I've written time and time again about consciously spending on the things you love. For me, since I'd be driving the car for a long time, I wanted to pick one that I really enjoyed driving. And like a dutiful Indian son, I love not having to worry about it breaking down.

- **RESALE VALUE.** One of my friends bought a $20,000 Acura Integra, drove it for about seven years, and then sold it for 50 percent of the price. That means she got a fantastic deal on driving a new car for seven years. To check out how your potential cars will fare, visit www.whatcar.com/car-depreciation-calculator/ and calculate resale prices in five, seven, and ten years. You'll be surprised how quickly most cars depreciate and how others (Toyotas and Hondas especially) retain their value.

- **INSURANCE.** The insurance rates for a new and used car can be pretty different. Even if they're only slightly different (say, £25/month), that can add up over many years.

- **FUEL EFFICIENCY.** With gas prices on a roller-coaster ride, you may want to hedge your bets and consider a very fuel-efficient, or even a hybrid, car. This could be an important factor in determining the value of a car over the long term.

- **THE DOWN PAYMENT.** This is important. If you don't have much cash to put down, a used car is more attractive because the down payment (i.e., money you have to pay when you buy the car) is typically lower. And if you put £0 down, the interest charges on a new car will be much more. In my case, I had cash available to put down.

- **INTEREST RATE.** The interest rate on your car loan will depend on your credit, which is why having a good credit score matters (see page 16). If you have multiple sources of good credit, your interest rate will be lower. This becomes more important over a longer-term loan. Each car dealership will negotiate differently. Don't be afraid to walk out if the dealer tries to change the finance terms on you at the last minute. This is a common trick.

CONQUERING CAR SALESPEOPLE BY OUTNEGOTIATING THEM

I've seen more than my share of negotiations—including watching my dad negotiate with car dealers for multiple days. I think we actually ate breakfast at a dealership once.

You must negotiate mercilessly with dealers. I have never seen as many people make bad purchasing decisions as when they're in a car dealer's office. If you're not a hardball negotiator, take someone with you who is. If possible, buy a car at the end of the year, when dealers are salivating to beat their quotas and are far more willing to negotiate. Their saliva is your salvation!

I recommend using Parker's price guide to find out how much your car should be worth new and also what its target price should be (that is, how much of a discount you should be able to negotiate (What Car has a similar service on its website). I used www.fightingchance.com in the United States, which told me exactly how much dealers were paying for my car—including details about little-known "dealer withholding." For instance, I spent a month on the site researching and planning and then bought my car for $2,000 *under invoice*. The service also provided specific tips for how to negotiate from the comfort of your sofa. You don't even have to set foot in a dealership until the very end.

Here's how I did it:

When I decided to buy—at the end of December, when salespeople are desperate to meet their quotas—I faxed seventeen car dealers and told them exactly which car I wanted. I said I was prepared to buy the car within two weeks and, because I knew exactly how much profit they would make off the car, I would go with the lowest price offered to me. The same day, as I sat back with a cup of Earl Grey tea and a Taco Bell burrito, faxes started rolling in from the dealers. After I had all the offers, I called the dealers, told them the lowest price I'd received, and gave each of them a chance to beat it. This resulted in a bidding war that led to a downward spiral of near-orgasmic deals.

In the end, I chose a dealer in Palo Alto who sold me the car for $2,000 under invoice—a nearly unheard-of price. I didn't have to waste my time going to multiple dealerships, and I didn't have to bother with slimy car salesmen. I went into only one dealer's office: the winning one.

> **I HAVE NEVER SEEN AS MANY PEOPLE MAKE BAD PURCHASING DECISIONS AS WHEN THEY'RE IN A CAR DEALER'S OFFICE.**

BORING BUT PROFITABLE: MAINTAINING YOUR CAR

I know that keeping your car well maintained doesn't sound sexy, but it will make you rich when you eventually sell your car. So take your car's maintenance as seriously as your retirement savings: As soon as you buy your car, enter the major maintenance checkpoints into your calendar so you remember them. Here's a hint: The average UK car is driven about ten thousand miles per year. You can use that number as a starting point to calculate a maintenance schedule based on the car manufacturer's instructions.

Of course, you also need to have regular oil changes, watch your tire pressure, and keep your car clean. I keep a record of each service I have, along with any notes. When I sell my car, I'll show the documentation to the buyer to prove how meticulous I've been (and charge the buyer accordingly). People often forget this and slap their foreheads when they go to sell their car, only to be negotiated down (by someone like me) for not keeping detailed maintenance records. Don't let yourself get outmaneuvered by a lack of paperwork.

The Biggest Big-Ticket Item of All: Buying a House

If I asked people, "Hey, would you like to make a hundred thousand pounds in one year?" who wouldn't say yes? And if I sweetened the offer by saying you'd have to spend only ten hours per week that year to do it, I guarantee every single person I asked would go for it. So why don't people spend that amount of time researching the biggest purchase of their lives? By doing the research that 99 percent of other people don't, you can save tens of thousands of pounds on your house over the life of your loan. That's why, when I hear about people who "fell in love" with a house and then "had to have it on the spot," I am reminded why I wish I could pull a red wagon full of tomatoes everywhere I go.

Buying a house is the most complicated and significant purchase you'll make, so it pays to understand everything about it beforehand. I mean *everything*. This isn't a pair of pants at The Gap. When you buy a house worth hundreds of thousands of pounds, you should be an expert on the tricks and common mistakes most home buyers make. You should know all the common real estate terms, and how to push and pull to get the best deal. And you should understand that houses are primarily for living in, not for making huge cash gains.

Look, if you buy a house without opening up a spreadsheet and entering some numbers, you are a fool. Remember, if you can save £10,000 or £30,000 over the entire course of a twenty-five-year loan just by educating yourself a little, it's certainly worth your time. I'm going to help you figure out if buying a house is right for you, and then I'm going to give you an overview of the things you'll need to do over the next few months—at least three months, probably twelve—to prepare to buy. I can't cover all the tips here, but I'll get you started with the basics.

WHO SHOULD BUY A HOUSE?

From our earliest days, we're taught that the American dream is to own a house, have 2.5 kids, and retire into the sunset. In fact, I have friends who graduated from college and the first major purchase they wanted to make was a house. What the hell? No budget, no pension, but they wanted to buy a house? When I ask my younger friends why they want to buy a house, they stare at me blankly. "They're a good investment," they reply like brainless automatons who are at risk of being smacked by me.

Actually, houses really aren't very good investments in general. But I'll cover that in a minute. Back to who should buy:

First and foremost, you should buy a house only if it makes financial sense. In the olden days, this meant that your house would cost no more than 2.5 times your annual income, you'd be able to put at least 20 percent of the purchase price down, and the total monthly payments (including the mortgage, maintenance, insurance, and taxes) would be about 30 percent of your gross income. If you make £50,000 per year before taxes, that means your house would cost £125,000, you'd put £25,000 down, and the total monthly payments would be £1,250 per month. Yeah, right. Maybe if you live in the sticks.

Things are a little different now, but that doesn't explain the stupidity of people who purchase houses for ten times their salaries with zero money down. Sure, you can stretch those traditional guidelines a little, but if you buy something you simply can't afford, it *will* come around and bite you in the ass.

Let me be crystal clear: Can you afford at least a 10 percent down payment for the house (25 percent will give you a better choice of mortgages)? If not, set a savings goal and don't even think about buying until you reach it. Even if you've got a down payment, you still need to be sure you make enough money to cover the monthly payments. You might be tempted to think, "Oh, I'm paying £1,000/month for my apartment, so I can definitely afford £1,000 for a house!" Wrong. First off, chances are you'll want to buy a nicer house than you're currently renting, which means the monthly payment will likely be higher. Second, when you buy a house, you'll owe stamp duty, insurance, and maintenance fees that will add hundreds per month. If the garage door breaks or the toilet needs repairing, that's coming out of your pocket, not a landlord's—and home repairs are ridiculously expensive. So even if your mortgage payment is the same £1,000/month as your rental, your real cost will be about 40 to 50 percent higher—in this case, more like £1,500/month when you factor everything in.

THE BOTTOM LINE: BUY ONLY IF YOU'RE PLANNING TO LIVE IN THE SAME PLACE FOR TEN YEARS OR MORE.

Bottom line: If you don't have enough money to make a down payment and cover your total monthly costs, you need to set up a savings goal and defer buying until you've proven that you can hit your goal consistently, month after month.

Next thing to think about: Are the houses you're looking at within your price range? It's funny how so many people I know want to live only in the grandest possible house. Sure, your parents may live in one of those now, but it probably took them thirty or forty years to be able to afford it. Unless you're already loaded, you need to readjust your expectations and begin with a starter house. They're called that for a reason—they're simple houses that require you to make trade-offs but allow you to get started. Your first house probably won't have as many bedrooms as you want. It won't be in the most amazing location. But it will let you get started making consistent monthly payments and building equity.

Finally, will you be able to stay in the house for at least ten years? Buying a house means you're staying put for a long time. Some people say five years, but the longer you stay in your house, the more you save.

There are a few reasons for this: If you sell through a traditional estate agent, you pay one to two percent in fees. Add in stamp duty and it's quite a whack. Divide that by just a few years, and it hits you a lot harder than if you had held the house for ten or twenty years. There are also the costs associated with moving. And depending on how you structure your sale, you may pay a significant amount in taxes. The bottom line here: Buy only if you're planning to live in the same place for ten years or more.

I have to emphasize that buying a house is not just a natural step in getting older. Too many people assume this and then get in over their heads. Buying a house changes your lifestyle forever. No matter what, you have to make your monthly payment every month—or you'll lose your house and watch your credit tank. This affects the kind of job you can take and your level of risk tolerance. It means you'll need to save for a six-month emergency plan in case you lose your job and can't pay your mortgage. In short, you really need to be sure you're ready for the responsibility of being a home owner.

Of course, there are certainly benefits to buying a house and, like I said, most Americans will purchase one in their lifetime. If you can afford it and you're sure you'll be staying in the same area for a long time, buying a house can be a great way to make a significant purchase, build equity, and create a stable place to raise a family.

THE TRUTH: REAL ESTATE IS A POOR INVESTMENT FOR INDIVIDUAL INVESTORS

Americans' biggest "investments" are their houses, but real estate is also the place where Americans lose the most money. Realtors (and most home owners) are not going to like me after this section, but in truth, real estate is the most overrated investment in America. It's a purchase first—a very expensive one—and an investment second.

As an investment, real estate provides mediocre returns at best. First, there's the problem of risk. If your house is your biggest investment, how diversified is your portfolio? If you pay £2,000 per month to a mortgage, are you investing £6,000 elsewhere to balance your risk? Of course not. Second, the facts show that real estate offers a very poor return for individual investors. Yale economist Robert Shiller found that "from 1890 through 1990, the return on residential real estate was just about zero after inflation."

I know this sounds crazy, but it's true. We fool ourselves into thinking we're making money when we're simply not. For example, if someone buys a house for £250,000 and sells it for £400,000 twenty years later, they think, "Great! I made £150,000!" But actually, they've forgotten to factor in important costs like stamp duty, maintenance, and the opportunity cost of not having that money in the stock market. The truth is that, over time, investing in the stock market has trumped real estate quite handily—even now—which is why renting isn't always a bad idea.

I'm not saying buying a house is always a bad decision. It's just that you should think of it as a purchase, rather than as an investment. And, just as with any other purchase, you should buy a house and keep it for as long as possible. Do your homework and then negotiate. And know your alternatives (like renting).

BUYING VS. RENTING: THE SURPRISING NUMBERS

I want to show you why renting is actually a smart decision for many people, especially if you live in an expensive area like New York or San Francisco. But first, let's get rid of the idea that renters are "throwing away money" because they're not building equity. Any time you hear clichés like that—from *any* area of personal finance—beware. It's just not true, and I'll show you the numbers to prove it.

The total price of buying and owning a house is far greater than the house's sticker price. Take a look at this research from the Office of Federal Housing Enterprise Oversight (opposite).

When you rent, you're not paying all those other assorted fees, which effectively frees up tons of cash that you would have been spending on a mortgage. *The key is investing that extra money.* If you do nothing with it (or, worse, spend it all), you might as well buy a house and use it as a forced savings account. But if you've read this far, chance are good that you'll take whatever extra money you have each month and invest it.

Of course, like buying, renting isn't best for everyone. It all depends on your individual situation. The easiest way to see if you should rent or buy is to use an online calculator. There are several to choose from: MSN Money has one at http://money.uk.msn.com/mortgages/calculate/rent_buy_calculator.aspx and there's a test you can take to see if your personality is more suited to renting or buying at http://www.teamtechnology.co.uk/loans-guidebook/rent-vs-buy-questionnaire.html

THE COST OF BUYING A HOME OVER 25 YEARS

	2007
Purchase Price	£200,000
Interest @ 5% over 25 years	£250,000
Stamp duty	£2,500
Council Tax & Insurance (£1,840/year)	£46,000
Major Repairs & Maintenance	£50,000
Total Costs	**£548,500**

Assumes a 25-year interest-only mortgage

BECOMING A HOME OWNER: TIPS FOR BUYING YOUR NEW HOUSE

Like any area of personal finance, there are no secrets to buying a house. But it does involve thinking differently from most other people, who make the biggest purchase of their lives without fully understanding the true costs. Although I may be aggressive with my asset allocation, I'm conservative when it comes to real estate. That means I urge you to stick by tried-and-true rules, like 25 percent down, a 5-year fixed-rate mortgage, and a total monthly payment that represents no more than 30 percent of your gross pay. If you can't do that, wait until you've saved more. It's okay to stretch a little, but *don't* stretch beyond what you can actually pay. If you make a poor financial decision up front, you'll end up struggling—and it can compound and become a bigger problem through the life of your loan. Don't let this happen, because it will undo all the hard work you put into the other areas of your financial life.

If you make a good financial decision when buying, you'll be in an excellent position. You'll know exactly how much you're spending each month on your house, you'll be in control of your expenses, and you'll have money to pay your mortgage, invest, and take vacations, buy a TV, or whatever else you want to do.

Here are some of the things you'll need to do to make a sound decision.

Myths About Owning a Home

"PRICES ALWAYS GO UP IN REAL ESTATE" (OR, "THE VALUE OF A HOUSE DOUBLES EVERY TEN YEARS"). Not true. We can see this now in a very obvious way with the recent real estate crash. But most insidiously, net house prices haven't increased when you factor in inflation, taxes, and other homeowner fees. They appear to be higher because the sticker price is higher, but you have to dig beneath the surface.

"YOU CAN USE LEVERAGE TO INCREASE YOUR MONEY." Home owners will often point to leverage as the key benefit of real estate. In other words, you can put £20,000 down for a £100,000 house, and if the house climbs to £120,000, you've effectively doubled your money. Unfortunately, leverage can also work against you if the price goes down. If your house declines by 10 percent, you don't just lose 10 percent of your equity—it's more like 20 percent once you factor in the 6 percent realtor's fees, the closing costs, new furniture, and other expenses.

"I CAN ALWAYS TRADE DOWN AND USE MY PROPERTY AS MY PENSION." Be careful. This isn't nearly as easy as it looks. If you're going to trade down you'll still need to live somewhere and realistically it's probably going to be impossible to trade down to a small enough (or cheap enough) home to make enough money to keep going for even a couple of years once you reach retirement. By the time you've paid your estate agent's fees, stamp duty (on both the property you're selling and the one you're buying), lawyer's fees and removal costs, you might have very little to show for it.

1. Check your credit score. The higher your score, the better the interest rate on your mortgage will be. If your credit score is low, it might be a better decision to delay buying until you can improve your score. (See page 17 for details on bettering your score.) Good credit translates into not only a lower total cost, but lower monthly payments. The table on the next page from www.checkmyfile.com shows how interest rates are affected by your credit score on a twenty-five-year interest-only mortgage.

HOW CREDIT SCORES AFFECT WHAT YOU PAY

On a £200,000 25-year interest only mortgage, if your credit score is . . .	. . . your APR (interest rate) might be . . .	. . . with interest, you'll pay a total of . . .
851–1000 (best range)	2.5%	£125,000
7081–850	2.75%	£137,000
620–780	3.0%	£150,000
450–699	4.5%	£225,000
0–499 (worst range)	You probably wouldn't get a mortgage	

Source: checkmyfile.com, based on a base interest rate of 0.5%

2. Save as much money as possible for a down payment. Traditionally, you had to put 5 to 10 percent down. In recent years, people were allowed to put as little as zero down—but it's become all too clear that that was a very bad idea. If you can't save enough to put 25 percent down, you may have to pay a higher lending charge (HLC), which serves as insurance against your defaulting on your monthly payments. The HLC can cost around 7.5 percent of the amount over 75 percent that you want to borrow, although some lenders only pass the cost onto borrowers if you take out a higher loan-to-value mortgage (say 85 percent and above). But the real reason for saving a higher deposit is that you'll be able to qualify for a lower mortgage rate. If you save 25 percent or more, you should be able to access the most competitive deals. If you can't even save 10 percent, how will you afford an expensive mortgage payment, plus maintenance and taxes and insurance and furniture and renovations and . . . you get the idea. Set a savings goal (page 106) for a down payment, and don't start looking to buy until you reach it.

3. Calculate the total amount of buying a new house. Have you ever gone to buy a car or mobile phone, only to learn that it's way more expensive than advertised? I know I have, and most of the time I just bought it anyway because I was already psychologically set on it. But because the numbers are so big when purchasing a house, even small surprises will end up costing you a ton of money. For example, if you stumble across an unexpected cost for £100 per month, would you really cancel the paperwork for a new home? Of course not. But that minor charge would add up to £30,000 over the lifetime of a twenty-five-year loan—plus the opportunity cost of investing it. Remember that the costs associated with completing the deal and moving in are usually between 2 and 5 percent of the house price. So on a £200,000 house, that's £10,000. Keep in mind that ideally the total price shouldn't be much more than three times your gross annual income. (It's okay to stretch here a little if you don't have any debt.) And don't forget to factor in insurance, maintenance, and renovations. If all this sounds a little overwhelming, it's telling you that you need to research all this stuff before buying a house. In this particular case, you should ask your parents and other home owners for their surprise costs or check out www.direct.gov.uk/en/MoneyTaxAndbenefits/ManagingMoney/ PlanningYourPersonalFinances/DG_10013610.

4. *Get the most conservative, boring loan possible.* I like fixed rate mortgages, and you should fix for the first five years if you've never owned property before (the only exception is if fixed rates have increased sharply and you know they're going to come down soon, in which case you might consider a mortgage that tracks the Bank of England base rate, but gives you the option to fix without penalty at any time). Get a loan that lets you make overpayments.

5. *Watch out for fees.* Over the last few years, mortgage arrangement and booking fees have risen dramatically. In the past they could be a few hundred pounds, now they can add up to thousands. Don't get seduced by the interest rate and ignore the fees. The smaller the mortgage, the higher the effect of fees on the real cost of the loan. Some lenders price their mortgages with two different rates, depending on the fee you're prepared to pay. Compare different mortgage deals at www.charcol.co.uk and www.lcplc.co.uk.

6. *Use online services to comparison shop.* You may have heard about www.mouseprice.com, which is a rich source of data about home prices all over in the United Kingdom. Also check out private sale sites so you can negotiate directly with the seller (ones to try include www.

houseweb.co.uk, www.propertybroker.co.uk and www.houseladder.
co.uk). If you want to find out whether prices where you want to buy are
rising or falling, try www.housepricecrash.co.uk. And to save money on
insurance try comparison sites like www.comparethemarket.com or www.
moneysupermarket.com.

How to Tackle
Future Large Purchases

We've covered weddings, cars, and houses, but there are plenty
of other major expenses that people don't plan ahead for—just
think about having kids! The problem is that, as we've seen,
if you don't plan ahead, it ends up costing you much more in the end.
The good news is that there is a way to anticipate and handle almost any
major expense you'll encounter in life.

*1. Acknowledge that you're probably not being realistic about how much
things will cost—then force yourself to be.* If you've read this whole book
(and taken even half of my advice), you're probably better at your finances
than 95 percent of other people, but you're still human. Sorry, but your
wedding will be more expensive than you planned. Your house will
have costs you didn't account for. Having a head-in-the-sand approach,
however, is the worst thing you can do. Bite the bullet, sit down, and
make a realistic plan of how much your big purchases will cost you in the
next ten years. Do it on a napkin—it doesn't have to be perfect! Just spend
twenty minutes and see what you come up with.

2. Set up an automatic savings plan. Because almost nobody will take my
recommendation to make a budget to forecast major purchases, I suggest
just taking a shortcut and setting up an automatic savings plan (see page
133). Assume you'll spend £20,000 on your wedding, £15,000 on a car,
£15,000 for the first two years of your first-born kid, and however much
you'll need for a typical down payment for a house in your city. Then figure
out how much you need to save. If you're twenty-five, and you're going to
buy a car and get married in seven years, that's £35,000 ÷ 84 months =
£416 per month. "But Ramit," you might say in an annoying whine, "that's

more than four hundred pounds per month. I can't afford that!" Okay, can you afford £150? If so, that's £150 more than you were doing yesterday.

3. You can't have the best of everything, so use the P word. Priorities are essential. Like I said, it's human nature to want the best for our wedding day or first house, and we need to be realistic about acknowledging that. But we also need to acknowledge that we simply can't have the best of everything. Do you want the filet mignon or an open bar at your wedding? Do you want a house with a backyard or a neighborhood with better local schools? If you have the costs down on paper, you'll know exactly which trade-offs you can make to keep within your budget. If you haven't written anything down, there will appear to be no trade-offs necessary. And that's how people get into staggering amounts of debt.

For the things you decide aren't that important, beg, borrow, and steal to save money: If you're getting married, use a public park instead of a ballroom, ask your baker friend to make the cake. If you're buying a car, cut out the sunroof so you can get the model you want. And whatever you do, negotiate the hell out of big-ticket purchases. This is where, if you plan ahead, time can take the place of money.

A Rich Life for You—and Others

If I've been successful, the end of this book is the beginning of a rich future for you. We know that being rich isn't just about money. We know that most people around us have strong opinions about money, yet are clueless with their own. And we know that conscious spending can be fun (especially when it's automated). But now that you know how money really works, there's one other thing: Not enough people know about being rich. It's not some mythical thing that happens only to Ivy League grads and lottery winners. *Anyone* can be rich—it's just a question of what rich means to you. In my definition, I've always believed in getting really good at something, then passing it on to others. You're great at managing your finances and goals now. Would you do me a favor and pass the word along to your friends to help them focus on their goals, too? A rich life is about more than money. It starts by managing your own. And it continues by helping others become rich.

INDEX